BEGINNING JAVA™ 5
GAME PROGRAMMING

JONATHAN S. HARBOUR

UNIVERSITY OF ADVANCING TECHNOLOGY

D1413866

THOMSON
™
COURSE TECHNOLOGY
Professional ■ Technical ■ Reference

ISBN: 1-59863-150-0

Library of Congress Catalog Card Number: 2006923227

Printed in the United States of America

06 07 08 09 10 PH 10 9 8 7 6 5 4 3 2 1

THOMSON

COURSE TECHNOLOGY

Professional ■ Technical ■ Reference

Thomson Course Technology PTR,
a division of Thomson Learning Inc.
25 Thomson Place
Boston, MA 02210
http://www.courseptr.com

Publisher and General Manager, Thomson Course Technology PTR:
Stacy L. Hiquet

Associate Director of Marketing:
Sarah O'Donnell

Manager of Editorial Services:
Heather Talbot

Marketing Manager:
Heather Hurley

Senior Acquisitions Editor:
Emi Smith

Project Editor:
Jenny Davidson

Technical Reviewer:
John Flynt

PTR Editorial Services Coordinator:
Elizabeth Furbish

Copy Editor:
Kim Benbow

Interior Layout Tech:
Jill Flores

Cover Designer:
Mike Tanamachi

CD-ROM Producer:
Brandon Penticuff

Indexer:
Sherry Massey

Proofreader:
Sara Gullion

For Kaitlyn Faye

ACKNOWLEDGMENTS

I thank God for the many opportunities that have come my way this year, such as the chance to write this book and for the apparent talent needed to make something tangible of it.

I am grateful to my family for their ongoing encouragement: Jennifer, Jeremiah, Kayleigh, Kaitlyn, Mom and Dad, Grandma Cremeen, Dave and Barbara, Grandma and Grandpa Schleiss, my extended family at Vision Baptist Church, and Pastor Michael Perham and his family—Jennifer, Ashley, Bryce, and Sage—who have been such a blessing this past year.

Thank you to the students, faculty, and staff at UAT for contributing to such a wonderfully creative environment for learning. I would like to thank the inaugural Alpha Squad team of 2006, who had some influence on this book (and even helped to solve a few coding problems with *Galactic War*): Roy Evans, Stewart Johnston, Peter Pascoal, Travis Eddlemon, Daniel Muller, Daniel Stirk, Patrick Cissarz, David Coddington, Marc Kirschner, and Jeffrey Woodard; to the rest of the team: Jonathan Allmen, Levi Bath, Douglas Cannon, Joshua Gertz, Justin Hair, Adam Knight, Eric Lacerna, Daryl Lynch, and Kevin McCusker; and to the faculty sponsors: Rebecca Whitehead, Brian Fabiano, Michael Eilers, and Arnaud Ehgner.

I owe thanks to two UAT students, Mark Walker and Andrew Hawken, for introducing me to the angular velocity code used in this book, which was the basis for *Galactic War*.

I am also very thankful for the beautiful artwork featured in this book, provided by Ari Feldman (www.flyingyogi.com), Reiner Prokein (www.reinerstileset.de), and Edgar Ibarra. Without their wonderful graphics, *Galactic War* would not exist (or—*shudder*—it would feature *programmer art!*).

I am grateful and offer my sincere thanks to the tireless folks who made this book happen: Jenny Davidson, Emi Smith, Kim Benbow, John Flynt, Jill Flores, Sara Gullion, Sherry Massey, Brandon Penticuff, and Mike Tanamachi.

ABOUT THE AUTHOR

JONATHAN S. HARBOUR is a senior instructor of game development at the University of Advancing Technology in Tempe, Arizona (www.uat.edu), where he teaches a variety of courses, from handhelds to consoles to game engines. When not teaching others about games, writing about games, or playing games, he enjoys audio/video editing and working in the garage. His favorite game development tools are DarkBASIC Pro, Allegro, and DirectX. Jonathan is the author of three upcoming revisions: *DarkBASIC Pro Game Programming, Second Edition*; *Beginning Game Programming, Second Edition*; and *Game Programming All In One, Third Edition*, all from Course Technology. He lives in the Arizona desert with his wife, Jennifer, and children, Jeremiah, Kayleigh, and Kaitlyn. He can be reached via the Web at www.jharbour.com.

CONTENTS

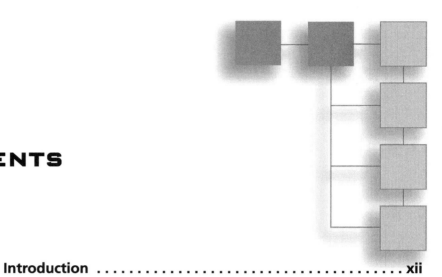

INTRODUCTION

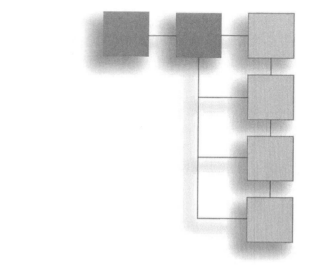

This book will teach you how to write Java games that will run as applets in a Web browser. The goal is to develop games for the casual game market. Game programming is a challenging subject that is not just difficult to master, it is difficult just to get started. This book takes away some of the mystery of game programming by explaining each step along the way, from one chapter to the next. I assume that you have a *little* Java programming experience, but even if you have never used Java before, you should be able to keep up if you keep a Java primer or reference book handy. This book does not teach the Java language.

First, you will learn how to write a simple Java program. From there, you will learn the details of how to write games that will run in a Web browser. I explain source code that is easy to understand, at a pace that will not leave you behind. After you have learned enough to write a simple game, you will do just that! You will see a simple vector-based game evolve from one chapter to the next into a fully featured sprite-based game by the end of the book. And I'm not talking about some half-baked wannabe *simulation* posing as a game. I'm talking about a *real* game that is retail quality, suitable for publishing in the casual game market.

There are hundreds of thousands of casual gamers who are paying to download games of this type from the many casual game sites on the Web today—such as Real Arcade (www.realarcade.com). By learning how to create a casual game, you may even be preparing for a career in the game industry, developing games for Microsoft Xbox Live Arcade and other commercial endeavors.

It all begins here! Are you serious about this subject and willing to learn? As a senior instructor of game development, I am scrutinized daily by students who eat, drink, and breathe video games. I cannot create something that *stinks*, or I'll never hear the end of it!

So I am as motivated here to teach you cutting-edge game development techniques as I am in a real classroom setting filled with students who are paying a lot more than the retail cost of this book to learn these concepts. In fact, this book will probably end up being used as a textbook in one of my own classes. So you are guaranteed high-quality material in these pages that will not be a waste of your time. If you are an instructor considering this text for your Java course, we should have instructor resources available for this title, including PowerPoint lectures. You may browse this book's support Web site at http://www.courseptr.com/ptr_detail.cfm?isbn=1598631500 and visit http://www.jharbour.com/begjava5 for up-to-date information and any corrections. In addition to this Web page, there is a discussion forum on my site where you may discuss Java game programming and get help for programming problems.

What Will You Learn in This Book?

This book will teach you the difference between Java applications and applets (which run in a Web browser). You will then learn about Java's graphics classes and begin writing graphics code. You will learn how to get input from the user, as well as how to play sound effects and music—all within the context of an online game. From there, the sky's the limit! Figure 1 shows the game you will learn to create in this book. Starting with the basics (and I'm talking about *extreme* basics here!), you will write a simple 2-D game using vector graphics (that is, using lines and filled polygons).

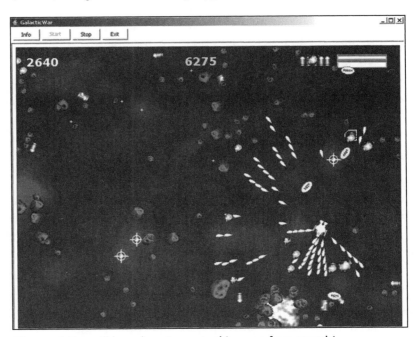

Figure 1 You will learn how to create this game from scratch!

You will then learn new techniques in each new chapter, such as how to load a bitmap file and render it on the 2-D applet window using the Graphics and Graphics2D classes. You will eventually put the handful of game-related classes together in an event-driven game library. As you can see from Figure 1, the final game uses some attractive artwork and is chock full of small details! You will learn about simple bitmaps, and then sprites, before getting into animation. Along the way you will learn how to use Java's advanced 2-D library to rotate graphics in any direction; and I'll show you some interesting code that moves bullets, powerups, asteroids, and other game objects on the screen smoothly and realistically. The end result is a professional sprite-based game engine that packs a serious punch! By learning how to create this retail-quality *casual game*, you will have learned enough to create your own games, suitable for sale in the casual game market (where games are played over the Web).

Because this book is dedicated to teaching the basics of game programming, it will cover a lot of subjects very quickly, so you'll need to be on your toes! I use a casual writing style to make the subjects easy to understand and use repetition rather than memorization to nail the points home. You will learn by practicing, and you will not need to struggle with any one subject because you will use each of them several times throughout the book. Each chapter builds on the one before. The game framework developed in Chapter 11 refers back to previous chapters, so I recommend reading one chapter at a time, in order, to fully understand everything that is going on.

If you skip a chapter here or there, you may not understand where some portions of code come from in later chapters, or you may be confused about how some code works. I tend to just *use* code after explaining how it works the first time, and often I do not explain something over and over again because the book moves along at a brisk pace. We have a lot to cover in a limited amount of space, so I recommend reading the book one chapter at a time, from start to finish.

Which Compiler Should You Use?

This book uses the Java language, and all examples are compiled with the JDK (Java Development Kit) version 1.5, release 6. While later versions of the JDK will certainly compile the code in this book without complaint, an older version of the JDK may very well fail to compile the programs. So I recommend you download the latest version of the JDK from http://java.sun.com for best results. You will be able to compile the programs in this book using the javac.exe program, and you will run the programs using appletviewer.exe on any platform—Windows, Linux, or Mac.

However, this book also uses a professional IDE (Integrated Development Environment)—Borland JBuilder 2005—the best tool for writing Java programs in my opinion. Specifically, I explain how to use the Foundation Edition, which is freely downloadable from Borland's Web site at http://www.borland.com/downloads/download_jbuilder.html.

If you have the full version of JBuilder 2005 or 2006, or even some other IDE entirely, then you should still be able to compile and run the programs in this book because I write standard Java source code. At the time of this writing, JBuilder 2005 Foundation can be downloaded and used for free (for non-commercial or educational use) from www.borland.com, and the JBuilder 2006 trial edition is also available. A 30-day trial version of JBuilder 2006 is included on the companion CD-ROM in the back of this book. I have tested the code in this book with older versions of JBuilder as well without incident.

What About the Programming Language?

This book focuses on the Java language; however, it is not a primer on the Java language. Rather, this book makes use of this very capable, high-level language to write games. The examples and source code are all Java. As such, you *should* already know Java in advance. We discuss game programming material in this book, not basic Java programming.

If this is your first experience with the Java language, then you may struggle with the source code in this book. If you feel that you are up to the challenge, then you *might* be able to read the Java code and make some sense out of it. But I don't spend very much time trying to teach anything about the Java language! We simply don't have enough pages to cover the basics of the Java language *and* cover game programming concepts as well.

This book is about game programming, and it assumes that you already know at least *some* Java. I recommend that you acquire a Java primer to read before delving into this book, or keep one handy for those parts that may confuse you. For starters, you can pick up *Java Programming for the Absolute Beginner*, by Joseph P. Russell (Course Technology PTR). If I lose you halfway through, I'll apologize in advance and can only say in my defense that we don't have enough pages to teach Java *and* build a complete game!

Conventions Used in This Book

The following styles are used in this book to highlight portions of text that are important. You will find these highlighted boxes here and there throughout the book.

note

This is what a Note looks like. Notes are additional information related to the text.

tip

This is what a Tip looks like. Tips give you pointers about the current tutorial being covered.

caution

This is what a Caution looks like. Cautions provide you with guidance as to what to do or not do in a given situation.

PART I

JAVA FOR BEGINNERS

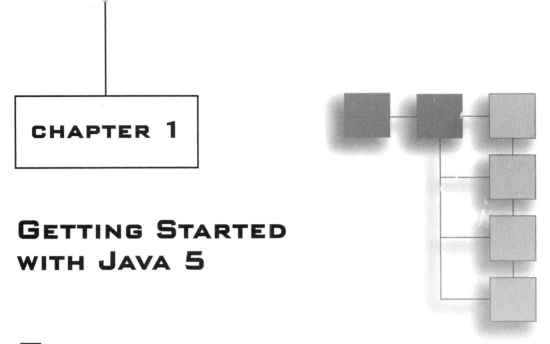

CHAPTER 1

GETTING STARTED WITH JAVA 5

Java is not the easiest programming language to learn, but it is probably the least expensive (it's free!) and most rewarding language you could invest time learning. This chapter will help you to get started with the basics of Java, and will be especially helpful if you have had no prior experience with this language. This chapter explains what you need, where to get it, and how to configure your system to prepare it for building Java-based games.

Here are some of the questions that will be answered in this chapter:

- What is the casual games boom all about?
- How much experience do I need to learn Java?
- What development tool should I use?
- What is the Java Development Kit and where can I get it?
- How do I compile a Java program from the command line?
- How do I create a Java applet?

What's New in Gaming?

I don't want to talk about the latest new features in Java, despite the title "What's New?" Instead, I'd like to focus on game design from a bird's-eye view. What truly has changed in the world of gaming since the "good old days"? By that term I am referring to the infancy of the game industry that entertains the world today, back in the 1980s. Most readers were probably *born* in the 1980s and have no recollection of the games of that era, except perhaps those that were ported to the second-generation consoles of the early 1990s (Nintendo SNES, Sega Genesis, Atari Jaguar). You have seen the various anthology collections from Namco, Atari, Midway, and Taito, featuring classics such as *Joust*, *Dig Dug*, *Pac-Man*, *Space Invaders*, *Defender*, and others (some of which date back to even the 1970s).

note

> Nintendo has not jumped onto the bandwagon yet of re-publishing an anthology collection of their classic games, such as *Donkey Kong*. Instead, Nintendo has given these classics an overhaul and released them on the extraordinary Game Boy Advance platform. Good move! Not only are some classics, like the original *Super Mario Bros.*, outselling most other handheld games, re-releases, such as *The Legend of Zelda: A Link to the Past* (don't you just love the play on words in this game title?), have outsold most console and PC games.

The game industry is advanced by gamers, not by marketing and business executives, which makes this industry somewhat unique in the world of entertainment. Isn't it obvious that professional sports (NFL, NBA, NHL, and MBA here in the states) are not advanced or directed by the fans? On the contrary, the fans are often derided and ignored by not only the team franchises but by the organizations themselves. This is an example of how centralized management can lead to problems. Unfortunately for sports fans, they are more than willing to put up with the homage paid to them in boxes of derision because they love the sport. This is a level of loyalty that simply doesn't exist in any other industry. If you love sports, you ignore all the problems and just enjoy the games, but it doesn't change the fact that it's a seller's market (although, digital entertainment is drawing fans away from professional sports).

How is the game industry a buyer's market (meaning, gamers have a lot of influence over the types of games that are created)? Most games are created specifically for a consumer segment, not for the general public. The decision makers at game publishing companies choose projects that will reach as many core constituents as possible, while also trying to reach casual gamers and hardcore fans of other game genres. For instance, Blizzard Entertainment (a subsidiary of Vivendi Universal Games, which also owns Sierra Entertainment) targets two game genres exclusively:

- Real Time Strategy (RTS) Games: *WarCraft* series, *StarCraft*
- Role-Playing Games (RPGs): *Diablo* series, *World of Warcraft*

Can you think of a game that Blizzard has published that does not fit into these two genres? *StarCraft Ghost* comes to mind, though it has not been released at the time of this writing. This game is a first-person stealth/action game from the point of view of a *StarCraft* character (the Ghost unit), so I prefer to categorize it as a derivative of an RTS game (a subsidiary title, if you will).

Blizzard has consistently hit the mark dead center with their games in terms of target audience, quality, polish, and subsequent mass appeal. *World of Warcraft* has sold 600,000 copies during its first year, with up to 200,000 simultaneous players supported on its servers. *WarCraft III* has sold over five million units (including the add-ons), while the entire *WarCraft* series has sold twelve million units since its debut in 1994. *StarCraft* has sold nine million copies since 1998 (including add-ons).

Why do you suppose Blizzard has been so successful? Certainly not through aggressive advertising campaigns! Gamers have traditionally been immune to marketing, relying primarily on word-of-mouth recommendations from friends, online review sites, and bloggers for their game purchase decisions. If any of Blizzard's games had not been up to par with the gamers, they would not have continued to play the game. But the sales figures shown here reveal products that have had a very long shelf life due to continued sales.

I could go into other companies with equally impressive success stories as well as those that have been dismal failures. But my goal is to demonstrate to you that the game industry is indeed a buyer's (gamer's) market. It's not dictated and ruled by the board of directors of one company or another or by marketing people, who have been stymied by the reluctance of gamers to go along with traditional promotional theories. In other words, gamers are a tough audience! It's an empowering position to be in, knowing that your personal preferences and tastes are shared by millions of others who demand excellence and innovative gameplay, and that these demands are met, more or less. Companies that produce excellent games are rewarded by gamers, while those that fall short quickly close up shop and move on.

Would you like another real-world example? A few years ago, a new publisher emerged in the game industry by the name of Eidos. This company's bank account was padded by millions of PlayStation owners who had all fallen in love with Lara Croft. Eidos seems to have misinterpreted the market, believing that gamers loved the *image* and *motif* of this Bond-esque heroine. Eidos created a new hot-shot team in Texas made up of some industry veterans in an endeavor called *Ion Storm*. The belief was that marketing the "Rock-n-Roll" hype of these developers would lead to millions of pre-order sales for their games (coming from the successes of the two *Tomb Raider* sequels).

Eidos failed to recognize that gamers bought into Lara Croft because the games were fun, not because of the image. When *Ion Storm* was launched, Eidos printed two-page spreads in major game magazines showing the team, along with the phrase "John Romero wants to make you his b---ch." I've met John and chatted with him on many occasions; he is the nicest guy I have ever met, hands down. Marketing ruined that game, not its producer, as he has since moved on to more successful projects. The developers of *Daikatana* were not able to keep up with the marketing explosion, and were derided for producing an average game that would have been well received were it not blacklisted by gamers because "The Man" had created it. The impression was very strong that it was all about sales, not a gaming experience, and gamers rejected that notion. Eidos has moved on from the experience too, having published my favorite console game of 2005, *LEGO: STAR WARS* (see Figure 1.1).

Figure 1.1 LEGO: STAR WARS is the best two-player co-op game I've ever played.

What's Old School?

In my experience, the fun factor of video games has risen exponentially in the last two decades along with the complexity of modern games. Let's face it, you can only play *Pac-Man* for an hour or so until it becomes tedious. The same applies to most of the classic arcade games. At one time, you could fit every video game in existence in a single room, and those quarter-fueled machines were housed in stand-up cabinets. Since that time, there have been about a half million games created, though we might narrow down that figure to a few thousand good games, out of which we find a few hundred "Hall of Fame" greats.

The Casual Boom

Believe it or not, I haven't been just reminiscing over the last few pages while talking about games. In the last two years a new genre has arisen in the game industry called "casual games." This genre has been relegated to secondhand status for many years, while the numbers of gamers has risen from the hardcore "geek" fans to include more and more people. The average gamer plays games for a few hours a week, while the hardcore gamer spends 20+ hours playing games every week (like a part-time job). Casual gamers, on the other hand, will only spend a few minutes playing a game now and then; perhaps every day, but not always. The casual gamer does not become addicted to any game the way a hardcore gamer does, with games such as *World of Warcraft*, *Star Wars Galaxies*, *The Matrix Online*, *EverQuest*, and so on.

So, what is a casual game anyway? A casual game is any game that can be played in a short time frame and requires no instructions on how to play. In this context, almost every classic arcade game ever made falls into this category. It is only recently that publishers and game industry pundits have begun to realize that gamers really don't want the long, drawn-out experience of installing a game, downloading a patch, and spending eight hours learning how to play it. Sometimes it is refreshing to just fire up a game and play for 10 or 20 minutes without having to screw with it all evening! This was a gripe of mine for a long time. It is why I spend far more time playing console games than PC games, and I'm sure many readers share that sentiment.

Yes, there are some PC games that are so compelling or innovative that they are worth the effort to get them installed and running. The best example of late is *World of Warcraft*. I have spoken to many gamers who claim that if Blizzard's games were not so darned much fun, they would boycott Blizzard altogether! (How's that for a contradiction?) The impression I get is that these gamers have a love/hate relationship with Blizzard and many other game publishers as well. Case in point, I recently purchased a new computer (Sony Vaio S590, Pentium M 2.0 GHz, GeForce Go 6400, 128MB) and could not install *World of Warcraft* on it. First, the installer locked up on a file called texture.mpq, and a subsequent install attempt reported an error on disc two. I got around these issues by copying all four discs to the hard drive and installed it from there with no more problems. However, as soon as I fired up the game and logged in to my account, it dropped out to download a 260 MB update to the game. When that was done, three more small updates were installed just to bring the game up to the latest version. Are these problems tolerable? Yes and no. On the one hand, this is the most advanced and complex MMORPG (massively multiplayer online role playing game) ever created, and Blizzard has a full-time team continually creating new content and improving the game, which I applaud. But on the other hand, that sure was a lot of work just to get the game installed, and it took three hours of my time (which is why hardcore gamers tend to have more than one PC).

Would a casual gamer be willing to devote that much time just to install a game that will end up requiring hundreds of hours of gameplay in order to rise through the ranks within the game world? Most casual gamers do not have the time or patience to jump through so many hoops for Blizzard. Such is the target audience for casual games! Have you ever given serious thought to this issue? If you are an IT (information technology) professional or a hardcore gamer, you are used to dealing with computer problems and cope with them without incident. But do you ever wonder, if you—a smart, experienced, knowledgeable computer expert—are having problems with a game, how on earth will Joe Q. Public figure out these problems? Well, the answer is, they don't, which accounts for most game returns.

Casual Gamers

Casual gamers include professionals (doctors, lawyers, janitors, and other service jobs), executives (CEOs, VPs, and other management leaders), as well as everyone else. Casual games attract people from all cultures, classes, genders, religions, ethnicities, and political orientations. (Yes, it's true, here in the states, we have Democrat and Republican gamers; Republican gamers accuse Democrat gamers of playing only politically-correct games like *Deer Avenger*, while Democrat gamers accuse Republican gamers of only playing "god" games like *Black & White*).

Given that most *potential* game players are not willing or able to cope with the issues involved in PC games, is it any wonder that this burgeoning market has been inevitable for several years now? While casual games are currently played mainly in a Web browser using technology like Java and Flash, the console systems are featuring online gameplay as well, and this trend will continue to gain popularity.

Casual Games

The casual game market was no market at all a few years ago. Only recently has this subject started to show up on the radar of publishers, schools, and retail stores, even though gamers have been playing casual games for two decades. (I predicted casual games would take off a few years ago, but my dog ate that article.) Casual games are a win-win situation because they are just as easy to create as they are to play; so the developer is able to create a casual game in a short time frame, and the gamer has an enjoyable experience with a lot of choices. Casual games have a very simple distribution model (most are put up on a Web site for online play), a respectable compensation model (developers receive a percentage of net sales or a single lump sum), an often meager development cycle measured in weeks or a few months, and almost no testing is required. As a casual game developer, you can come up with an innovative game idea, develop the game, and get it onto store shelves (i.e., a Web site) all within the time frame of just the concept art stage of a full-blown retail game.

Jay Moore is an evangelist for Garage Games who promotes the Torque Game Engine around the country at conferences and trade shows. He spoke at the 2005 Technology Forum at the University of Advancing Technology where he addressed the possibility of earning a living as a casual game developer. Garage Games' Torque engine has been ported to Xbox, and they have published two games on Xbox Live Arcade that you can download and play if you are a Live user. *Marble Blast* is one such game, shown in Figure 1.2, and Garage has many more games planned for release on Live and through retail channels. In fact, when you purchase the entire Torque Game Engine for $100, you have the option of publishing through Garage Games, which does the contractual work and provides you with a contract (subject to quality considerations, of course).

Figure 1.2 *Marble Blast* is a Torque game published on Xbox Live Arcade.

Microsoft has really embraced casual games by making it possible for independent developers to publish games directly on Live (for both Xbox and Xbox 360) without going through retail channels. Xbox 360 is the first console video game system in history to provide downloadable games right out of the box without first purchasing retail software. If you are interested in casual games, you can enjoy playing on Live Arcade without buying a retail game at all, as many games are available for free trial and purchase on Live Arcade.

I attended the Austin Game Conference 2005 this year, and the entire show was consumed with the overall subject of "casual games." Microsoft's booth was titled "Microsoft Casual Games," and they were giving away USB flash drives with the MSN Messenger SDK and showcasing some of the Live Arcade games. So if you've ever wanted to play *Solitaire* in high definition, now is your chance!

One of the most impressive games available on Live Arcade is *RoboBlitz*, shown in Figure 1.3. This game was built using the Unreal Engine 3 (which Epic Games is building for *Unreal Tournament 2007*). *RoboBlitz* also makes use of the impressive Ageia PhysX physics engine to produce realistic gameplay.

Figure 1.3 *RoboBlitz* is a download-only Xbox Live Arcade game for Xbox 360 that uses the awesome Unreal Engine 3 and Ageia PhysX engines.

Another innovative game coming to Xbox Live Arcade from the creators of *Project Gotham Racing* is *Geometry Wars*, shown in Figure 1.4. This game is unique and compelling, with gameplay that involves gravity and weapons that resemble geometric shapes.

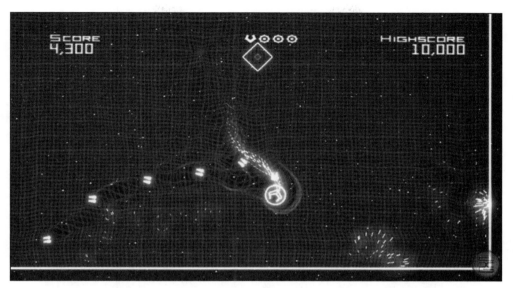

Figure 1.4 *Geometry Wars* is a download-only game for Xbox 360 with intriguing gameplay.

If you feel as if I've been leading you along a train of thought, you would be right to trust your feelings. The focus of this book is about programming games using Java, and we will learn shortly to do just that. Since Java is the pioneer language of casual game development, I will be emphasizing this aspect of gaming while creating games in the chapters to come.

Let's Get to the Point: Java

As you might have guessed, Java games run in a Web browser—Internet Explorer and Mozilla FireFox work equally well for running Java games. Java programs can also run on a desktop system locally without going to a Web site. These types of programs are called Java applications and require the Java Runtime Environment (JRE) to be installed. The Web browser JRE is not the same as the desktop application JRE, which must be installed, while the Web browsers include a browser-based version of the Java Runtime automatically. You can update the JRE associated with a Web browser to the latest JRE by simply installing a newer version, since the installer identifies the Web browsers installed on your system and upgrades them for you. So if you write a Java game using features from Java 5, the JRE might need to be updated before it will run the game properly. In some cases, the compiled Java program (which ends up being a file with an extension of .class or .jar) will run on older Runtime versions, because some updates to the Java language have no impact on the resulting compiled files. Figure 1.5 shows the game you will create in Chapter 5, "Creating Your First Java Game."

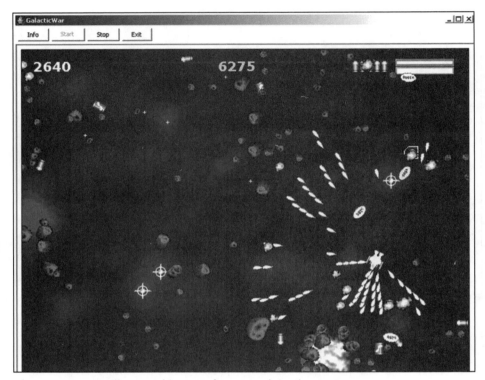

Figure 1.5 You will create this game from scratch in Chapter 5.

No Experience Required

I am assuming that you have no experience with the Java language, even though some of you may be accomplished Java developers. I am starting at the beginning because it's easier to teach a course on the subject of Java programming without any prerequisites, and this book will be used in many middle school, high school, and college courses. While not leaving anyone behind, we also will not limp along in the slow lane of this highway for long. While covering some of the basics over the next two chapters, you'll have created a complete casual game in Java that runs in a Web browser, which will be a milestone as well as a measure of your own skill level at that point.

So how will you be able to get the most out of this subject when I am adopting the Marine Corps policy of "leave no man behind"? Very carefully! Actually, I'll build a logical progression of subjects, one upon another, from one prerequisite skill after another, until you have the breadth of information needed to delve into the subjects covered in the last few chapters of the book. First, I'll help you develop the foundational knowledge needed to construct the frame of a game, after which we'll add electrical wiring, plumbing, and then put on the finishing touches.

Development Tools

I am using the best development tool there is for writing Java games: Borland JBuilder 2005 Foundation. This is a completely free version of JBuilder that you can download and install without limitations on its use (see Figure 1.6). You will need to visit www.borland.com to download JBuilder 2005 Foundation, and then register the software to receive a free registration key before you can use it.

Figure 1.6 Borland JBuilder 2005 Foundation is a free Java compiler and IDE.

Why do you suppose Borland is just giving away this compiler? JBuilder Foundation is a trial version of JBuilder without an expiration date, meaning you can continue to use it as long as you want for non-commercial uses. You cannot compile a game using JBuilder Foundation, and then sell the game online. You also cannot use JBuilder Foundation on a business computer owned by your employer to produce software for your company. JBuilder Foundation is for evaluation purposes to determine if JBuilder is a tool that will meet your needs, as an individual or as a corporation. Figure 1.7 shows the interface of JBuilder 2005.

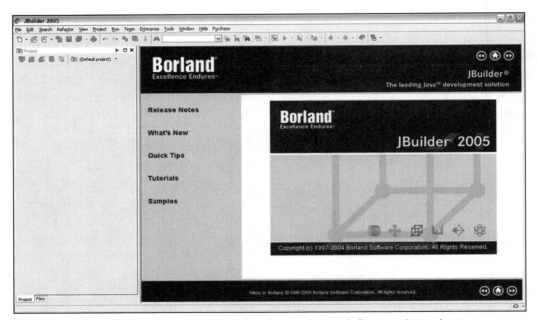

Figure 1.7 The JBuilder IDE is an attractive interface packed with features devoted to Java development.

There are three versions of JBuilder available:

1. JBuilder Foundation is a basic Java IDE that is free.
2. JBuilder Developer also supports Web and mobile applications as well as performance profiling.
3. JBuilder Enterprise includes additional support for CORBA, Web services, and client/server performance management; it is also suitable for large projects.

I will be using this tool throughout the book because it is, in my opinion, the easiest tool to use when you are just getting started programming with Java. If you are using a platform other than Windows, you will be happy to learn that Borland is a multi-platform company (unlike some software companies that shall go unnamed), so JBuilder is available for all of the following platforms:

- Windows
- Mac OS X
- Linux
- Solaris

Installing the Latest JDK

JBuilder 2005 comes with the Java Development Kit 1.4.2 (i.e., "Java 1.4"). At the time of this writing, the latest version, JBuilder 2006, is available, but not as the Foundation edition, only as the 30-day Enterprise trial edition. So we'll continue to use JBuilder 2005 Foundation, since a newer free "Foundation" version is not available. You must download JBuilder separately from the Java Development Kit, because JBuilder is a Borland product, while the JDK was created by Sun Microsystems. First, download and install JBuilder by visiting http://www.borland.com. After that, visit http://java.sun.com and download the latest JDK (at the time of this writing, it is 1.5.0 Release 6). Next, I'll explain how you can attach the latest JDK to JBuilder (so you won't be stuck using JDK 1.4, which is bundled with JBuilder).

tip

> If you happen to own a newer version of JBuilder already, that's terrific, you should be good to go with the JDK 1.5 packaged along with it. The core features of JBuilder have not changed much in the 10 years since the first version came out, so everything discussed in this book that is related to JBuilder should be relevant to any newer version.

One of the best features of JBuilder is the ability to upgrade the JDK whenever a new version is released by Sun Microsystems. You can check for the latest version of the JDK by browsing to http://java.sun.com/. At the time of this writing, the latest JDK version is 1.5.0 Release 6, and you can replace the existing JDK used by JBuilder with this new JDK by following these steps.

1. Run JBuilder. Open the Tools menu and select Configure, then JDKs, as shown in Figure 1.8.

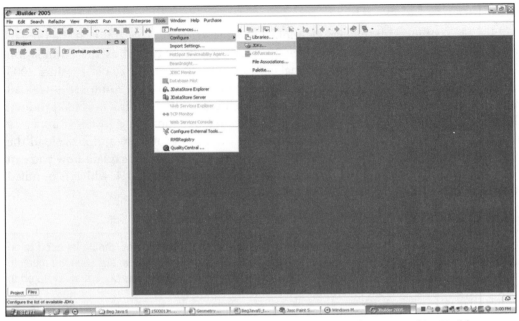

Figure 1.8 Use the Tools, Configure, JDKs menu option to upgrade the JDK used by JBuilder.

2. This menu item brings up the Configure JDKs dialog box, shown in Figure 1.9.

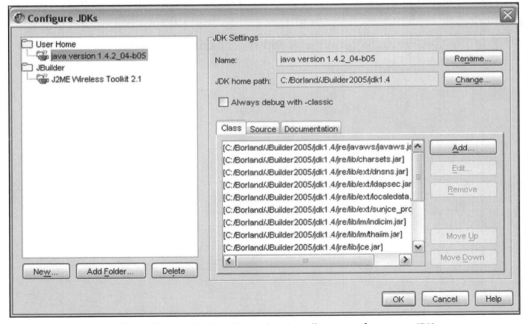

Figure 1.9 The Configure JDKs dialog box is used to install support for a new JDK.

3. Now select User Home in the treeview on the left side of this dialog, and then click the New button at the bottom (see Figure 1.10).

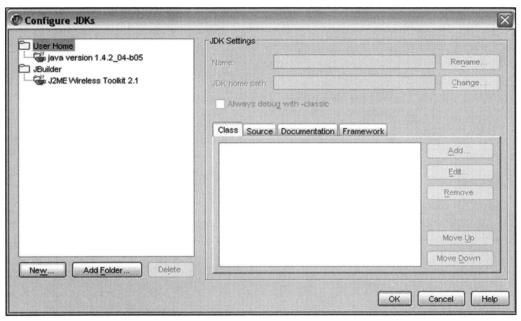

Figure 1.10 Preparing to install a new JDK version.

4. This brings up the New JDK Wizard dialog box, shown in Figure 1.11. Click the ellipsis button next to the Existing JDK Home Path field.

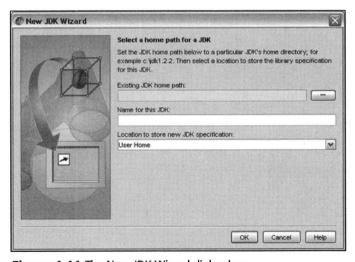

Figure 1.11 The New JDK Wizard dialog box.

5. Browse to the location of the new JDK that you would like JBuilder to adopt. This is usually found in the main Java folder on your system (which is in C:\Program Files\Java by default), and then select the jdk subfolder, as shown in Figure 1.12. Click OK to select the folder.

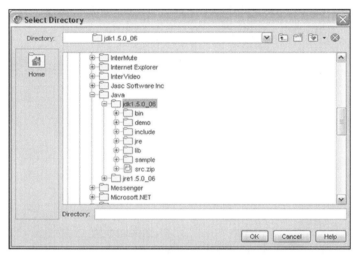

Figure 1.12 Selecting the folder location for the new JDK.

6. The folder location will be pasted into the New JDK Wizard dialog box, as shown in Figure 1.13. Click OK to continue.

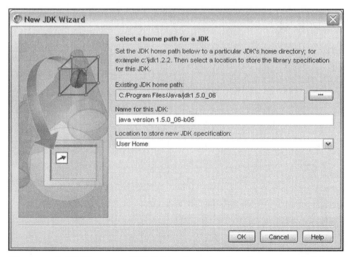

Figure 1.13 The new JDK folder location has been entered into the New JDK Wizard dialog field.

7. The Configure JDKs dialog box will show the newly associated JDK that you selected. You may delete the older JDK if you wish (1.4.2 in this example). See Figure 1.14.

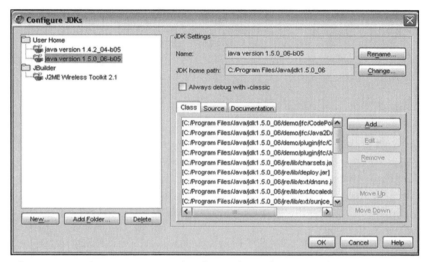

Figure 1.14 The new JDK 1.5.0 has been plugged into JBuilder.

Version Numbers and Revision Woes

Java's versioning is a confusing subject (and needlessly so), but it's something you might want to understand. The official latest version of Java at the time of this writing is "Java 2 Platform Standard Edition (J2SE) 5.0 Update 6." However, the actual version number is 1.5.0. The computer industry is anything but consistent, given the extraordinary changes that have taken place on the Internet and in software development in general. But one thing has been agreed upon in the computer industry regarding versioning. The first release of a software product is version 1.0. Often a revision or build number will be appended, such as 1.0.8392, which helps technical support or call center personnel identify the version of software that a customer is using when a problem arises. The revision number is, in every case, not part of the retail packaging and product name, but rather a tracking tool.

The Java team members, however, have decided to come up with their own versioning standard for the Java Development Kit (JDK) and Java Runtime Environment (JRE), as revealed in Table 1.1.

Table 1.1 Java Version History

Version	Marketed Name	Description
1.0	Java 1.0	Initial public release version, not quite proven yet
1.1	Java 1.1	First major revision, improvements throughout
1.2	Java 2	Second major revision/release
1.3	Java 2	New improvements, added features (i.e. "Java 3")
1.4	Java 2	Major revision, significant changes (i.e. "Java 4")
1.5	Java 5	Many new features, classes, and improvements

The interesting thing about this table is that it is very consistent in the first column (Version), but chaos ensues in the second column (Marketed Name), which is not a great surprise since marketing campaigns seldom make sense. If you were to follow the progression from one version to the next and tally them, you might note that there have been six major versions of Java. My theory is that, since Java was derived from C++, the versions are zero-based, so it was "Java 0." To maintain one's sanity, I recommend going with the flow, accepting the fact that Java's version numbering is a segmented fiasco without any harm being done (except for those of us who suffer from Obsessive-Compulsive Disorder).

tip

Product branding is a very expensive and time-consuming process, which is why businesses defend their brand names so viciously. Java 2 was "cool" when it first came out, and it became a recognized brand name for Sun Microsystems (with popular "standard" J2SE and "enterprise" J2EE), which is reluctant to retire the name and move on. As a software professional, I have often disagreed with the methods employed by marketing with regard to branded software. For instance, did you know that Windows XP is actually the 10th version of Windows since its inception (by my estimation, at least)? It's refreshing to find software with a simple progression of versions released over the years without the meddling of marketing people.

I believe a certain amount of momentum was in play here, which is why the versioning is so messed up. When Sun released Java 2 as a trademarked/branded name, it caught on, and unfortunately, the version we are using now, "Java 5," is still known internally as "Java 2" version 1.5, even though there was no "Java 2" version 1.0. Are you confused yet? It might make sense to have a "brand name" or "product name," and then a new version starting with 1.0 for the new product. But Java 2 started with version 1.2. Since I am somewhat obsessive about details, I'd like to verify that we're still using Java 1, according to the version displayed by the JDK:

```
java version "1.5.0_06"
Java(TM) 2 Runtime Environment, Standard Edition (build 1.5.0_06-b05)
Java HotSpot(TM) Client VM (build 1.5.0_06-b05, mixed mode, sharing)
```

Java fans love these quirks, which are not flaws but endearing traits, and it's not a problem once you understand how it has evolved over the past decade.

Compiling from the Command Line

Many Java programmers prefer to use the Java command-line tools to build and run Java programs instead of using an IDE like JBuilder. If you already have experience programming in Java and have your own preferred code editor, you may use that tool if you wish. I will simply be listing source code in this book and not relying too much on JBuilder. However, since JBuilder is available for just about every operating system there is, I can't really imagine why anyone would want to use something else; to each his own. The source code will be provided in .java files, compiled into .class files, and the JBuilder project files (.jpx) are also provided on the CD. If you prefer to use the JDK command-line tools, you can use the javac.exe compiler program to build any .java file introduced in the book. But as a *Beginning* title, I am focusing on the JBuilder IDE.

To run a Java .class file that you have successfully compiled, use the java.exe program. You will likely have to set up a path to C:\Program Files\Java\jdk1.5.0_06\bin (substitute the current version you are using here) in order to invoke these programs. Since all of the Java programs in this book are *applets*, they must be run with the appletviewer.exe program instead of java.exe (which is used to run Java applications and services). JBuilder creates a host Web file for each project it builds, so you may open the associated .html file (such as GalacticWar.html in upcoming chapters) to run a particular example program on the CD-ROM.

caution

You can't simply run a .class file with appletviewer; you must pass the html Web host file (containing a link to the applet) to appletviewer.exe.

I want to show you how to set up your system so you can use the command-line tools for building and running a Java program because we'll be writing a short test program here in a few minutes to test the installation of the JDK on your computer to make sure it's working.

The Java Development Kit (JDK) is installed by default to C:\Program Files\Java\jdk1.5.0_06 (assuming you are using the same version; substitute the folder pathname if necessary). Inside this folder is a folder called bin, which is where the Java programs like javac.exe, appletviewer.exe, and java.exe are located. You want to add this folder to the system search path so you can run them from anywhere using the command line. To set up your system in this way, perform the following steps:

1. Open the Windows Control Panel from the Start menu. Open the Control Panel applet called System. This brings up the System Properties dialog. Select the Advanced tab, as shown in Figure 1.15.

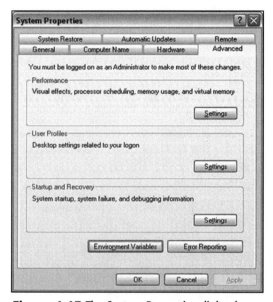

Figure 1.15 The System Properties dialog box is accessed from the Control Panel.

2. Click the button Environment Variables to bring up the Environment Variables dialog box, shown in Figure 1.16.

Figure 1.16 The Environment Variables dialog box.

3. Scroll down in the second list to a System variable called Path, then click the Edit button. A text entry dialog will pop up, allowing you to modify the path of folders where the command prompt searches when you type in a program name that it can't find. Add the following text to the *end* of the path text so that it resembles Figure 1.17, and don't forget the semi-colon in front of it.

caution

You don't want to *replace* the path, just add the new entry to the *end* of it!

```
;C:\Program Files\Java\jdk1.5.0_06\bin
```

Figure 1.17 Editing the Path variable.

4. You can close all of the windows to save the newly changed path. At this point, any time you open the Command Prompt, the JDK bin folder will be visible so that you can run javac.exe and java.exe.

tip

You can open a Command Prompt window by clicking Start, Run, and typing in **cmd.exe**.

Writing Your First Java Program

I want to take you through the steps of creating a new Java program to test the JDK and a Java applet project to test Web-browser integration before moving on to the next chapter. Let's start at the very beginning so that when you have written a full-featured game down the road, you'll be able to look back and see where you started.

The DrinkJava Program

The following program, shown in Figure 1.18, is called DrinkJava. Type it in and save the file as DrinkJava.java.

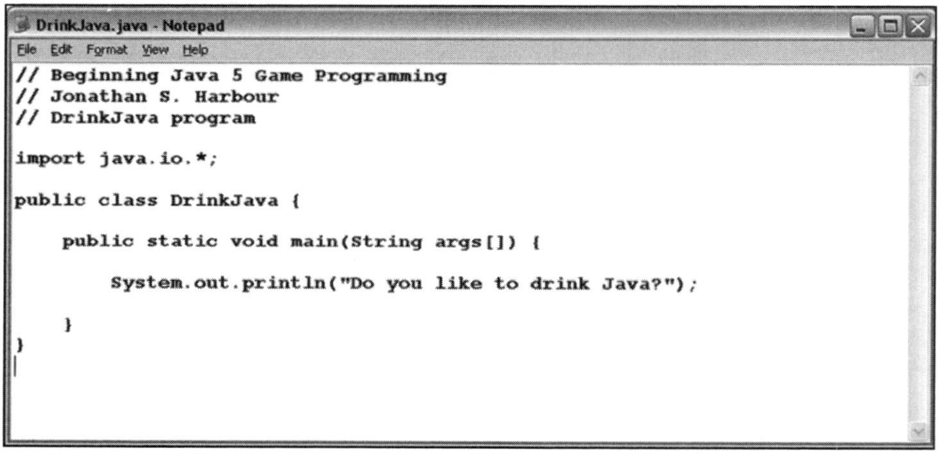

```
🗎 DrinkJava.java - Notepad
File  Edit  Format  View  Help
// Beginning Java 5 Game Programming
// Jonathan S. Harbour
// DrinkJava program

import java.io.*;

public class DrinkJava {

    public static void main(String args[]) {

        System.out.println("Do you like to drink Java?");

    }
}
```

Figure 1.18 The DrinkJava program can be edited and saved using Notepad.

Now let's compile the program to see if the JDK has been installed correctly, as well as to see if you set the environment path correctly. To compile the program, you'll need to open a Command Prompt window. Use the CD command to change to the folder where you saved the .java file. For instance, CD \chapter01\DrinkJava. Once in the correct folder, you can then use the javac.exe program to compile your program:

```
javac DrinkJava.java
```

The Java compiler (javac.exe) should spend a few moments compiling your program, and then return the command prompt cursor to you. If no message is displayed, that means everything went okay. You should then find a new file in the folder called DrinkJava.class. You can see the list of files by typing `dir` at the command prompt, or just open Windows Explorer to browse the folder graphically.

To run the newly compiled DrinkJava.class file, you use the java.exe program:

```
java DrinkJava
```

Note that I did not include the .class extension, which would have generated an error. Let Java worry about the extension on its own. By running this program, you should see a line output onto the command prompt like this:

```
Do you like to drink Java?
```

Without realizing it, what you have done here is create a Java "application." This is one of the two types of Java programs you can create. The other type is called an "applet," which describes a program that runs in a Web browser and is really the goal of what we want to do in order to create Java games. You can certainly write a Java game as an application and run it on a local system, but the real point of Java game programming is to create Web-based games.

The Appletizer Program

Now let's use JBuilder to create a Java applet that will run in a Web browser. JBuilder includes a number of standard project templates you can use for a new project, including applet projects.

Fire up JBuilder if it isn't already running. Open the File menu and select New. Note that I didn't ask you to select New Project, just New. The New Project option doesn't give you the selection of project templates that you need to create an applet. When you select New, you will get the Object Gallery dialog box, which is really just a list of project templates (see Figure 1.19).

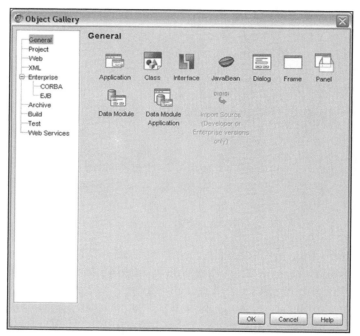

Figure 1.19 The Object Gallery dialog box displays the project templates available in JBuilder.

Take some time to browse the different types of project templates available in this dialog box. Note that if you are using JBuilder Foundation, not all of the project templates are available (such as those under Enterprise and Web Services, which are disabled). The template we want is under the Web list item. Selecting this presents a list of Web-based projects, and the only one that is visible (for JBuilder Foundation users) is Applet. This is just the one you want, so go ahead and select it (see Figure 1.20).

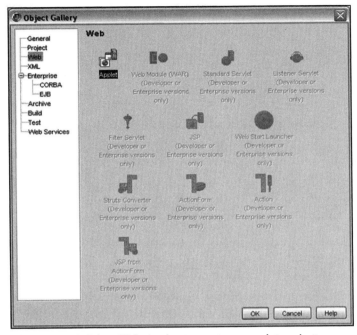

Figure 1.20 Select Web, Applet to create an applet project.

Creating the Project

There are two wizards that run when you create a new Java Applet project in JBuilder. The first wizard configures the project, where you specify the project folder, project name, JDK version, and so on. Here are the steps you'll want to follow:

1. First, type in the Project Name, Directory, and select Default Project for the Template field, as shown in Figure 1.21. Click Next.

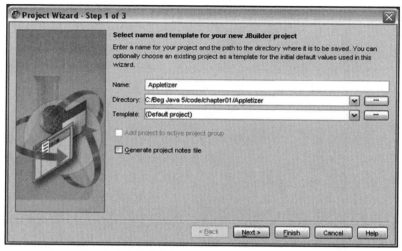

Figure 1.21 The Project Wizard, Step 1.

2. Next, select the JDK version you want to use, if it isn't already shown in the JDK field. You can leave the rest of the fields alone. See Figure 1.22. Click Next.

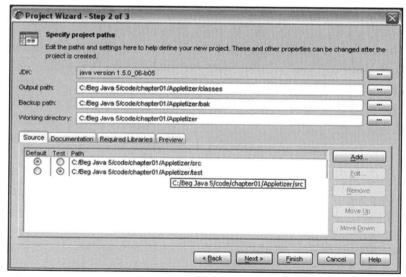

Figure 1.22 The Project Wizard, Step 2.

3. The next step (Step 3) contains optional information used by JavaDoc, and you can ignore it. Click Finish.

4. The project is then created, and the Applet Wizard comes up. Step 1 of 4 is shown in Figure 1.23. Note that I have named this project "Appletizer." The third field down is Base Class; note that java.applet.Applet is already filled in. The Applet class is the basis for a Java Applet program. Click Next.

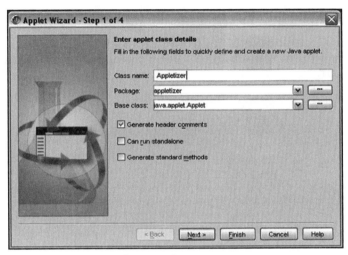

Figure 1.23 The Applet Wizard, Step 1.

5. Step 2 of the Applet Wizard comes up, allowing you to specify applet parameters (which are passed to the applet via the Web URL); skip it by clicking Next.

6. Step 3 of the Applet Wizard (shown in Figure 1.24) allows you to modify some of the properties of the applet, such as the width and height of the applet window and the alignment. The width and height are important things to consider when writing a game, and it's good to stick to a standard resolution like 640 x 480 or any reasonable size, as long as it is not too small or too large. I would never go over 800 x 600 for an applet, as it's very possible that it will not be rendered correctly in the Web browser of low-res users.

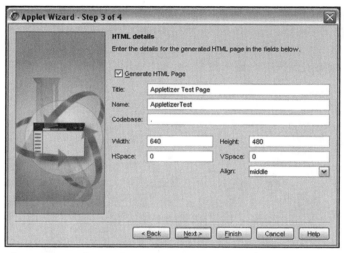

Figure 1.24 The Applet Wizard, Step 3.

7. You can click Finish at this point because you don't need to be concerned with Step 4, setting the runtime configuration. The Appletizer project is now ready for your handiwork (see Figure 1.25).

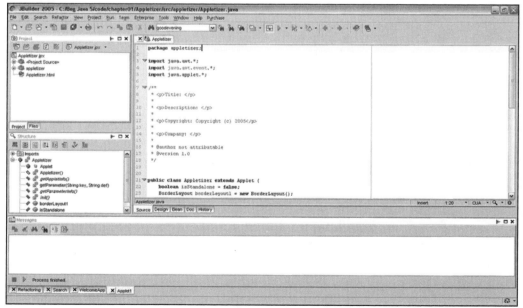

Figure 1.25 The new Java Applet project has been created and is ready to go.

Typing Some Source Code

This applet template is fully functional and includes a ready-to-use HTML Web page for testing the applet. JBuilder can also run the applet using an applet test program. Either method works just fine.

Let's type in some code to get this applet to do something useful, even if it is only to display a message. Scroll down to the bottom of the Appletizer.java source code file, and insert some code just before the final closing brace for the class. Type in the following code:

```
public void paint(Graphics g) {
    g.drawString("This is my first Java Applet!", 20, 30);
}
```

Figure 1.26 shows the final result of the code added to the Appletizer.java file.

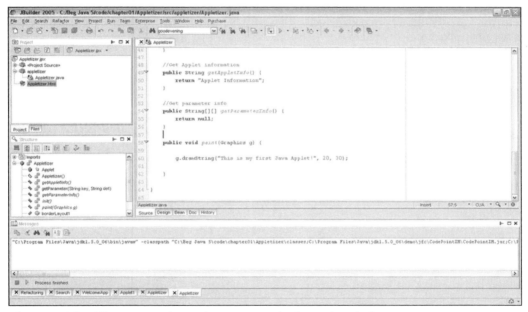

Figure 1.26 Adding some code to print a message in the applet window.

Running the Program

Now let's run the program. You can press F9 or click the Run Project icon on the toolbar (looks like a green arrow). JBuilder will compile the source code and run the applet in JBuilder's applet viewer as a standalone window, shown in Figure 1.27.

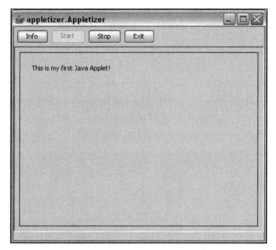

Figure 1.27 The applet is running in a standalone applet viewer window.

If you want to compile the program to check for errors before you try to run it, you have that option as well—by pressing Ctrl+F9 or by going through the Project menu for a list of build options.

Another alternative to the applet viewer is to use the Appletizer.html file that the Project Wizard created automatically for you. The file is shown in the Project manager window on the left side of the JBuilder interface. Right-click the Appletizer.html file, and select Run Using Appletizer from the pop-up menu. This will parse the html file and open the applet using the Java Applet Viewer, as shown in Figure 1.28.

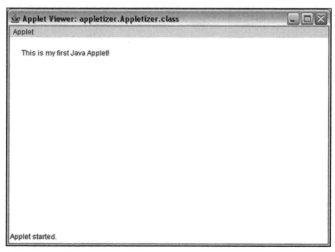

Figure 1.28 The applet is running in the Java Applet Viewer.

Finally, there is a third way to test your applet. Using Windows Explorer, locate the folder containing your project. Then look inside the class folder that JBuilder created for the Appletizer.html file, and open it to invoke Internet Explorer, Mozilla FireFox, or whatever browser you are using.

What You Have Learned

Well, this has been a pretty heavy chapter that covered a lot of material, but my goal was to get the basics covered so that we can jump right into Java game programming in the next chapter. You learned about:

- Casual games, what they are, and their importance
- The Java Development Kit (JDK) and Java versions
- JBuilder Foundation
- Standalone Java application and Java applets

Review Questions

The following questions will help you to determine how well you have learned the subjects discussed in this chapter.

1. What does the acronym "JDK" stand for?
2. What version of the JDK are we focusing on in this book?
3. What is the name of the company that created JBuilder?
4. Where on the Web will you find the free version of JBuilder 2005?
5. What is the free version of JBuilder called?
6. Where on the Web is the primary download site for the JDK?
7. What type of Java program do you run with the java.exe tool?
8. What type of Java program runs in a Web browser?
9. What is the name of the command-line tool used to run a Web-based Java program?
10. What is the name of the parameter passed to the paint() event method?

On Your Own

1. Modify the Appletizer program so that it displays your own message on the screen below the current message.
2. See if you can figure out where System.out.println output goes when run from an applet project, since the text is not displayed in the applet window.

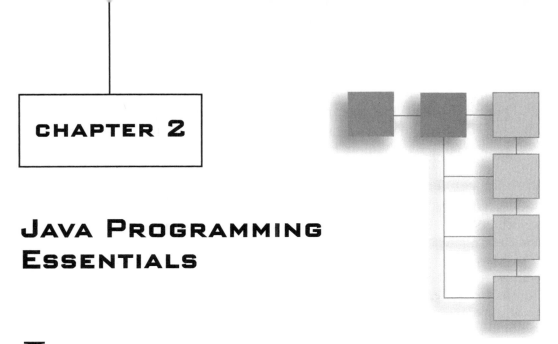

CHAPTER 2

JAVA PROGRAMMING ESSENTIALS

Java is a mature programming language today, offering a diverse set of features and capabilities that make it popular on many different computer systems. Java is used the most on Linux server machines and mainframes, but a lot of programmers enjoy using Linux as a regular operating system for their PCs—and Java is often their development tool of choice. If you are just getting started as a Java programmer, then this chapter will help you gain some familiarity with the Java language. You will learn most of the basics in this chapter that you will need to get through all of the remaining chapters. There is a lot more to the Java language than what you will learn about in this chapter—and in the book in general—but rest assured, you will learn enough in this chapter to write your own Web-based games.

Here are some of the things you will learn in this chapter:

- Writing Java code using applets
- How to use the Java data types
- The basics of object-oriented programming
- Writing Java classes

Java Applets

There are two different types of programs you can compile with Java: an application or an applet. A Java application is a program compiled to run on a computer as a standalone application (hence, the name). A Java applet, on the other hand, is compiled specifically to run in a Web browser. Java applications are usually written to run as server programs, while applets run as client programs in a networked environment.

For example, Java Web Server (JWS) is a Java application that hosts Web page files to a Web browser (such as Internet Explorer or Mozilla FireFox), and it is comparable to Microsoft's Internet Information Server (IIS) Web server and the open-source Apache Web server.

Web Server Technology Explained

The main difference is that Microsoft's Web server (IIS) and the Apache Web server were written in C++, while JWS was written in Java. JWS can host regular HTML Web pages and custom Java Server Pages (JSP), which are custom Web server programs written in Java. A Java applet is different: an applet is a client-side program that runs entirely in the Web browser, not on the Web server. A Java Server Pages application literally runs on the Web server and sends content to the Web browser, while an applet runs only in the Web browser. For this reason, we say that server programs run on the "back end," while applets run on the "front end."

Microsoft's IIS Web server has gained in popularity and market share in recent years thanks in part to the new .NET ("dot net") technology. The latest version of IIS hosts Active Server Pages .NET (ASP.NET) pages, which are similar to Java Server Pages (JSP) in concept; but ASP.NET pages are written in Visual Basic or C# (a new Microsoft language pronounced "see-sharp").

note

If you don't know much about Web servers and Web applications, don't worry, because we will not be focusing much attention on the subject in this book.

I built my personal Web site in ASP.NET (shown in Figure 2.1), and I've been updating this site for the last few years by adding new controls and features to it. The menu at the top was sourced from www.skmmenu.com; I like this ASP.NET menu control because it is based on XML data, so I can make changes to the menu without recompiling the web site.

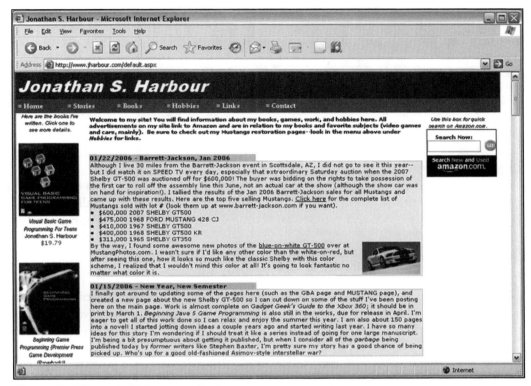

Figure 2.1 The main Web page at jharbour.com.

The content in the middle of the page is contained in a custom CollapsablePanel control sourced fromwww.eworldui.net, and all of the data is contained in an XML file; so when I want to modify the content of my page, I just edit the XML file. The book images on the left side of the page are provided by a custom control I wrote that communicates with Amazon.com's Web service; once I've plugged in a product's ISBN or ASIN into the control, it is automatically updated because the data is all brought over from Amazon.com, including the book cover images. Furthermore, clicking on a book brings up another custom control I developed (see Figure 2.2) that displays details, such as the publisher, average customer rating, release date, and even reviews.

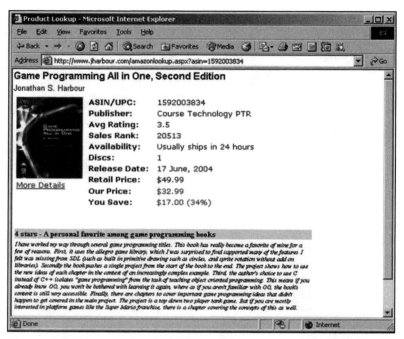

Figure 2.2 This custom control displays information about a specific book with information drawn from Amazon.com's free Web service.

tip

You can build Java Web services that are hosted on a Web server to provide data to Web sites using the Enterprise Edition of Borland JBuilder 2005 or 2006. This is just one of the many enterprise-level application development features available. For more information, visit www.borland.com.

I prefer ASP.NET over traditional HTML or PHP for my Web site because I spent several years building ASP.NET database applications and Web sites, and also because I teach several courses in .NET development at UAT, so it is something I do well. You might prefer to create a Web site entirely with Java or Flash or PHP; it's a matter of what you do well, and when you are good at something, you will tend to enjoy doing it.

Hosting Java Applets

If you really find that you enjoy Java after reading this book (or *while* reading it), then you may come up with a plan to create your own Web site (or update your current Web site) using Java applets. You can build an entire Web site as one large applet, or you can embed many different applets inside a standard HTML page to enhance your Web site.

One of the strong suits of Java is that you don't need any special type of Web server in order to use Java on your Web site. Java has been around for about 10 years now, and Web browsers have been supporting Java for most of that time. Microsoft Internet Explorer and Mozilla FireFox (the two most popular browsers) both support the latest versions of Java, so you can put up a complete site or just small applets on any old Web server. A more recent technology like ASP.NET requires special support on the Web server in order to host ASP.NET Web pages. I can't just throw my jharbour.com site up on any Web server; it must support ASP.NET and the .NET framework.

The Java Language

Let's talk about the Java language itself for a while. I'm going to assume that you might have no experience with Java at all, and I will try to explain all of the code you need to write in order to create the games in later chapters. There are thousands of classes in Java, but we will only be using a few of them to build applets that will run in a Web browser. Now then, I suppose even a word like "class" might be a mystery if you are new to programming. Do you have any experience with the C or C++ languages? They are used synonymously quite often, which is incorrect because C and C++ are quite different languages. Java was based on the C++ language. The Sun Microsystems programmers who developed the Java specification created a language that is more of an evolution than something created. C++ is a powerful language, and it is used to build operating systems and advanced software, such as device drivers (for devices like your video card).

Java is innovative enough to be called a new language, but it was heavily influenced by C++. Java is significantly easier to program than C++. Java automatically handles memory management for you—all you do is allocate memory for new variables and objects, and then you don't really need to worry about freeing up the memory afterward. Java uses a technology called *garbage collection* to remove unused things from memory that your program no longer needs. To give you an analogy, in the realm of Java, you don't even need to carry the trash can out to the street for pickup because the garbage collector just picks up all the trash thrown about in your house. The garbage collector is sort of like a little robot that scurries about the house searching for trash to pick up. When you are done with your Chinese take-out, just pitch the container and your napkin, and the little trash robot will find it and clean it up for you.

There is a drawback to garbage collection: you can't tell it specifically *when* to pick up the trash (variables and objects that are no longer used), only that there is trash to be picked up. (This analogy follows the real-world metropolitan waste handlers fairly closely in my experience.)

Java is an easy language to learn because most of the complexity in C++ has not been brought over to this evolutionary language. For example, you can write your own classes (and then create objects in your programs using those classes), and the syntax of a Java class is very similar to a C++ class.

Java Data Types

I think it would be helpful now to go over the basic data types available in a Java program because you will be using these data types throughout the book (and presumably, for the rest of your programming career, should you choose to pursue work as a Java programmer).

Integer Numbers

Java supports many data types, but probably the most basic data type is the *integer*. Integers represent whole numbers, which are numbers that have no decimal point. Table 2.1 shows the different types of integers you can use and their attributes.

Table 2.1 Integer Data Types

Type	Size in Bits	Range
byte	8 bits	−128 to 127
short	16 bits	−32,768 to 32,767
int	32 bits	−2,147,483,648 to 2,147,483,647
long	64 bits	−9,223,372,036,854,775,808 to 9,223,372,036,854,775,807

Since Java programs can run on a wide variety of computer systems (this is called *cross-platform development*), you might be wondering if these data type values will be the same on every system. After all, a Java program can run on a little cell phone or it can run on a supercomputer like a Cray Red Storm system.

tip

For more information about supercomputers, I refer you to www.top500.org, which lists the top 500 supercomputers on the planet. The site's Top10 list is particularly interesting. At the time of this writing, the most powerful computer on the planet is IBM's BlueGene/L, which has 131,072 processors running in parallel to achieve a mind-numbing 280 trillion operations per second. This awesome machine (which was commissioned by the U.S. Department of Energy) is three times faster than the runner-up in the #2 spot.

Java gets around the irritating data type inconsistency in C and C++ by defining that data types will be exactly the same, regardless of the computer system the Java program is running on. It's the job of the Java Runtime Environment (JRE) to determine at runtime how the current computer system will handle the data types your Java program is trying to use, and it does this seamlessly behind the scenes.

Floating-Point Numbers

There are two data types available in Java for working with floating-point numbers. A floating-point represents a decimal value. The float data type stores a 32-bit single-precision number. The double data type stores a 64-bit double-precision number. Table 2.2 shows the specifics of these two data types.

Table 2.2 **Floating-Point Data Types**

Type	Size in Bits	Range
float	32 bits	1.4E-45 to 3.4028235E+38
double	64 bits	4.9E-324 to 1.7976931348623157E+308

The easiest way to determine the range for a numeric data type is to use the MIN_VALUE and MAX_VALUE properties of the base data type classes. Although we use lowercase to specify the type of a numeric variable (byte, short, int, long, float, and double), these base numeric types are actually instances of Java classes (Byte, Short, Integer, Long, Float, and Double). Therefore, we can take a peek inside these base classes to find some goodies. The MIN_VALUE and MAX_VALUE properties will give you the range of values for a particular data type.

I have written a program called DataTypes that displays these values in an applet window. The output is shown in Figure 2.3 and the source code listing follows. This program is on the CD-ROM in the \sources\chapter02\DataTypes folder.

Figure 2.3 The DataTypes program displays the range for each numeric data type.

```
import java.awt.*;
import java.applet.*;
public class DataTypes extends Applet {
    //paint on the applet window
    public void paint(Graphics g) {
        //select a nice font
        g.setFont(new Font("Courier New", Font.PLAIN, 12));

        //display minimum and maximum values for numeric data types
        g.drawString("Byte   : " + Byte.MIN_VALUE + " to "
            + Byte.MAX_VALUE, 5, 20);
        g.drawString("Short  : " + Short.MIN_VALUE + " to "
            + Short.MAX_VALUE, 5, 35);
        g.drawString("Int    : " + Integer.MIN_VALUE + " to "
            + Integer.MAX_VALUE, 5, 50);
        g.drawString("Long   : " + Long.MIN_VALUE + " to "
            + Long.MAX_VALUE, 5, 65);
        g.drawString("Float  : " + Float.MIN_VALUE + " to "
            + Float.MAX_VALUE, 5, 80);
        g.drawString("Double : " + Double.MIN_VALUE + " to "
            + Double.MAX_VALUE, 5, 95);
    }
}
```

Characters and Strings

There are two data types in Java for working with characters data: char and String. Note that char is a base data type, while String is automatically recognizable as a class (due to the uppercase first letter). Java tries to make programming easy for C++ programmers by using many of the same basic data types in order to make it easier to convert C and C++ programs to Java. So we have a base char and a String class; of course, as you now know, every data type in Java is a class already.

You define a char variable like this:

```
char studentgrade;
char examscore = 'A';
```

The char data type can only handle a single character, not an entire string. Note that a character is identified with single quotes ('A') rather than double quotes, necessary for strings.

The String data type (or rather, class) is very easy to use and is used by many of the Java library methods (remember, a method is a function). For instance, you have seen a lot of the Graphics class so far in this chapter because it is the main way to display things (like text) in an applet window. Here are a couple of different ways to create a string:

```
String favoritegame = "Sid Meier's Civilization IV";
String username;
username = "John" + " R. " + "Doe";
```

In addition to supporting the plus operator for combining strings (something that C programmers look upon with envy), the String class also comes equipped with numerous support methods for manipulating strings as well. I won't go over every property and method in the String class here because that is the role of a Java reference book, to cover every single detail.

tip

If you are enjoying Java so far and think you will stick with it, you will definitely need a good Java language reference book. I recommend Herbert Schildt's *Java: The Complete Reference, J2SE 5 Edition* (McGraw-Hill Osborne Media, 2004).

One good example of a function we've been using in this chapter is Graphics.drawString. This function has many overloaded versions available (overloading is explained later in this chapter in the section, "Object-Oriented Programming") that give you a lot of options for printing text to the applet window, but the main version I use is this:

```
drawString(String str, int x, int y)
```

note

We have just scratched the surface of the Graphics class (and the Graphics2D inherited class). This will be the focus of most of Part II, covering Chapters 6 through 12. You will learn about class inheritance later in this chapter.

Table 2.3 lists just *some* of the useful methods in the String class. This is by no means a complete list.

Table 2.3 String Class Methods

Method	Description
contains	Returns true if one string is contained in another string
endsWith	Returns true if the string ends with a certain string
equalsIgnoreCase	Compares strings without considering upper or lower case
length	Returns the length of the string
replace	Replaces all occurrences of a sub-string with another sub-string in a string
trim	Removes blank spaces from the start and end of a string

If you want to see all of the properties and methods in a class (such as String), the easiest way to get a list, aside from using a reference book, is to create an instance of a class (such as String s) and then use the dot operator (.) to cause JBuilder to bring up the contents of the class. This built-in "look" feature works with the Java language classes as well as classes you have written yourself, as shown in Figure 2.4.

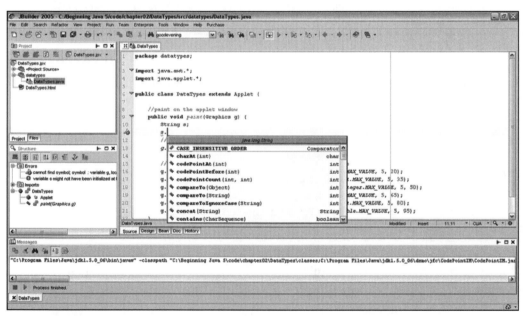

Figure 2.4 JBuilder displays the contents of a class with a pop-up window.

Booleans

The boolean data type can be set to either *true* or *false*, and it is useful as a return value for methods. For instance, in some of the example programs you've seen so far, there have been methods that returned a boolean based on whether the code succeeded or not. You can declare a boolean variable like so:

```
boolean gameover = false;
```

Here is a short method that returns a boolean value based on whether a value is within a boundary of a minimum and maximum value:

```
public boolean checkBounds(long val, long lower, long upper) {
    if (val < lower || val > upper)
        return false;
    else
        return true;
}
```

Here is an example of using the checkBounds method to determine whether a sprite's position on the screen (in the horizontal orientation) is within the screen's boundary:

```
spriteX = spriteX + 1;
if (checkBounds(spriteX, 0, 639) == true)
    spriteX = 0;
```

This short example assumes that the spriteX variable has already been declared earlier in the program. The sprite's X position on the screen will wrap around to the left edge any time the sprite moves off the right edge of the screen. This boolean method can also be written like this, where the == true is assumed in the if statement:

```
if (checkBounds(spriteX, 0, 639)) ...
```

Note that I have left out the == true in this line of code. This is possible because Java evaluates the return value of the checkBounds method and replaces the method call with the return value when the program is running. Thus if the checkBounds method returns true, the if statement becomes this:

```
if (true) ...
```

This is why we can leave the == true out of the equation. On the converse, when you want to test for a false return value, you can insert == false in the if statement, or you can use the logical negative operator (!) in the statement:

```
if (!checkBounds(spriteX, 0, 639)) ...
```

The result is that if checkBounds returns false, the if statement will execute the code that follows, otherwise the code is not executed. Speaking of which, you may include a single line of code after an if statement, or you may include a code block enclosed in curly braces as follows. This is especially helpful if you want to do more than one thing after a conditional statement returns true or false:

```
public boolean checkBounds(long val, long lower, long upper) {
    if (val < lower || val > upper) {
        ...
        return false;
    } else {
        ...
        return true;
    }
}
```

The use of curly braces in this new version of checkBounds might not change anything, but it does allow you to add more lines of code before each of the return statements (for instance, you may want to display a message on the screen before returning).

note

As the Introduction to the book disclaimed, this is not a comprehensive Java programming book—it is a book dedicated to *Java game programming*. There are not nearly enough pages in this book to provide a comprehensive reference to the Java language. (There are 1000+ page books on the language alone!) In general, I must assume that you have at least *some* Java programming experience.

If you have none whatsoever, I'll repeat here what I mentioned in the Introduction: this book is *not* an introduction to the Java language for a complete novice. We have a lot of game programming material to cover as it is! Please refer to Appendix B, "Recommended Books and Web Sites," for a list of recommended Java primers and reference books.

I will do my best to explain all of the *key* classes, properties, and methods you will need as we come to them, but I will not provide an exhaustive treatment of every nuance of the Java language.

This chapter should provide you with the basics to at least get you through the book without being *completely* lost.

Arrays

An *array* is a collection of variables of a specific data type that are organized in a manageable container. That's the most descriptive definition I can come up with, but I'm sure Herbert Schildt has a more academic definition for an array in his masterful reference book!

An array is created using one of the base data types, a Java library class, or one of your own classes. To tell Java that you want an array, attach brackets to the data type in your variable declaration:

```
int[] highScoreList;
```

But there are *two* steps to creating an array because an array must first be defined and *then* memory must be allocated for it. First, you define the data type and array variable name, then allocate the array by specifying the number of elements in the array with the new operator:

```
int[] studentGrades;
studentGrades = new int[30];
```

Note that I have allocated enough memory for this array to hold 30 elements in the studentGrades array. You can also define a new array with a single line of code:

```
int[] studentGrades = new int[30];
```

I don't know about you, but I get an endorphin high from writing beautiful code like this. Am I just weird, or is that a really cool way to create an array? I get a chill when writing code like this because my imagination starts to take off with visions of scrolling backgrounds and spaceships and bullets and explosions, all of which are made possible with arrays.

But the real power of an array is made obvious when you start iterating through an array with a loop. If you need to update the values of this array, you might access the array elements individually like this:

```
studentGrades[0] = 90;
. . .
studentGrades[29] = 100;
```

tip

> By the time you get to Chapter 10, arrays will be obsolete because the *Galactic War* example game will have become too complex for this construct. Instead, we'll explore how to use a *linked list* to manage the game's complexity.

If you truly need to set each element in an array individually, then an array can still help to cut down on the clutter in your program. And an array will always benefit from processing in a loop when it comes to things like printing out the contents of the array or storing it in a data file, or any other purpose you may have for the array. Let's set all of the elements in an array to a starting value of zero (this is good programming practice):

```
long[] speed = new long[100];
for (int i = 0; i < 100; i++) {
    speed[i] = 0;
}
```

There is another way to create an array by setting the initial values of the array right at the definition. This array of five floats is defined and initialized in memory with starting values at the same time.

```
float[] radioStations = { 88.5, 91.3, 97.7, 101.5, 103.0 };
```

You can also create multi-dimensional arrays. An array with more than one dimension will have a multiplicative number of elements (based on the number of elements in each dimension) because for every one element in the first dimension there are N elements in the next dimension (based on the size of the next dimension). In my own experience writing games, I seldom use more than one dimension for an array because it is possible (and more efficient) to use a single-dimensioned array, and then index into it creatively to deal with multiple dimensions.

Here is an example two-dimensional array that stores the values for a game level. The pound characters (#) represent walls (or any other object you want in your game) while the periods (.) represent dirt, or grass, or any other type of image. I presume that this is a level for a tile-based game, where each character in the array is drawn to the screen as a tile from a bitmap file.

```
char[][] gameLevel = {
    {'#','#','#','#','#','#','#','#','#','#'},
    {'#','.','.','.','.','.','.','.','.','#'},
    {'#','.','.','.','.','.','.','.','.','#'},
    {'#','.','.','.','.','.','.','.','.','#'},
    {'#','.','.','.','.','.','.','.','.','#'},
    {'#','.','.','.','.','.','.','.','.','#'},
    {'#','#','#','#','#','#','#','#','#','#'}
};
```

Another common practice is to create a game level with just numbers (such as 0 to 9). Some programmers prefer to use character-based levels because they sort of *look* more like a game level, and are, therefore, easier to edit. I tend to prefer integer-based game levels because I am a big fan of a level editing program called Mappy, which exports levels as a comma-delimited array of numbers. Here is how Mappy might export the same level with numeric data:

```
2, 2, 2, 2, 2, 2, 2, 2, 2, 2,
2, 1, 1, 1, 1, 1, 1, 1, 1, 2,
2, 1, 1, 1, 1, 1, 1, 1, 1, 2,
2, 1, 1, 1, 1, 1, 1, 1, 1, 2,
2, 1, 1, 1, 1, 1, 1, 1, 1, 2,
2, 1, 1, 1, 1, 1, 1, 1, 1, 2,
2, 2, 2, 2, 2, 2, 2, 2, 2, 2
```

tip

Mappy has been included on the book's CD-ROM. Look in the \software\Mappy folder. You can find out more information about this great level-editing tool at www.tilemap.co.uk.

Can you make out the similarity between the two game levels shown here? It's all the same data, just represented differently. When Mappy exports a level like this, it sends the data to a text file that you can then open and paste into your game's source code. To make it work, you would define an array to handle the data like this:

```
int[][] gameLevel = {
    {2, 2, 2, 2, 2, 2, 2, 2, 2, 2},
    {2, 1, 1, 1, 1, 1, 1, 1, 1, 2},
    {2, 1, 1, 1, 1, 1, 1, 1, 1, 2},
    {2, 1, 1, 1, 1, 1, 1, 1, 1, 2},
    {2, 1, 1, 1, 1, 1, 1, 1, 1, 2},
    {2, 1, 1, 1, 1, 1, 1, 1, 1, 2},
    {2, 2, 2, 2, 2, 2, 2, 2, 2, 2}
};
```

tip

Don't forget the semicolon at the end of an array declaration, or you will get some very strange errors from the Java compiler.

However, I prefer to treat a game level (or other array-based data sequence) as a single-dimensioned array because data like this is easier to work with as a 1-D array. Here is how I would define it:

```
int[] gameLevel = {
    2, 2, 2, 2, 2, 2, 2, 2, 2, 2,
    2, 1, 1, 1, 1, 1, 1, 1, 1, 2,
    2, 1, 1, 1, 1, 1, 1, 1, 1, 2,
    2, 1, 1, 1, 1, 1, 1, 1, 1, 2,
    2, 1, 1, 1, 1, 1, 1, 1, 1, 2,
    2, 1, 1, 1, 1, 1, 1, 1, 1, 2,
    2, 2, 2, 2, 2, 2, 2, 2, 2, 2
};
```

Do you see the subtle difference between this 1-D array and the 2-D array defined before? All I need to know is the width and height of the array data, and then I don't need multiple dimensions. In this example, this game level is 10 tiles wide and 10 tiles deep, for a total of 100 tiles. (A tile is a small bitmap used to build a game world in a 2-D scrolling game, and it very closely resembles the analogy of floor tiles in the way they are used.)

The Essence of Class

In case you haven't noticed, I've been talking about "classes" a lot. That's because you can't really get around the subject when writing a Java program. The main part of a Java source code file itself is a class. You might have seen a C program before and might already be familiar with the main() function. Here is a simple C program:

```
int main(int argc, char argv[]) {
    printf("I am a C program.\n");
    return 0;
}
```

Let's take a look at the same program written in pure C++:

```
#include <iostream>
using namespace std;
int main(int argc, char argv[]) {
    cout << "I am a C++ program." << endl;
    return 0;
}
```

Now take a look at the same program written in Java:

```
import java.io.*;
public class SampleJava {
    public static void main(String args[]) {
        System.out.println("I am a Java program.");
    }
}
```

Do you see any similarities among these programs? You should because they are listed in evolutionary order. Now I don't want to get into an argument with anyone about whether Java is truly an evolutionary leap ahead of C++ because I'm not sure if I believe that in the strictest sense (with a feature comparison). But I do like to think of Java as the next logical step above C++; it is easier, less prone to error, but not as powerful. Doesn't that describe any system that tends to evolve over time? Take the computer industry itself, for instance. The earliest computers were built with thousands of vacuum tubes which were difficult to maintain and very prone to error; and as far as power consumption goes, I think the computers of old were definitely more powerful than the computers we commonly use today—but let's not talk about performance, which is no contest.

The C program is quite simple and maybe even readable by a non-programmer (who may not understand anything other than the `printf` line, and even then with much confusion). The C++ program is so much gobbledygook to anyone but a programmer. But those of us with a C++ background often describe C++ code as beautiful and elegant, with a powerful, perhaps even *intimidating* lure. The Java program is very similar to the C and C++ programs. Like the C++ program, the Java program must "get something" from "somewhere else" in the form of the `import java.io.*` statement. This java.io is a library that provides access to the `System.out` class, which is used for printing out text (as you probably guessed). But the biggest difference is that the Java program is located inside a class. This class is called `SampleJava`, and inside this class (enclosed with curly braces) is a main function very similar to the main functions found in the C and C++ program.

What is this `SampleJava` class, you may ask? The truth is, *everything* in Java is a class, and it is not possible to do anything useful in Java without using a class. All source code that you write in Java will be enclosed inside a class definition.

The main Function

The core of a Java application is the `main` function (note that applets typically don't have a `main` function, as I'll explain shortly). The `main` function has this basic format:

```
public static void main(String args[]) {
}
```

The parameter (`String args[]`) allows you to pass information to the Java program, and is only practical when developing a Java application (rather than an applet), to which you *can* pass parameters, presumably from a command prompt or shell. You can pass parameters to a Java applet, but that is not done very often. I once worked for a company that built vehicle tracking systems using GPS (global positioning system), and my job was to maintain the Java program that displayed a map with all the vehicles in the state of Arizona moving along their routes. This Java program received vehicle tracking information from a server, and then displayed it in an applet.

caution

Java applets typically don't use a `main` function because there are several *events* that are used in an applet instead (such as `init` and `paint`).

Let's dissect the `main` function to help you better understand what it does. The term `public` specifies that this function is visible outside the class (remember, every Java program runs inside a class). The `static` term specifies that the function definition never changes and is not to be inherited (borrowed for use in another function). The `static` keyword is optional and not often used in an applet. The `void` term means that the function does not return a value. Every Java application you write will have a `main` function, just like every C and C++ program. However, a Java applet, which runs in a Web browser, contains events instead and is not in complete control in the same way that a standalone Java application (with a main method) is.

However, you *can* write Java classes that *don't* have a `main` function. Why would you want to do that? A class is usually created to perform a specific task, such as the handling of sprites in a game. You might write a sprite class that knows how to load a bitmap file and draw a sprite on the screen; then the main Java program (with the `main` function) will *consume* or use the sprite class, which itself has no `main` function. A class has its own variables and functions, some of which are hidden inside the class itself and invisible outside the class. What I'm describing here are some of the key aspects of object-oriented programming, or OOP. In some cases, as when developing an applet, you may just use the `paint` event rather than use a `main` function (more on that later).

Object-Oriented Programming

There are four main concepts involved in OOP, though you may not use all of them in every class you write:

- Data hiding
- Encapsulation
- Inheritance
- Polymorphism

I'll briefly talk about each of these concepts because you will be dealing with these throughout the book. I don't spend a lot of time discussing advanced concepts like these while writing Java games, and this book is not intended as a primer on the Java language. Hundreds of books have been written about Java programming, including some very complex textbooks on the subject used in college courses. I refer you to Appendix B for a good primer on the Java language that will provide a more thorough tutorial.

Data Hiding

Data hiding is a key concept of OOP because it provides a way to protect data within an object at runtime from direct manipulation. Instead of providing access to certain pieces of data, a class definition will include functions (often called *methods* or *accessors/mutators* in OOP lore) for retrieving and changing data (often called *properties*) that is hidden within the class definition. An accessor function retrieves a hidden variable; a mutator changes a hidden variable.

This way, the programmer can specify exactly what changes can be made to a private variable through the built-in mutator functions and return custom-formatted data through the accessor functions. For instance, if you want to make sure that a birth date is valid, the mutator function can restrict changes to a certain range (such as 0 to 120). The following source code demonstrates the concept of data hiding. I have intentionally kept the code listing simpler by not including any comments.

```java
public class vehicle {
    private String make;
    private int numwheels;

    public String getMake() {
        return make;
    }
    public boolean setMake(String newmake) {
        if (newmake.length() > 0) {
            make = newmake;
            return true;
        } else {
            return false;
        }
    }


    public int getNumWheels() {
        return numwheels;
    }
    public boolean setNumWheels(int count) {
        if (count > 0 && count < 20) {
            numwheels = count;
            return true;
        } else {
            return false;
        }
    }
}
```

Encapsulation

Encapsulation is related to data hiding in that it describes how information and processes are both handled internally by a class. These two concepts are often used interchangeably, depending on the opinion of the programmer. (I prefer to use the term encapsulation rather than data hiding.) I would suggest that encapsulation involves modeling a real-world entity, while data hiding describes the ability to use private variables in a class. It's common to encapsulate a real-world entity by writing a class that describes the data and functions for working with that data. In the vehicle class example, I have encapsulated the specifications for a basic vehicle inside a class with hidden (or private) data members and public functions (or methods).

Inheritance

Inheritance describes the ability to reuse class definitions and to make changes to a sub-class that relies on a base class. For instance, the vehicle class might be used as a basis for many sub-classes covering a wide range of vehicles, from two-wheel motorcycles to 18-wheel semi trucks. When you are writing the code for a class, it is best to put each class inside its own source code file. Java allows us to inherit from a single base class.

note

Although C++ allows us to inherit from multiple base classes, this feature often causes more problems than it solves, so it is seldom used. Instead of multiple inheritance, Java allows us to use multiple interfaces—which are guidelines for the properties and methods that should be found within a particular class.

For instance, the SimpleClass program in \sources\chapter02 on the CD-ROM includes the source code listing for the vehicle class, and it is stored in a file called vehicle.java. Also included in the SimpleClass project is the main source code file called SimpleClass.java—and this file "consumes" or uses the vehicle class defined in the vehicle.java file. Additional classes can be written and saved in their own source files.

To add a new class to your project, just open the File menu and select New Class. It's as simple as that. Let's take a look at the steps involved in creating a new class for the SimpleClass project. Figure 2.5 shows the Class Wizard dialog box that appears when you choose File, New Class. For the Class Name field, I have typed in "truck," and for the Base Class field I have typed "vehicle." This will cause my new truck class to inherit any public properties or methods from the vehicle class.

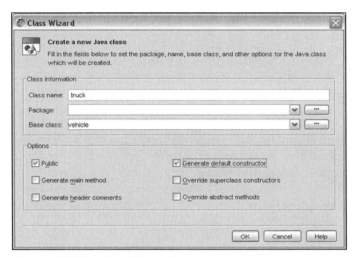

Figure 2.5 The Class Wizard dialog box.

As far as options go, I have selected Public and Generate Default Constructor but none of the other options. This second option requires a little explanation. A constructor is a function (method) that is called on whenever you create a new class in your program. I'm not talking about typing in a new class, but when a class is instantiated into an object at runtime. When a new class is created (with the `new` operator), the class definition is used to construct an object. See where the key word comes in here? The new object is "constructed" when it is being created at runtime; the class is a blueprint used to build or construct the object at runtime.

definition

Instantiate means to create, or to construct. Within the context of object-oriented programming, new objects are instantiated when they are created at runtime from the blueprint specified in a class definition (such as the `vehicle` class).

When I click the OK button on the Class Wizard dialog box, a new file is added to my project called truck.java, and it contains this source code:

```java
public class truck extends vehicle
{
    public truck()
    {
    }
}
```

This is a nice clean starting point for a new class. Note that this class inherits from the vehicle class (extends vehicle), and it includes a simple constructor (public truck()). This constructor is called whenever you use new to create a new truck object using code like this:

```
truck silverado = new truck();
```

The constructor is specified after the new operator in this line of code, and this is called an *empty constructor*. If you want to pass parameters to a constructor, you can do so by defining another version of the constructor, which is a topic that needs to be covered in the next section on polymorphism.

Polymorphism

Polymorphism is a complex word that, when broken down, equates to poly ("many") and morph ("shape"); therefore, polymorphism means "many shape" or "many shapes." Java allows you to write many versions of a function (or method) with different sets of parameters. When you write more than one version of a method, you have *overloaded* that method. Overloading is a technical programming term that describes polymorphism at work.

tip

I have been using the terms *function* and *method* together up to this point. I will refer to *method* from this point forward. Just note that a method is the same as a function, and this applies to accessor/mutator functions as well (terms that are commonly discussed among C++ programmers).

The complete truck class source code listing demonstrates polymorphism. Note the constructor, truck(), which has been overloaded once with an alternative version with the following syntax:

```
public truck(String make, String model, String engine, int towing)
```

You will probably not pass all of the data to a class in this manner all at once, as it is not usually very practical. You may pass any values to the constructor that you think will help with the initialization of the object that is being instantiated, but keep in mind that there are methods available for reading and changing those variables (or properties) as well.

Do you see how the default constructor includes several method calls to set the private variables to some initial values? This is a good practice to do when creating a class definition, as it eliminates the chance of a null-pointer runtime error from occurring—which is common when working with strings that have not yet been set to a value. I've decided not to include a string length check in the set functions to make the source code easier to read, but this sort of built-in error handling is a good idea.

```java
public class truck extends vehicle {
    private String model;
    private String engine;
    private int towingcapacity;

    public truck() {
        setMake("make");
        setNumWheels(4);
        setModel("model");
        setEngine("engine");
        setTowingCapacity(0);
    }

    public truck(String make, String model, String engine, int towing) {
        setMake(make);
        setModel(model);
        setEngine(engine);
        setTowingCapacity(towing);
    }

    public String getModel() {
        return model;
    }
    public void setModel(String newmodel) {
        model = newmodel;
    }

    public String getEngine() {
        return engine;
    }
    public void setEngine(String newengine) {
        engine = newengine;
    }

    public int getTowingCapacity() {
        return towingcapacity;
    }
    public void setTowingCapacity(int value) {
        towingcapacity = value;
    }
}
```

Now let's make some changes to the main source code in the SimpleClass.java file. This is the part of the program that consumes, or uses, the vehicle and truck classes. Here is the complete listing:

```java
import java.lang.*;
import java.applet.*;
import java.awt.*;

public class SimpleClass extends Applet {
    vehicle car;
    truck lightning;

    public void init() {
        //initialize a vehicle object
        car = new vehicle();
        car.setMake("Ford");
        car.setNumWheels(4);
        //initialize a truck object using a constructor
        lightning = new truck("Ford SVT", "F-150 Lightning", "5.4L Triton V8", 7700);
    }

    public void paint(Graphics g) {
        //let's use a nice big font
        g.setFont(new Font("Verdana", Font.BOLD, 12));

        //display the car info
        g.drawString("Car make: " + car.getMake(), 20, 20);
        g.drawString("Number of wheels: " + car.getNumWheels(), 20, 40);

        //display the truck info
        g.drawString("Truck make: " + lightning.getMake(), 20, 70);
        g.drawString("Truck model: " + lightning.getModel(), 20, 90);
        g.drawString("Truck engine: " + lightning.getEngine(), 20, 110);
        g.drawString("Truck towing capacity: " +
                        lightning.getTowingCapacity(), 20, 130);
    }
}
```

What is the most significant part of this program that might seem unusual or surprising? Well, take a look at those last few lines of code where the truck information is displayed on the screen. The truck is using a method called getMake() that is not even defined in the truck class; this is a method found only in the vehicle class, from which the truck class was inherited. That is the real power of inheritance, the ability to reuse functionality while enhancing existing classes.

I have added the truck class to the SimpleClass program, which is where the vehicle class may also be found. You can open the SimpleClass project from the CD-ROM in the \sources\chapter02 folder. Figure 2.6 shows the output from the current version of the program up to this point.

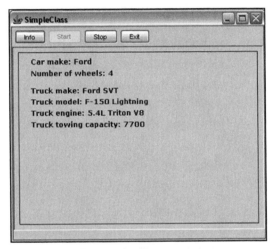

Figure 2.6 The SimpleClass program now demonstrates inheritance with the truck class.

What You Have Learned

This chapter provided an overview of the basics of Java programming. You learned about the differences between a Java application and a Java applet, and how to write programs of each type and then compile and run them. You learned the basics of object-oriented programming and many other Java programming issues that will be helpful in later chapters. Specifically, this chapter covered:

- How to write a Java application
- How to write a Java applet
- How to compile a Java program
- How to create a new project using Borland JBuilder

Review Questions

The following questions will help you to determine how well you have learned the subjects discussed in this chapter.

1. What is the name of the JDK tool used to compile Java programs?
2. Which JDK command-line tool is used to run a Java application?
3. Which JDK command-line tool is used to run a Java applet?
4. What version of Borland JBuilder did you learn about in this chapter?
5. Encapsulation, polymorphism, and inheritance are the keys to what programming methodology?
6. What's the main difference between a Java application and an applet?
7. Which method of the Graphics class can you use to print a text message on the screen?
8. How many bits make up a Java integer (the *int* data type)?
9. How many bits are there in a Java long integer (the *long* data type)?
10. What programming language was Java based on?

On Your Own

1. Write your own Java class and then use it to extend an inherited class to try out the concepts of inheritance and encapsulation.
2. Modify your new class by adding some methods that demonstrate the concept of polymorphism by writing several versions of the same method with different sets of parameters.

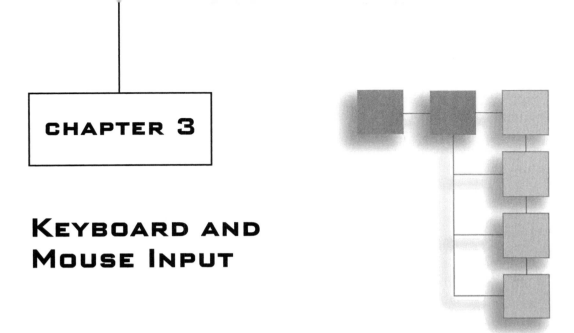

CHAPTER 3

KEYBOARD AND MOUSE INPUT

The keyboard and mouse are the only realistic devices for user input in a Web-based game developed as a Java applet. But even when considering a standard Windows-based game developed in DirectX or another library, the keyboard and mouse are by far the most common forms of user interaction with a game. This chapter covers the important subject of handling user input. Although we have only touched upon the graphics capabilities of Java and have not delved into 2-D programming in any depth yet, I think you will appreciate the value of covering user input at this point rather than putting it off for later. For one thing, when you have a solid understanding of user input right from the start, you are able to write example *games* rather than example graphics demos without any user interaction. I don't know about you, but I will take a playable game over a simple demo any day.

Here is what you will learn in this chapter:

- Listening for keyboard events
- Testing keyboard input
- Displaying key presses
- Reading mouse motion
- Detecting mouse buttons
- Testing mouse input

Listening to the User

Java provides an interesting way to interact with users through a series of *listener* methods. You tell Java that you would like to listen to keyboard input events, and then Java sends keyboard events to your own listener methods, at which point you can check the key codes to figure out which keys have been pressed or released. The way Java tells your program that a key has been pressed (or that the mouse has moved) is through an interface that your program uses—or rather, *implements*.

Your program must use the *implements* key word to use an interface class. This is a type of class that just includes methods your program needs to use (or implement); the class doesn't really have any functionality on its own. This type of class is called an *interface* because it represents a blueprint of the methods your program must use.

Keyboard Input

The `KeyListener` interface listens for events generated by the keyboard and sends those events to the callback methods implemented in your program. These methods are called `keyPressed`, `keyReleased`, and `keyTyped`, and these three methods all have a single parameter called `KeyEvent`.

When writing a program to use the `KeyListener`, you modify the class definition of your program using the `implements` key word:

```
public class KeyboardTest extends Applet implements KeyListener
```

tip

The interesting thing about the implements feature of Java classes is that you can implement multiple interfaces in your program by separating the interface class names with a comma.

Listening for Keyboard Events

Your program needs to then call the `addKeyListener` method to initialize the keyboard listener so that key events will be sent to your program by the Java Runtime Environment. The sole parameter of this method is the instance of your program's class, represented by the key word `this`. You use `this` as a way to identify the current class in a block of code without referring to that class specifically by name. It is usually best to call `addKeyListener(this)` in the init method within your program (recall that init is automatically called when your applet-based program starts running).

Next, you must implement the three keyboard events in your program to satisfy the `KeyListener` interface:

```
public void keyPressed(KeyEvent e)
public void keyReleased(KeyEvent e)
public void keyTyped(KeyEvent e)
```

There are two ways of determining the key that has been pressed or released using the KeyEvent parameter. If you want to determine the character code of a key, you can use the getKeyChar method which returns a char. If you want to know whether a key has been pressed based on the key code instead of the character, you can use the getKeyCode method instead. If your program is listening to the keyboard and you press the A key, then getKeyChar will return "a" (or "A" if you are holding down Shift) while getKeyCode will return a virtual key code called VK_A. All of the virtual key codes are contained in a class called KeyEvent. Table 3.1 shows a partial list of virtual key codes with the most commonly used keys for a game.

note

When you want to get the keys being typed for use in a chat message, for instance, then you will want to use the keyTyped event. Most of your game's input will come from the keyPressed event. For a listing of virtual key codes, highlight the KeyEvent class somewhere in your source code and press F1 to bring up a help file in JBuilder. This applies to all of the Java language classes and methods.

Table 3.1 Virtual Key Codes (Partial List)

Key Code	Description
VK_LEFT	Left arrow
VK_RIGHT	Right arrow
VK_UP	Up arrow
VK_DOWN	Down arrow
VK_0. . .VK_9	Numeric keys
VK_A. . .VK_Z	Alphabetic keys
VK_F1. . .VK_F12	Function keys
VK_KP_LEFT	Numeric keypad left
VK_KP_RIGHT	Numeric keypad right
VK_KP_UP	Numeric keypad up
VK_KP_DOWN	Numeric keypad down
VK_ENTER	Enter key
VK_BACK_SPACE	Backspace key
VK_TAB	Tab key

Testing Keyboard Input

Now let's write a program to test keyboard input so you will have a complete example of how this works with Java code. For the purpose of review, I'll go over the steps to create a Java Applet project in Borland JBuilder 2005 again (one last time). I understand that you may not even be using Windows, preferring to compile the Java code using the command-line tools. If you are a Linux or Mac user, you may still use JBuilder because Borland provides versions of the tool for those platforms. Feel free to skip this short tutorial if you are already familiar with compiling Java programs.

Creating the KeyboardTest Project

The blank interface of JBuilder 2005 is shown in Figure 3.1. This is your starting point for building new Java programs.

Figure 3.1 Borland JBuilder 2005 with an empty IDE.

Click the File menu and select New. If you have any open projects, go ahead and close them first because the New option brings up a different dialog if you already have a project open; you want to start with an empty IDE. The Object Gallery will appear when you select File, New, and this is shown in Figure 3.2.

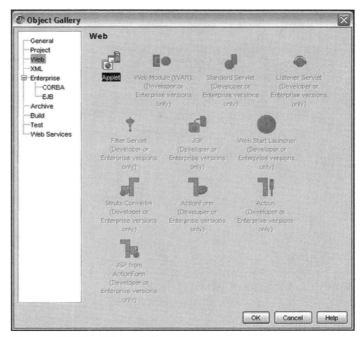

Figure 3.2 The Object Gallery dialog box.

The Object Gallery dialog box shows the different types of Java projects you can create. Some projects are not available with the Foundation edition of JBuilder, such as CORBA, Enterprise Java Beans (EJB), XML, Archive, and Web Services projects. These projects are available with the Developer or Enterprise editions of JBuilder. In fact, even the Web project category is very limited in JBuilder 2005 Foundation, with just a single project type available: Applet. Fortunately, that is the type of project we need, so go ahead and select the Applet project type.

The Project Wizard

The Project Wizard is where you enter the name of your new Java Applet project and specify the folder where the project will be saved. This dialog box is shown in Figure 3.3.

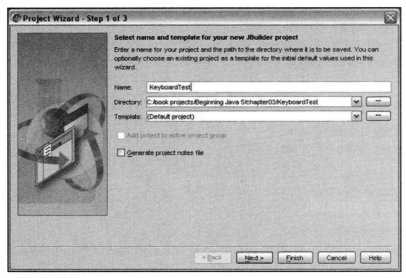

Figure 3.3 The Project Wizard dialog box.

Clicking Next brings up the next dialog box for the Project Wizard (Step 2). There is a problem with the project configuration on this dialog box, as shown in Figure 3.4.

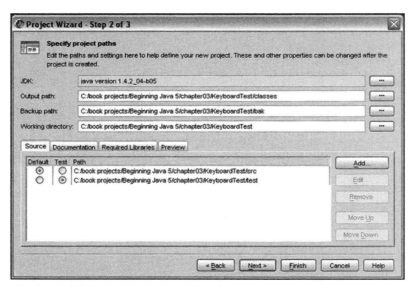

Figure 3.4 Step 2 of the Project Wizard.

Take a look at the JDK field: it shows "java version 1.4.2_04-b05." This is an old version of the Java Development Kit (JDK) that was packaged with JBuilder 2005. As you'll recall, you learned how to install the latest JDK back in Chapter 1, "Getting Started with Java 5." So, let's change it. Click the ellipsis (...) to the right of the field, and then choose the latest JDK you have installed, as shown in Figure 3.5. If you don't see a newer version of the JDK in this dialog, then return to Chapter 1 to learn how to add the JDK 1.5 to your project.

Figure 3.5 Selecting a different version of the JDK.

Next, verify that the correct JDK is now displayed in the JDK field of the Project Wizard dialog box. Your version may be different than the one shown in Figure 3.6, but the important thing is that you are using the JDK 1.5 (your revision will probably be different). You can click the Finish button at this point.

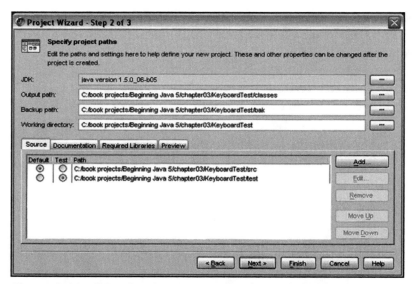

Figure 3.6 Verifying that the correct JDK has been selected for this new project.

The Applet Wizard

After the Project Wizard dialog box closes, another dialog box will appear to help you configure the project you have chosen to create. This new wizard will differ, depending on the type of project you have selected. In this instance, the Applet Wizard dialog box appears (see Figure 3.7). Give your new applet an appropriate name, and then click the Finish button. You don't need to change any of the other project default settings.

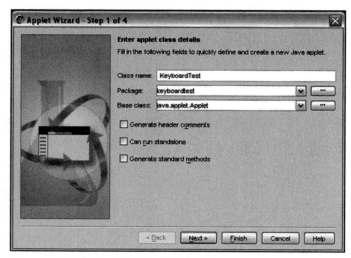

Figure 3.7 The Applet Wizard dialog box.

Writing Some Code

JBuilder provides a lot of code for a stock applet project, and you don't need some of the code JBuilder adds for you. For instance, there's a property called `isStandalone`, a `BorderLayout` class, and several methods (`getParameter`, `jbInit`, `getAppletInfo`, `getParameterInfo`, and the `KeyboardTest` constructor) that you don't need, so just delete that code. You might normally think that the `KeyboardTest` constructor would be useful, and often it is, but we have the applet's `init` event method that is called at the start of the program, and that will suffice. Speaking of which, go ahead and delete the code inside `init` as well. Your KeyboardTest project source code should resemble the following when you are done stripping out the unneeded portions.

```
package keyboardtest;

import java.awt.*;
import java.awt.event.*;
import java.applet.*;

public class KeyboardTest extends Applet {
    //Initialize the applet
    public void init() {
    }
}
```

The first line of the program is a package definition. This is an important aspect of Java programming when you are writing code that will be reused. For instance, if you build your own Java game engine using the code in this book, you might use a package called MyGameEngine or any name you like. JBuilder actually stores the source code file inside a folder called keyboardtest. This package name is completely optional, and actually adds some problems when loading media files (images, sounds, etc). So I recommend deleting the package name in the New Project dialog when creating new projects. This is the direction I'll be taking in future chapters, and the way the projects are configured on the CD-ROM.

tip

If you don't want to use a default package, you have the option of deleting the package name when you create a new project in JBuilder.

Now, let's add `KeyListener` support to our new KeyboardTest project. Modify the source code listing so it incorporates the `KeyListener` interface and related event methods as follows. I have highlighted the changes in bold.

```
package keyboardtest;

import java.awt.*;
import java.awt.event.*;
import java.applet.*;

public class KeyboardTest extends Applet implements KeyListener {

    //Initialize the applet
    public void init() {
        addKeyListener(this);
    }

    public void keyPressed(KeyEvent e) {
        int keyCode = e.getKeyCode();
        if(keyCode == KeyEvent.VK_LEFT) {
            //left arrow key was pressed
        }
    }
    public void keyReleased(KeyEvent e) {
    }
    public void keyTyped(KeyEvent e) {
        char keyChar = e.getKeyChar();
        switch(keyChar) {
            case 'a': {
                //'a' key was pressed
            }
        }
    }
}
```

This is the bare minimum code you need to provide keyboard support to your Java programs, so you might want to jot down this page number for future reference (or save the code in a file that you can easily find).

Displaying Key Presses

Now I'd like to modify the KeyboardTest program one more time to give you a functional program. You will be able to use this program to display the key code and character for every key press. You can then use this information in your own Java programs directly, or you can look up the virtual key codes in the KeyEvent class. I sometimes find it easier to just use the numeric key code as displayed by this program, but that makes the source code more difficult to read unless you include comments. For instance, the virtual key code for the left arrow is 37; but Java defines this key as VK_LEFT. Obviously, VK_LEFT is easier to read in source code.

tip
___
A virtual key code is a platform-neutral value for a key. When you write code to work with a certain virtual key code (such as VK_LEFT), you can be certain that the key will be detected on any platform (Windows, Linux, Mac, Solaris, etc).
___

The complete KeyboardTest program displays the key code and key character for each key press, as shown in Figure 3.8. Following is the listing for the completed KeyboardTest program that displays key code and character values in the applet window. I've highlighted important parts in bold.

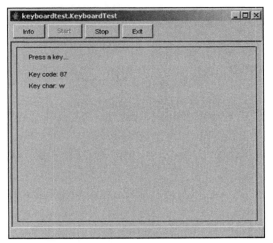

Figure 3.8 Output from the KeyboardTest program.

tip
___
The *init()* method is a special method in an applet that you will not find in a standalone Java program (i.e. an *application*). The init() method is the first thing that runs when an applet starts up. There are several other events in an applet, such as paint(), that I will explain as we go along. Suffice it to say, the paint() event refreshes the applet window, so this is often where programmers will write all of the code for a game.
___

```java
public class KeyboardTest extends Applet implements KeyListener {
    int keyCode;
    char keyChar;

    //Initialize the applet
    public void init() {
        addKeyListener(this);
    }

    public void paint(Graphics g) {
        g.drawString("Press a key...", 20, 20);
        g.drawString("Key code: " + keyCode, 20, 50);
        g.drawString("Key char: " + keyChar, 20, 70);
    }

    public void keyPressed(KeyEvent e) {
        keyCode = e.getKeyCode();
        keyChar = ' ';
        repaint();
    }

    public void keyReleased(KeyEvent e) {
    }

    public void keyTyped(KeyEvent e) {
        keyChar = e.getKeyChar();
        repaint();
    }
}
```

tip

I recommend you remember the steps involved in creating the KeyboardTest project because I will skip most of the steps from this point forward and just provide basic Java applet-based source code listings. Pausing to go through the new project creation steps tends to break the flow of the topic at hand, when a source code listing alone enhances a train of thought.

Mouse Input

Tapping into the mouse handler in Java is similar to the process of programming the keyboard, as you might have suspected. Java handles mouse input using events that are generated by the Java Runtime Environment (JRE) and passed to your program when you implement a mouse listener.

tip

The Java Runtime Environment, or JRE, is a subset of the Java Development Kit (JDK) that is designed to allow you to have access to an essential set of classes that you can use to run Java programs.

The first step you must take to incorporate mouse event handling in your program is to call two functions that will tell the JRE to begin sending your program mouse events. Since we'll be dealing with two interfaces for the mouse, you must initialize both mouse handlers. This is similar to the function you learned about for initializing the keyboard handler. You put these functions in the applet's init event method so that they are sure to be called when the program starts up. You'll recall from the keyboard section earlier in this chapter that the this key word represents the current program; in more technical terms, this represents the primary object that was created based on the main class definition in your program.

tip

An object is not a class, it is the result of a class. Think of a class as a blueprint for a product, and an object as the product itself that has been constructed.

```
public void init() {
    addMouseListener(this);
    addMouseMotionListener(this);
}
```

Reading Mouse Motion

Java provides an interface class for mouse motion and button press events that is similar to the keyboard interface. The MouseListener class is an *abstract* class that provides your program with an interface, or blueprint, with five methods that you must implement in your program (whether you will use all of them or not):

- public void mouseClicked(MouseEvent e)
- public void mouseEntered(MouseEvent e)
- public void mouseExited(MouseEvent e)
- public void mousePressed(MouseEvent e)
- public void mouseReleased(MouseEvent e)

The MouseListener interface keeps track of the mouse buttons, the mouse position in the applet window, and the mouse location when the mouse cursor moves *into* the applet window and *out of* the applet window.

There is another, completely different interface class for mouse *movement*. You can read the mouse's position during a button or enter/leave event with a MouseListener, but to receive events for actual mouse *motion* on the window requires another interface. To receive events for the mouse's movement across the applet window, you must use the MouseMotionListener interface. There are two events in this interface:

- public void mouseDragged(MouseEvent e)
- public void mouseMoved(MouseEvent e)

Detecting Mouse Buttons

Some of these events report when a mouse button is clicked, pressed, or released. The only methods that do not deal with the mouse buttons are mouseEntered, mouseExited, and mouseMoved, all of which deal with the mouse's position and motion, regardless of button status. The remaining events (mouseClicked, mousePressed, mouseReleased, and mouseDragged) all have to do with the buttons.

As you might have noticed, all of these events have a single parameter called MouseEvent. This parameter is actually a class, and the JRE fills it with information for each mouse event. You can look inside this class to get the mouse's position and button values. For the mouse's X and Y position values, you can use MouseEvent.getX() and MouseEvent.getY(). The parameter is usually defined as (MouseEvent e), so in actual practice you would use e.getX() and e.getY() to read the mouse's current position.

Likewise, MouseEvent tells you which button was pressed. Inside MouseEvent is a method called getButton() that will equal one of the following values depending on which button is being pressed:

- BUTTON1
- BUTTON2
- BUTTON3

The getButton() method is useful if you only care about detecting a single button press. If, for whatever reason, you need to know when two or three mouse buttons are being pressed at the same time, you can use a different method in the MouseEvent class called getModifiers(). This function will report multiple events in the MouseEvent class, such as the following:

- BUTTON1_MASK
- BUTTON2_MASK
- BUTTON3_MASK

There are many more masked values (that is, values that are bit-packed into a single variable) in the MouseEvent class that you can examine using the getModifiers() method. But if all you care about is the usual left-click and right-click events, you can make use of getButton().

Testing Mouse Input

I would like to show you a program called MouseTest that demonstrates all of the mouse events that you have just learned about. To build this program, you should create a new Web Applet project called MouseTest, and then remove all of the automatically generated code to be replaced with the following code listing instead. This program uses the Graphics class' drawString method and a bunch of variables to display the status of all the mouse events individually. Figure 3.9 shows what the program output looks like. Note the important parts of the code listing in bold.

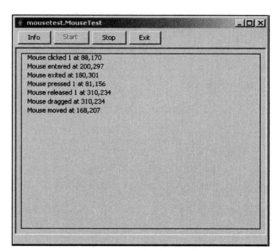

Figure 3.9 Output from the MouseTest program.

The first part of the program includes the applet's class definition (with the needed interfaces following the implements keyword) and variable declarations.

```
package mousetest;
import java.awt.*;
import java.awt.event.*;
import java.applet.*;

public class MouseTest extends Applet
        implements MouseListener, MouseMotionListener {

    //declare some mouse event variables
    int clickx, clicky;
    int pressx, pressy;
    int releasex, releasey;
    int enterx, entery;
    int exitx, exity;
    int dragx, dragy;
    int movex, movey;
    int mousebutton;
```

The init() event method is the first method that gets run in an applet. So this is where you would initialize your game objects and variables, and this is also where we add the listeners for any input devices the program needs to use. If your program ever seems to be ignoring the keyboard or mouse, check init() to make sure you have added the appropriate listener.

```
    //initialize the applet
    public void init() {
        addMouseListener(this);
        addMouseMotionListener(this);
    }
```

The paint() event method is called whenever the applet needs to refresh the window. Since paint() comes with a parameter (Graphics g), we can use this object to draw onto the screen. In this program, I've used the Graphics.drawString() method to display text on the applet window.

```
    //redraw the applet window
    public void paint(Graphics g) {
        g.drawString("Mouse clicked " + mousebutton + " at " +
            clickx + "," + clicky, 10, 10);
```

```
        g.drawString("Mouse entered at " + enterx + "," +
            entery, 10, 25);
        g.drawString("Mouse exited at " + exitx + "," + exity,
            10, 40);
        g.drawString("Mouse pressed " + mousebutton + " at " +
            pressx + "," + pressy, 10, 55);
        g.drawString("Mouse released " + mousebutton + " at " +
            releasex + "," + releasey, 10, 70);
        g.drawString("Mouse dragged at " + dragx + "," + dragy,
            10, 85);
        g.drawString("Mouse moved at " + movex + "," + movey,
            10, 100);
    }
```

The next portion of code includes the checkButton() method, which I have written to support the mouse event handler in the program. This checkButton() method checks the current button that is being pressed and sets a variable (mousebutton) to a value representing the pressed button.

```
    //custom method called by mouse events to report button status
    private void checkButton(MouseEvent e) {
            //check the mouse buttons
            switch(e.getButton()) {
            case MouseEvent.BUTTON1:
                mousebutton = 1;
                break;
            case MouseEvent.BUTTON2:
                mousebutton = 2;
                break;
            case MouseEvent.BUTTON3:
                mousebutton = 3;
                break;
            default:
                mousebutton = 0;
            }
    }
```

The mouseClicked() event is part of the MouseListener interface. When you implement this interface, you must include all of the mouse events defined in the interface or the compiler will generate some errors about the missing events. This event is called whenever you click the mouse button on the applet window—in which case both a press and release has occurred. This event is not usually needed when you program mousePressed() and mouseReleased() yourself.

```
public void mouseClicked(MouseEvent e) {
    //save the mouse position values
    clickx = e.getX();
    clicky = e.getY();

    //get an update on buttons
    checkButton(e);

    //refresh the screen (call the paint event)
    repaint();
}
```

The next two mouse event methods, mouseEntered() and mouseExited() are called whenever the mouse cursor enters or leaves the applet window. These events are not often needed in a game.

```
public void mouseEntered(MouseEvent e) {
    enterx = e.getX();
    entery = e.getY();
    repaint();
}
public void mouseExited(MouseEvent e) {
    exitx = e.getX();
    exity = e.getY();
    repaint();
}
```

The mousePressed() and mouseReleased() event methods are called whenever you click and release the mouse button, respectively. When these events occur, you can get the current position of the mouse as well as the button being pressed or released.

```
    public void mousePressed(MouseEvent e) {
        pressx = e.getX();
        pressy = e.getY();
        checkButton(e);
        repaint();
    }
    public void mouseReleased(MouseEvent e) {
        releasex = e.getX();
        releasey = e.getY();
        checkButton(e);
        repaint();
    }
```

The `MouseMotionListener` interface defines the next two events—mouseDragged() and mouseMoved(). These events are helpful when you just want to know when the mouse is moving over the applet window (and when it is moving while the button is being held down).

```
    public void mouseDragged(MouseEvent e) {
        dragx = e.getX();
        dragy = e.getY();
        repaint();
    }
    public void mouseMoved(MouseEvent e) {
        movex = e.getX();
        movey = e.getY();
        repaint();
    }
}
```

What You Have Learned

This chapter explained how to tap into the keyboard and mouse listeners in order to add user input to your Java programs.

- You learned how to detect key presses.
- You learned about key codes and character values.
- You learned how to read the mouse's motion and buttons.

Review Questions

The following questions will help you to determine how well you have learned the subjects discussed in this chapter. The answers are provided in Appendix A, "Chapter Quiz Answers."

1. What is the name of the method used to enable keyboard events in your program?
2. What is the name of the keyboard event interface?
3. What is the virtual key code for the Enter key?
4. Which keyboard event will tell you the code of a pressed key?
5. Which keyboard event will tell you when a key has been released?
6. Which keyboard event will tell you the character of a pressed key?
7. Which KeyEvent method returns a key code value?
8. What is the name of the method used to enable mouse motion events?
9. What is the name of the class used as a parameter for all mouse event methods?
10. Which mouse event reports the actual movement of the mouse?

On Your Own

Are you ready to put mouse and keyboard input to the test in a real game yet? These exercises will challenge your understanding of this chapter.

1. Modify the KeyboardTest program so that pressing numeric keys 1 to 9 will change the font size used to display the key code and character values. To do this, use the Graphics class in the paint event, which has a method called setFont that you can implement like this:

   ```
   g.setFont(new Font("Ariel", Font.NORMAL, value));
   ```

   I will give you a hint: the key code for "1" is 49, so you can subtract 40 from the key code to arrive at a good font size.

2. Modify the MouseTest program so that a point is drawn whenever the user presses a mouse button. You can use the Graphics class' fillRect method and the mouse position variables (just draw a rectangle with four corners that are one pixel apart). If you are feeling confident with your new Java programming skill, try using the setColor method to change the color of the points.

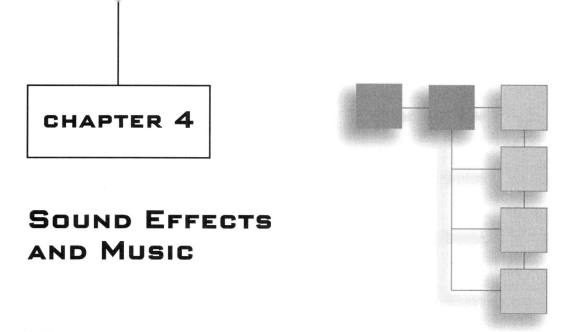

CHAPTER 4

SOUND EFFECTS AND MUSIC

Java has a rich set of features for recording, mixing, and playing sound samples and MIDI sequences using a variety of classes that you will learn about in this chapter. You will learn about Java's rich set of sound support classes for loading and playing audio files in a variety of formats through Java's sound mixer. You will then learn about MIDI files and how to load and play them through Java's MIDI sequencer. Here is a rundown on the key topics in this chapter:

Here is what you will learn in this chapter:

- Loading and playing audio files
- Loading and playing MIDI sequence files
- Writing some reusable audio classes

Playing Digital Sample Files

Java's Sound API provides a package for working with digital sample files, which has methods for loading a sample file (aiff, au, or wav) and playing it through the sound mixer. The package is called javax.sound.sampled and includes numerous classes, most of which we will ignore. Some of these classes provide support for recording sound and manipulating samples, so you could write a complete sound editing program that runs in a Web browser as an applet or just as a standalone Java application, with functionality that is similar to programs like Audacity, a freeware, open-source sound editor that is available for download at http://audacity.sourceforge.net (see Figure 4.1).

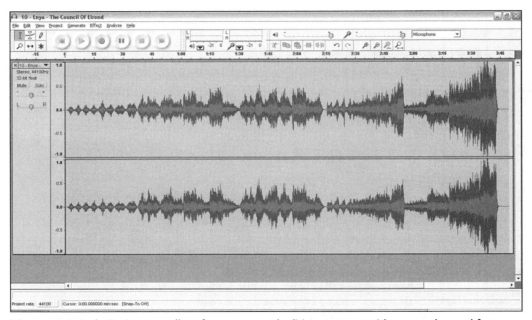

Figure 4.1 Audacity is an excellent freeware sound editing program with many advanced features.

The Java Sound API supports the three main audio file formats used in Web and desktop applications:

- AIFF
- AU
- WAV

The digital sample files can be 8-bit or 16-bit, with sample rates from 8 kHz to 48 kHz (which is CD quality). Java's Sound API includes a software sound mixer that supports up to 64 channels for both sound effects and background music for a Java applet.

tip

For the latest information about the Java Sound API, point your Web browser to http://java.sun.com/products/java-media/sound/.

Getting Started with Java Sound

The first step to writing some Java sound code is to include the `javax.sound.sampled` package at the top of your program:

```
import javax.sound.sampled.*;
```

If you are using JBuilder, you will see a pop-up menu appear to help you narrow down the class names within javax, which can be very educational. You'll see that when you type in `import javax.sound.`, JBuilder will show you the two classes available in `javax.sound.`, which are `sampled` and `midi`. By adding .* to the end of the import statement, you are telling the Java compiler to import every class within `javax.sound.sampled`, of which there are many.

In fact, when working with the sound system, you will need access to several classes, so it is convenient to import the associated packages at the start of a program so those classes are easier to use. For instance, without importing `javax.sound.sampled`, you would need to create a new sound sample variable using the full class path, such as:

```
javax.sound.sampled.AudioInputStream sample = javax.sound.sampled.AudioSystem.getAudio
   InputStream(new File("woohoo.wav"));
```

Could you imagine what it would look like if you had to write all of your code like this? It would be illegible for the most part. Here is what the code looks like after you have imported `javax.sound.sampled.*`:

```
AudioInputStream sample = AudioSystem.getAudioInputStream(
    new File("woohoo.wav"));
```

`AudioSystem` and `AudioInputStream` are classes within the `javax.sound.sampled` package and are used to load and play a sample in your Java applet. Later in this chapter when I show you how to do background music, you'll get the hang of using some classes in a package called `javax.sound.midi`.

caution

You may run into a problem with the audio portion of your game where your source code seems to be well written, without bugs, but you still get unusual errors. One of the most common sources of problems when working with audio data is an unsupported file format error. This type of exception is called `UnsupportedAudioFileException` and will be discussed later in this chapter.

If your program ever dies unexpectedly, you may want to add a breakpoint to the code (using the Run menu), and then run the program with debugging support (also using the Run menu, or Shift+F9). If the program's flow runs through the `UnsupportedAudioFileException` block in your error handler, then the audio file may be encoded with an unsupported file format. The other, more obvious, problem is that the file itself is missing.

You can check and convert audio files using the freeware Audacity program that I mentioned earlier. Just load up a wary audio file that you suspect is encoded in a weird format, and then save the file to a new format. Figure 4.2 shows the File Formats tab in the Audacity Preferences dialog box. Here you can change the default file format for exporting audio files from the File menu. If you choose the Other option in the drop-down list, you will be presented with *even more* audio formats, but most of them are obsolete (for instance, you can save to Creative Labs' old VOC format which was popular in MS-DOS games many years ago). Some of the custom formats require an additional download of a plug-in for that particular sound format.

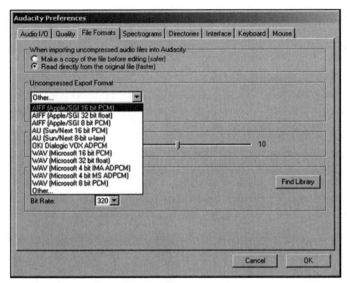

Figure 4.2 Changing the digital sample format settings in Audacity.

The key to sound programming is a class called AudioInputStream. This class is used to load a sound file (which can be an aiff, au, or wav file) from either a local file on the current Web server, where the applet is located, or from a remote URL anywhere on the internet. An input stream is a source of data. You can create a new instance of the class like so:

```
AudioInputStream sample;
```

This statement is usually specified as a global variable within the class, defined up at the top of the class before any methods. You can define this variable as private, public, or protected (the default, if you do not specify it, is public). In object-oriented terms, *public* specifies that the variable is visible to other classes outside the current class, *private* means the variable is hidden to the outside world, and *protected* is similar to private, except that sub-classes (through inheritance) have access to otherwise hidden variables defined as protected.

The code to load a sound from a file or URL is usually called from an applet's `init` method. The method used to load a sound is `AudioSystem.getAudioInputStream`. This method accepts a File, InputStream, or URL; there are two other ways to create an audio stream (AudioFormat and Encoding), neither of which is useful for our needs.

```
sample = AudioSystem.getAudioInputStream(new File("humbug.wav"));
```

Note that the return value of this method is an `AudioInputStream`. Also, since `getAudioInputStream` does not offer an overloaded version that just accepts a `String` for a filename, you must pass a `File` object to it instead. This is easy enough using a `new File` object, passing the filename to the File's constructor method. If you want to grab a file from a URL, your code might look something like this:

```
URL url = new URL("http://www.jharbour.com/test.wav");
sample = AudioSystem.getAudioInputStream(url);
```

Either way, you then have access to a sound file that will be loaded when needed. However, you can't just use an `AudioInputStream` to play a sound; as the class name implies, this is just a source of sample data without the ability to play itself. To play a sample, you use another class called Clip (`javax.sound.sampled.Clip`). This class is the return value of an `AudioSystem` method called `getClip`:

```
Clip clip = AudioSystem.getClip();
```

Since we don't need to pass a parameter to `getClip`, you might be wondering how this object knows what to play. There's actually one more step involved because at this point, all you have is a sound clip object with the *capability* to load and play an audio file or stream. This method actually returns a sound clip object from the default system mixer.

tip
_____

JBuilder 2005 has a built-in context-sensitive help system for the Java documentation. Click or highlight any key word in your source code, and then press F1 to bring up the JBuilder Help Viewer, which is shown in Figure 4.3. This feature is a huge timesaver because you can quickly and easily look up information about Java's libraries without opening a book or Web site.
_____

Loading Resources

The code presented here will load a sound file correctly when your Java program is running either on your local PC or in a Web browser. However, we need to use a slightly different method to load a file out of a Java archive. This is a subject that is covered in Chapter 12, "Deploying Java Games on the Web."

But I want to prepare you for distributing your Java programs on the Web *now*, so that your programs will *already* be ready for deployment. To that end, you must replace the new File() and new URL() methods to load a resource (such as an image or sound file) with the following code instead: this.getClass().getResource(). The getResource() method is found in the current class instance, this.getClass(). You will find it most useful if you use this.getClass().getResource() any time you need to build a URL. Here is a method I've written that accomplishes that goal:

```java
private URL getURL(String filename) {
    URL url = null;
    try {
        url = this.getClass().getResource(filename);
    }
    catch (Exception e) { }
    return url;
}
```

You will see the getURL() method used from here on any time a filename path is needed. Then, when you get to Chapter 12, the programs you've written will be ready for Web deployment in a compressed Java archive (JAR)! During your explorations of the Java language while writing games and other programs, you will likely come up with many useful methods like getURL(). You may want to store them in a reusable package of your own designation. The root package might be called jharbour, and then I would add subpackages to this, like jharbour.graphics, jharbour.util, and so on. Since getURL() is the only custom reusable method repeatedly used in the book, it is more convenient to just include it in every class.

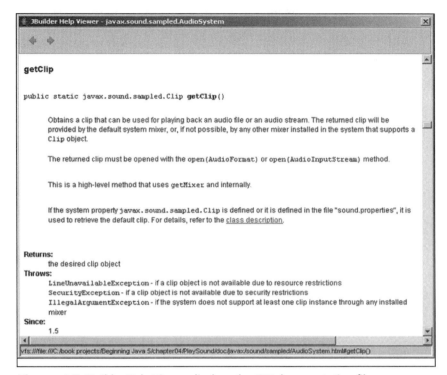

Figure 4.3 JBuilder Help Viewer displays the JDK documentation files.

Loading the Sound Clip

At this point, you have an AudioInputStream and a Clip, so you just need to open the audio file and play it. These steps are both performed by the Clip class. First, let's open the sound file:

```
clip.open(sample);
```

Playing the Sound Clip

Next, there are two ways to play a clip, using the Clip class. You can use the start() method or the loop() method to play a sample. The start() method simply plays the sound clip.

```
narrator.start();
```

On the other hand, the loop method provides an option that lets you specify how many times the clip will repeat, either with a specific number of repeats or continuously. Here is how you might play a clip one time using the loop method:

```
explosion.loop(0);
```

Remember, the parameter specifies the number of times it will replay, as it's a given that the clip will always play at least once using the `loop` method. Here's how you can play a clip continuously:

```
thrusters.loop(Clip.LOOP_CONTINUOUSLY);
```

You might use this option if you have a music track that you would like to play repeatedly for the sound track of the game. Keep in mind, though, that sample files (aiff, au, and wav) are quite large, so you wouldn't want the user to wait five minutes or longer (especially on dial-up) while the sound file is downloaded by your applet. This happens when you call the `open()` method, so if you try to open a huge sound file it will force the user to sit there and wait for an indeterminate length of time while the clip downloads. This is why I recommend using a MIDI sequence rather than a digital sound track for your game's background music.

tip

MIDI is the acronym for Musical Instrument Digital Interface. MIDI is a synthesized music format, not a sampled format, meaning that MIDI music was not recorded using an analog-to-digital converter (which is built into your computer's sound card). Professional music instruments use the MIDI format to record *notes* rather than *samples*.

You may feel free to use the `Clip` class' `start()` method to play a sound clip, but I recommend using `loop(0)` instead. This type of call will give you the same result, and it will be easy to modify the method call if you ever want to repeat a sound clip once or several times. For instance, you might use this technique to save some bandwidth. Instead of downloading a two-second explosion sound effect, go for a one-half second clip, and then repeat it four times. Always keep your mind open to different ways to accomplish a task, and look for ways to optimize your game.

tip

As you will learn in Chapter 12, "Deploying Java Games on the Web," the Java Runtime Environment (JRE) provides an attractive applet download screen with a progress bar when you use a Java archive (JAR) to store the applet and all of its media files.

Stopping the Sound Clip

Most of the time you will simply forget about a sound clip after it has started playing. After all, how often do you need to stop a sound effect from playing when there's a sound mixer taking care of all the details for you? Seldom, if ever. However, if you do need to stop a clip during playback, you can use the stop() method. I suspect the only time you will need this method is when you are looping a sample.

```
kaboom.stop();
```

Handling Errors

One interesting aspect of the sound classes is that they *require* that errors be caught. The compiler will refuse to build a program using some of the sound classes without appropriate try...catch error-handling blocks. Since this is a new concept, I'll quickly explain it.

Java errors are handled with a special error-handling feature called a try...catch block. This feature was simply borrowed from the C++ language, on which Java was based. Here is the basic syntax of a try...catch block:

```
try {
    //do something bad
} catch (Exception e) {
}
```

When you add error handling to your program, you are "wrapping" an error handler around your code by literally wrapping a try...catch block around a section of code that you need to track for errors. The Java sound classes require try...catch blocks with specific types of error checks. The generic Exception class is used to catch most errors that are not caught by a more specific type of error handler. You can have many catch blocks in your error handler, from the more specific down to the more generic in nature.

tip

In some cases, a try...catch error handler is *required* to handle exception errors that a particular method *throws* (on purpose). In those cases, your program *must* implement the appropriate error handler (such as IOException).

Another available version of the error handler is called `try...catch...finally`. This type of error-handling block allows you to put code inside the `finally` section in order to perform any clean-up or closing of files. The code in a `finally` block will be run *regardless* of whether an error occurred or not. It gets executed if there *are* errors and if there are *no errors*.

For instance, if you are loading a file, you will first check for an `IOException` before providing a generic `Exception` handler. The `AudioSystem`, `AudioInputStream`, and `Clip` classes require the following error handlers:

- `IOException`
- `LineUnavailableException`
- `UnsupportedAudioFileException`

Let me show you how to implement an error handler for the audio code you're about to write for the PlaySound program. The following code is found in the `Applet.init()` event:

```
public void init() {
    try {
        //source code lines clipped
    } catch (MalformedURLException e) {
    } catch (IOException e) {
    } catch (LineUnavailableException e) {
    } catch (UnsupportedAudioFileException e) {
    }
}
```

I'll be the first person to admit that this is some ugly code. Error handling is notoriously ugly because it adds all kinds of unpleasant-looking management methods and events around your beautifully written source code. However, error handling is necessary and prevents your program from crashing and burning. I like to think of a `try...catch` block as a rev limiter that prevents a car engine from blowing itself up when a foolish driver hits the accelerator too hard.

Wrapping Sound Clips

Since error handling is a necessary evil, it supports the argument that you may want to put some oft-used code into reusable methods of your own. A couple of methods to load and play a sound file would be useful (and that error-handling code could be bottled up out of sight). It would be logical to encapsulate the `AudioInputStream` and `Clip` objects into a new class of your own design with your own methods to load and play a sound file or URL. Later in this chapter you will find source code for a class called `SoundClip` that does just that.

Playing Sounds

The Java sound classes are not quite a "turn-key" programming solution, as you must perform several steps to load and play a sound file. I think it would be convenient to write a class that has a collection of sound clips you can load and play at any time from that single class, but I hesitate to "wrap" any Java code inside another class when it is such a heavily object-oriented language in the first place. Let's just write an example program to see how to put all this code to work. The resulting program, called PlaySound, is shown in Figure 4.4. The relevant code to this chapter is highlighted in bold.

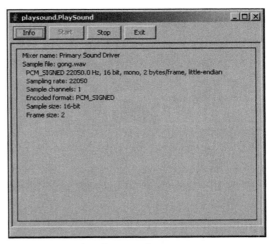

Figure 4.4 The PlaySound program demonstrates how to load and play a sound clip.

```
//this line is only needed if you specified a package
//when the project was created
package playsound;

import java.awt.*;
import java.applet.*;
import java.io.*;
import java.net.*;
import javax.sound.sampled.*;

public class PlaySound extends Applet {
    String filename = "gong.wav";
    AudioInputStream sample;
```

```
    private URL getURL(String filename) {
        URL url = null;
        try {
            url = this.getClass().getResource(filename);
        }
        catch (Exception e) { }
        return url;
    }
    //initialize the applet
    public void init() {
        try {
            sample = AudioSystem.getAudioInputStream(getURL(filename));
            //create a sound buffer
            Clip clip = AudioSystem.getClip();
            //load the audio file
            clip.open(sample);
            //play the sound clip
            clip.start();
    } catch (MalformedURLException e) {
        } catch (IOException e) {
        } catch (LineUnavailableException e) {
        } catch (UnsupportedAudioFileException e) {
        } catch (Exception e) { }
    }

    //the paint event handles the screen refresh
    public void paint(Graphics g) {
        int y = 1;
        g.drawString("Sample file: " + filename, 10, 15*y++);
        g.drawString("  " + sample.getFormat().toString(), 10, 15*y++);
        g.drawString("  Sampling rate: " +
            (int)sample.getFormat().getSampleRate(), 10, 15*y++);
        g.drawString("  Sample channels: " +
            sample.getFormat().getChannels() , 10, 15*y++);
        g.drawString("  Encoded format: " +
            sample.getFormat().getEncoding().toString(), 10, 15*y++);
        g.drawString("  Sample size: " +
            sample.getFormat().getSampleSizeInBits() + "-bit", 10, 15*y++);
        g.drawString("  Frame size: " +
            sample.getFormat().getFrameSize(), 10, 15*y++);
    }
}
```

Playing MIDI Sequence Files

Although using MIDI is not as popular as it used to be for background sound tracks in games, you have an opportunity to save a lot of bandwidth by using MIDI files for background music in a Web-based game delivered as a Java applet. On the Web, bandwidth is crucial, since a game that takes too long to load may cause a potential player to abandon the game and go elsewhere. For this reason, I would like to recommend the use of MIDI for in-game music when delivering a game through the Web. Java supports three types of MIDI formats:

- MIDI Type 1
- MIDI Type 2
- Rich Music Format (RMF)

Loading a MIDI File

Loading a MIDI file in Java is just slightly more involved than loading a digital sample file because a MIDI file is played through a sequencer rather than being played directly by the audio mixer. The Sequence class is used to load a MIDI file:

```
Sequence song = MidiSystem.getSequence(new File("music.mid"));
```

Although this code does prepare a MIDI file to be played through the sequencer, we haven't actually created an instance of the sequencer yet, so let's do that now:

```
Sequencer seq = MidiSystem.getSequencer();
```

Note that the Sequencer class can be accessed through MidiSystem directly, but it requires less typing in of code to create a local variable to handle the setup of the MIDI sequencer. Next, let's tell the Sequencer class that we have a MIDI file available (via the Sequence class):

```
seq.setSequence(song);
```

This line of code establishes a link between the sequencer and this particular MIDI sequence file. Now all that remains to do is actually open the file and play it:

```
seq.open();
seq.start();
```

At this point, the MIDI sequence should start playing when the applet window comes up.

Playing Music

The following program listing demonstrates how to load and play a MIDI file in a Java applet window. The PlayMusic program is shown in Figure 4.5. As you can see, there are some minor details about the MIDI file that are displayed in the applet window, which is basically just an easy way to determine that the MIDI file has been loaded correctly. The key portions of code are highlighted in bold.

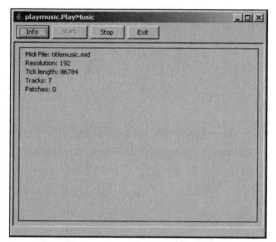

Figure 4.5 The PlayMusic program demonstrates how to load and play a MIDI sequence.

```
import java.awt.*;
import java.applet.*;
import java.io.*;
import java.net.*;
import javax.sound.midi.*;

public class PlayMusic extends Applet {
    String filename = "titlemusic.mid";
    Sequence song;

    private URL getURL(String filename) {
        URL url = null;
        try {
            url = this.getClass().getResource(filename);
        }
        catch (Exception e) { }
        return url;
    }
```

```
//initialize the applet
public void init() {
    try {
        song = MidiSystem.getSequence(getURL(filename));
        Sequencer sequencer = MidiSystem.getSequencer();
        sequencer.setSequence(song);
        sequencer.open();
        sequencer.start();

    } catch (InvalidMidiDataException e) {
    } catch (MidiUnavailableException e) {
    } catch (IOException e) { }
}

//repaint the applet window
public void paint(Graphics g) {
    int x=10, y = 1;
    if (song != null) {
        g.drawString("Midi File: " + filename, x, 15 * y++);
        g.drawString("Resolution: " + song.getResolution(), x, 15 * y++);
        g.drawString("Tick length: " + song.getTickLength(), x, 15 * y++);
        g.drawString("Tracks: " + song.getTracks().length, x, 15 * y++);
        g.drawString("Patches: " + song.getPatchList().length, x, 15 * y++);
    } else {
        g.drawString("Error loading sequence file " + filename, 10, 15);
    }
}
}
```

Reusable Classes

Now that you understand how to load and play sound clips and sequence files, let's put all of this useful (but scattered) code into two reusable classes that can be easily dropped into a project and used. Instead of dealing with all of the Java sound classes and packages, you will be able to simply create a new object from the SoundClip and MidiSequence classes, and then load up and play either a sample or sequence with a couple lines of code.

I should disclaim the usefulness of these classes for you, so you will know what to expect. Java's Sound API has a sound mixer that works very well, but we can't tap into the mixer directly using the Clip class that I've shown you in this chapter. The sound files that you load using the Clip class *do support mixing*, but a single clip will interrupt itself if played repeatedly. So, in the case of *Galactic War*, when your ship fires a weapon, the weapon sound is restarted every time you play the sound. However, if you have another clip for explosions (or any other sound), then it *will be mixed* with any other sound clips currently playing.

In other words, a single Clip object cannot mix *with itself*, only *with other sounds*. This process works quite well if you use short sound effects, but can sound odd if your sound clips are one second or more in length (they sound fine at up to about half a second, which is typical for arcade game sound effects). If you want to repeatedly mix a single clip, there are two significant options:

1. Load the sound file into multiple Clip objects (such as an array), and then play each one in order. Whenever you need to play this specific sound, just iterate through the array and locate a clip that has finished playing, and then start playing it again.

2. Load the sound file into a single Clip object, and then copy the sample bytes into multiple Clip objects in an array, and then follow the general technique described in #1 for playback. This saves time from loading the clip multiple times.

3. Write a threaded sound playback class that creates a new thread for every sound that is played. The thread will terminate when the sound has completed playing. This requires some pretty complex code and there is a lot of overhead involved in creating and destroying a thread for every single sound that is played. One way to get around this overhead is to create a thread pool at the start of the program and then re-use threads in the pool. Again, this is some very advanced code, but it is how professional Java games handle sound playback. If you write a great Java game suitable for publishing (such as *Galactic War*, which is started in the next chapter and developed throughout the book), I would recommend options 1 or 2 above as good choices for a simple game. You don't want to deal with the overhead (or weighty coding requirements) of a threaded solution, and an array of five or so duplicates of a sound clip can be played to good effect—with mixing.

The SoundClip Class

The SoundClip class encapsulates the AudioSystem, AudioInputStream, and Clip classes, making it much easier to load and play an audio file in your applets. On the CD-ROM there is a project called SoundClass that demonstrates this class. This class simply includes all of the code we've covered in the last two pages, combined into a single entity. Note the key portions of code that I've discussed in this section, which are highlighted in bold.

```java
import javax.sound.sampled.*;
import java.io.*;
import java.net.*;
public class SoundClip {
    //the source for audio data
    private AudioInputStream sample;

    //sound clip property is read-only here
    private Clip clip;
    public Clip getClip() { return clip; }

    //looping property for continuous playback
    private boolean looping = false;
    public void setLooping(boolean _looping) { looping = _looping; }
    public boolean getLooping() { return looping; }

    //repeat property used to play sound multiple times
    private int repeat = 0;
    public void setRepeat(int _repeat) { repeat = _repeat; }
    public int getRepeat() { return repeat; }

    //filename property
    private String filename = "";
    public void setFilename(String _filename) { filename = _filename; }
    public String getFilename() { return filename; }

    //property to verify when sample is ready
    public boolean isLoaded() {
        return (boolean)(sample != null);
    }

    //constructor
    public SoundClip() {
        try {
            //create a sound buffer
            clip = AudioSystem.getClip();
        } catch (LineUnavailableException e) {   }
    }
}
```

```
//this overloaded constructor takes a sound file as a parameter
public SoundClip(String audiofile) {
    this();  //call default constructor first
    load(audiofile); //now load the audio file
}

 private URL getURL(String filename) {
     URL url = null;
     try {
         url = this.getClass().getResource(filename);
     }
     catch (Exception e) { }
     return url;
}
//load sound file
public boolean load(String audiofile) {
    try {

        //prepare the input stream for an audio file
        setFilename(audiofile);
        //set the audio stream source
        sample = AudioSystem.getAudioInputStream(getURL(filename));
        //load the audio file
        clip.open(sample);
        return true;

    } catch (IOException e) {
        return false;
    } catch (UnsupportedAudioFileException e) {
        return false;
    } catch (LineUnavailableException e) {
        return false;
    }
}

public void play() {
    //exit if the sample hasn't been loaded
    if (!isLoaded()) return;

    //reset the sound clip
    clip.setFramePosition(0);
```

```
        //play sample with optional looping
        if (looping)
            clip.loop(Clip.LOOP_CONTINUOUSLY);
        else
            clip.loop(repeat);
    }

    public void stop() {
        clip.stop();
    }
}
```

The MidiSequence Class

The MidiSequence class is another custom class that makes it easier to work with the Java sound code. This class encapsulates the MidiSystem, Sequencer, and Sequence classes, making it much easier to load and play a MIDI file with just two lines of code instead of many. Take note of the key portions of code which have been highlighted in bold.

tip
_____

A complete project demonstrating this class is available on the CD-ROM in the \sources\ chapter04\MusicClass folder.

_____

```
import java.io.*;
import java.net.*;
import javax.sound.midi.*;

public class MidiSequence {
    //primary midi sequencer object
    private Sequencer sequencer;

    //provide Sequence as a read-only property
    private Sequence song;
    public Sequence getSong() { return song; }

    //filename property is read-only
    private String filename;
    public String getFilename() { return filename; }
```

```java
//looping property for looping continuously
private boolean looping = false;
public boolean getLooping() { return looping; }
public void setLooping(boolean _looping) { looping = _looping; }

//repeat property for looping a fixed number of times
private int repeat = 0;
public void setRepeat(int _repeat) { repeat = _repeat; }
public int getRepeat() { return repeat; }

//returns whether the sequence is ready for action
public boolean isLoaded() {
    return (boolean)(sequencer.isOpen());
}

//primary constructor
public MidiSequence() {
    try {
        //fire up the sequencer
        sequencer = MidiSystem.getSequencer();
    } catch (MidiUnavailableException e) {   }
}
//overloaded constructor accepts midi filename
public MidiSequence(String midifile) {
    this();   //call default constructor first
    load(midifile); //load the midi file
}

private URL getURL(String filename) {
    URL url = null;
    try {
        url = this.getClass().getResource(filename);
    }
    catch (Exception e) { }
    return url;
}

//load a midi file into a sequence
public boolean load(String midifile) {
    try {
        //load the midi file into the sequencer
        filename = midifile;
        song = MidiSystem.getSequence(getURL(filename));
```

```
            sequencer.setSequence(song);
            sequencer.open();
            return true;
        } catch (InvalidMidiDataException e) {
            return false;
        } catch (MidiUnavailableException e) {
            return false;
        } catch (IOException e) {
            return false;
        }
    }

    //play the midi sequence
    public void play() {
        if (!sequencer.isOpen()) return;
        if (looping) {
            sequencer.setLoopCount(Sequencer.LOOP_CONTINUOUSLY);
            sequencer.start();
        } else {
            sequencer.setLoopCount(repeat);
            sequencer.start();
        }
    }

    //stop the midi sequence
    public void stop() {
        sequencer.stop();
    }

}
```

What You Have Learned

This chapter explained how to incorporate sound clips and MIDI sequences into your Java applets. Game audio is a very important subject because a game is just no fun without sound. You learned

- How to load and play a digital sound file.
- How to load and play a MIDI sequence file.
- How to encapsulate reusable code inside a class.

Review Questions

The following questions will help you to determine how well you have learned the subjects discussed in this chapter. The answers are provided in Appendix A, "Chapter Quiz Answers."

1. What is the name of Java's digital sound system class?
2. What is the name of Java's MIDI music system class?
3. Which Java class handles the loading of a sample file?
4. Which Java class handles the loading of a MIDI file?
5. What type of exception error will Java generate when it cannot load a sound file?
6. Which method of the MIDI system returns the sequencer object?
7. What is the main Java class hierarchy for the audio system class?
8. What is the main Java class hierarchy for the MIDI system class?
9. What three digital sound file formats does Java support?
10. What rare exception error will occur when no MIDI sequencer is available?

On Your Own

Use the following exercises to test your grasp of the material covered in this chapter. Are you ready to put sound and music to the test in a real game yet? These exercises will challenge your understanding of this chapter.

1. Write your own sound-effects generating program to try out a large list of sound files. You can acquire sound files of various types by searching the Web. Have the program play a specific sound file by pressing keys on the keyboard.
2. Write a similar program for playing back multiple MIDI music sequence files by pressing various keys on the keyboard. For an even greater challenge, try combining this program with the one in Exercise 1 so that you can try out playing music and sound effects at the same time!

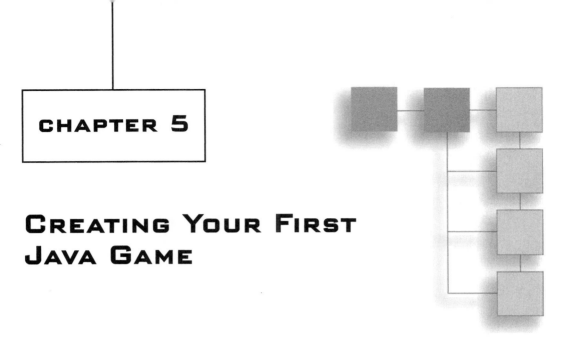

CHAPTER 5

CREATING YOUR FIRST JAVA GAME

Are you ready to create a complete Java game already? If not, then you'll get a crash course in this chapter. Although we haven't covered graphics programming yet, this chapter will give you a glimpse of what's coming in the next few chapters while teaching you some of the basics of game creation. The game featured in this chapter was inspired by the classic Atari game *Asteroids* from the 1980s. My first video game system was an Atari 2600, and *Asteroids* was one of my favorite games on that old system. In this chapter, you'll learn how to create a variation of this classic game, and this game will be the basis of a more advanced game that you'll learn to create throughout the rest of the book. This simple game will be enhanced in each new chapter until you have an exciting, high-quality version of the game called *Galactic War* in the final chapter. Here are the key topics in this chapter:

- Creating an Asteroids-style game
- Writing key classes: `BaseVectorShape`, `Ship`, `Asteroid`, and `Bullet`
- Writing the main source code
- Calculating velocities on the fly

About the Game Project

The Asteroids-style game we're building in this chapter will run in a Web browser window with a resolution of 640 x 480 and will be done entirely using vector graphics. It will feature sound effects, a music soundtrack, and many features that you have not yet learned about. All in good time! I want to expose you to some of the concepts up front in this chapter so that you'll recognize these concepts when we get to them in upcoming chapters. This is a good way to learn—you may not understand everything in the source code for the game at this point, but you will learn how it works in time. Figure 5.1 shows the completed game you will build in this chapter.

Figure 5.1 This Asteroids clone is the basis for a much more ambitious game.

As mentioned, the game is entirely based on vector graphics. The player's ship, the asteroids, and the bullets are all rendered as polygons, as shown in Figure 5.2.

tip

Vector graphic displays are different from our modern monitors in that they draw shapes based on entire lines instead of our modern displays which draw raster graphics based on pixels.

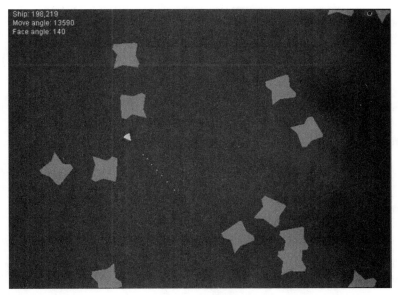

Figure 5.2 The objects in the game are all rendered as vector graphics.

All of the objects in the game are moved using an algorithm that calculates the X and Y velocity values, which are used to update the object's position on the screen. All of these values use floating-point math, and the result is fluid 2-D rotation animation and realistic movement (see Figure 5.3).

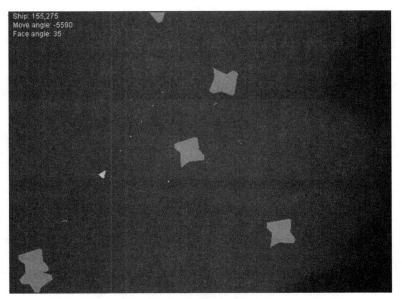

Figure 5.3 Floating-point math algorithms give the game a realistic look and feel.

Each of the vector shapes in the game has a built-in bounding rectangle that is used to simplify collision testing, which is a crucial aspect of the game. Without it, the bullets would not destroy the asteroids, and the ship would be invulnerable! Collision testing is what makes gameplay possible in a game.

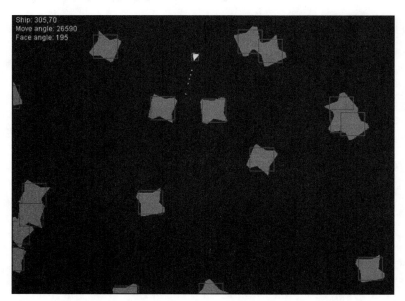

Figure 5.4 Bounding rectangles are used to detect when collisions occur.

The goal is to modify this game concept in each chapter until you have come up with a high-quality, polished game with a lot of interesting gameplay elements by the time you've finished the book. The final version of *Galactic War* is an arcade-style game with many different types of asteroids, animated explosions, and power-ups for the player's ship. Future versions of the game will make the transition from vector graphics (based on polygons) to rasterized graphics (based on bitmaps).

But before you can run, as the old saying goes, you have to learn how to walk. This chapter teaches you how to walk, and you will gradually improve the game a little at a time, starting with the next chapter.

Creating the Game

I will go over the source code for this game in detail in the following pages, explaining every key variable and method in the program. This game is divided into five classes. Does that seem like a lot of classes for just your first game? I thought about that for a while, considering this might be too much code all at once. But I think you will enjoy it.

This is a complete game, for the most part, so you can examine it, pore over the lines of code in Holmesian style (with a magnifying glass, if you wish) to learn the secrets of how a game is made.

This first version of the game is simple enough that I think you will enjoy updating it in each new chapter, adding new features as we go along. The main class, Asteroids, contains the main source code for the game. Four additional classes will be used (which will eventually be replaced with more advanced classes later on):

- BaseVectorShape
- Ship
- Bullet
- Asteroid

Creating the Project in JBuilder

You can type in the code for each of the classes (and the main source code file, Asteroids.java) and then compile each file into a .class file using the Java Development Kit (JDK) command-line tools. The compiler is called javac.exe. You can compile a file by simply typing

```
javac Asteroid.java
```

and likewise for the other source code files.

However, I strongly recommend you use JBuilder. You will want to create a new "Applet" project and call it "Asteroids." When you are given the option, delete the package name entirely so the project is not based on a package (the default will be called "asteroids"). If you include the package name in the project, then you will need to include the line

```
package asteroids;
```

in every source code file in the project. I am leaving this line out of the source code files because it will generate compiler errors if the project is not configured to use the package when you create the project. Just take note of this; if you get compiler errors about the package, you will need to include this line at the top of all source code files.

The BaseVectorShape Class

The three main objects in the game are all derived from the BaseVectorShape class. I originally wrote this game without the base class, and in the end, all three of the game objects (the player's ship, the bullets, and the asteroids) ended up sharing most of their properties and methods, so the BaseVectorShape class was a way to clean up the code. In the end, I put a lot of useful methods in this class for handling the needs of this vector graphics game. By doing this, I have used the object-oriented feature called *inheritance*, since the Asteroid, Ship, and Bullet classes are all based on BaseVectorShape.

For one thing, this game uses bounding rectangle collision detection, so each vector shape in the game includes its own bounding rectangle. While the getBounds() method is not found in the BaseVectorShape class for reasons I'll explain in a moment, this method does use the getX() and getY() methods from the base class to calculate the bounding rectangle. This class basically contains all the variables that will be used to move the objects around on the screen, such as the X and Y position, the velocity, the facing and moving angles, and the shape itself (which is a polygon).

tip

Whoa, what is *bounding rectangle collision detection*? This is one of about fifty things in this game that I am exposing you to prematurely. This subject is covered in detail in the next two chapters. To summarize, this phrase describes the process of detecting when objects collide with each other in the game (such as a bullet hitting an asteroid).

```
import java.awt.Shape;
/*******************************************************
 * Base vector shape class for game entities
 *******************************************************/
public class BaseVectorShape {
    //variables
    private Shape shape;
    private boolean alive;
    private double x,y;
    private double velX, velY;
    private double moveAngle, faceAngle;

    //accessor methods
    public Shape getShape() { return shape; }
    public boolean isAlive() { return alive; }
    public double getX() { return x; }
    public double getY() { return y; }
    public double getVelX() { return velX; }
    public double getVelY() { return velY; }
    public double getMoveAngle() { return moveAngle; }
    public double getFaceAngle() { return faceAngle; }
```

```
//mutator and helper methods
public void setShape(Shape shape) { this.shape = shape; }
public void setAlive(boolean alive) { this.alive = alive; }
public void setX(double x) { this.x = x; }
public void incX(double i) { this.x += i; }
public void setY(double y) { this.y = y; }
public void incY(double i) { this.y += i; }
public void setVelX(double velX) { this.velX = velX; }
public void incVelX(double i) { this.velX += i; }
public void setVelY(double velY) { this.velY = velY; }
public void incVelY(double i) { this.velY += i; }
public void setFaceAngle(double angle) { this.faceAngle = angle; }
public void incFaceAngle(double i) { this.faceAngle += i; }
public void setMoveAngle(double angle) { this.moveAngle = angle; }
public void incMoveAngle(double i) { this.moveAngle += i; }

//default constructor
BaseVectorShape() {
    setShape(null);
    setAlive(false);
    setX(0.0);
    setY(0.0);
    setVelX(0.0);
    setVelY(0.0);
    setMoveAngle(0.0);
    setFaceAngle(0.0);
}
}
```

The Ship Class

The Ship class handles the shape, position, and velocity of the player's ship in the game. It includes its own bounding rectangle, which is calculated based on the custom polygon shape for the ship. However, it is not automatically calculated—the bounding rectangle is based on the values in the X and Y vector arrays used to create the ship's polygon shape, which is different for each shape.

```
import java.awt.Polygon;
import java.awt.Rectangle;
/**********************************************************
 * Ship class derives from BaseVectorShape
 **********************************************************/
```

```java
public class Ship extends BaseVectorShape {
    //define the ship polygon
    private int[] shipx = { -6, -3, 0, 3, 6, 0 };
    private int[] shipy = { 6, 7, 7, 7, 6, -7 };

    //bounding rectangle
    public Rectangle getBounds() {
        Rectangle r;
        r = new Rectangle((int)getX() - 6, (int) getY() - 6, 12,12);
        return r;
    }

    Ship() {
        setShape(new Polygon(shipx, shipy, shipx.length));
        setAlive(true);
    }
}
```

The Bullet Class

The Bullet class defines the bullets fired from the ship. It is also derived from the BaseVectorShape class, so most of the functionality of this class is provided by the base class. All we really need to do for bullets in this game is to define a rectangle that is one pixel in width and height to create a tiny rectangle. This small shape is used to calculate the bounding rectangle returned in the getBounds() method.

```java
import java.awt.*;
import java.awt.Rectangle;

/**********************************************************
 * Bullet class derives from BaseVectorShape
 **********************************************************/
public class Bullet extends BaseVectorShape {

    //bounding rectangle
    public Rectangle getBounds() {
        Rectangle r;
        r = new Rectangle((int)getX(), (int) getY(), 1, 1);
        return r;
    }
```

```
    Bullet() {
        //create the bullet shape
        setShape(new Rectangle(0, 0, 1, 1));
        setAlive(false);
    }
}
```

The Asteroid Class

The Asteroid class also inherits from BaseVectorShape and provides three of its own new methods: getRotationVelocity, setRotationVelocity, and getBounds. The rotation velocity value is used to rotate the asteroids (which is a cool effect in the game). The getBounds method returns the bounding rectangle for the asteroid and is similar to the same method found in the Ship and Bullet classes.

```
import java.awt.Polygon;
import java.awt.Rectangle;

/***********************************************************
 * Asteroid class derives from BaseVectorShape
 ***********************************************************/
public class Asteroid extends BaseVectorShape {
    //define the asteroid polygon shape
    private int[] astx = {-20,-13, 0,20,22, 20, 12,  2,-10,-22,-16};
    private int[] asty = { 20, 23,17,20,16,-20,-22,-14,-17,-20, -5};

    //rotation speed
    protected double rotVel;
    public double getRotationVelocity() { return rotVel; }
    public void setRotationVelocity(double v) { rotVel = v; }

    //bounding rectangle
    public Rectangle getBounds() {
        Rectangle r;
        r = new Rectangle((int)getX() - 20, (int) getY() - 20, 40, 40);
        return r;
    }
```

```
//default constructor
Asteroid() {
    setShape(new Polygon(astx, asty, astx.length));
    setAlive(true);
    setRotationVelocity(0.0);
}
}
```

The Main Source Code File

The main source code file for this game is found in a file called Asteroids.java. I am providing the complete source code listing here so you can examine it in detail while reading my explanations of each method along the way. Since this is the first of many revisions for this game, I recommend you study it here to get a good feel for how this game works. If you don't understand everything, that's okay—we will be opening up this game project and enhancing it several more times.

```
/****************************************************
 * Beginning Java 5 Game Programming
 * Chapter 5 - ASTEROIDS GAME
 * by Jonathan S. Harbour
 ****************************************************/
package asteroids;
import java.applet.*;
import java.awt.*;
import java.awt.event.*;
import java.awt.geom.*;
import java.awt.image.*;
import java.util.*;


/****************************************************
 * Primary class for the game
 ****************************************************/
public class Asteroids extends Applet implements Runnable, KeyListener {
    //the main thread becomes the game loop
    Thread gameloop;
    //use this as a double buffer
    BufferedImage backbuffer;
    //the main drawing object for the back buffer
    Graphics2D g2d;
    //toggle for drawing bounding boxes
    boolean showBounds = false;
```

```
//create the asteroid array
int ASTEROIDS = 20;
Asteroid[] ast = new Asteroid[ASTEROIDS];

//create the bullet array
int BULLETS = 10;
Bullet[] bullet = new Bullet[BULLETS];
int currentBullet = 0;

//the player's ship
Ship ship = new Ship();

//create the identity transform (0,0)
AffineTransform identity = new AffineTransform();

//create a random number generator
Random rand = new Random();

// sound effects objects
SoundClip shoot;
SoundClip explode;
```

Applet init() Event

The applet init() event is run when the applet first starts up and is used to initialize the game. The code first creates a double buffer, upon which all graphics will be rendered in order to produce a smooth screen refresh without flicker. The player's ship and the asteroids are initialized, and then the key listener is started.

```
/*****************************************************
 * applet init event
 *****************************************************/
public void init() {
    //create the back buffer for smooth graphics
    backbuffer = new BufferedImage(640, 480, BufferedImage.TYPE_INT_RGB);
    g2d = backbuffer.createGraphics();

    //set up the ship
    ship.setX(320);
    ship.setY(240);
```

```
    //set up the bullets
    for (int n = 0; n<BULLETS; n++) {
        bullet[n] = new Bullet();
    }

    //set up the asteroids
    for (int n = 0; n<ASTEROIDS; n++) {
        ast[n] = new Asteroid();
        ast[n].setRotationVelocity(rand.nextInt(3)+1);
        ast[n].setX((double)rand.nextInt(600)+20);
        ast[n].setY((double)rand.nextInt(440)+20);
        ast[n].setMoveAngle(rand.nextInt(360));
        double ang = ast[n].getMoveAngle() - 90;
        ast[n].setVelX(calcAngleMoveX(ang));
        ast[n].setVelY(calcAngleMoveY(ang));
    }

    //load sound files
    shoot = new SoundClip("shoot.au");
    explode = new SoundClip("explode.au");

    //start the user input listener
    addKeyListener(this);
}
```

tip
___
The sound files, shoot.au and explode.au, are in the Sun Microsystems' file format (note the .au extension). You can also use .wav or .aiff formats for sound files if you wish. To convert among these file formats, I recommend the excellent audio editing software, Audacity. This is a freeware program and is included on the CD-ROM in \software\Audacity.

Applet update() Event

The applet's update() event is triggered whenever the screen needs to be refreshed. This game does not call the update() method from the game loop yet, although a future version of the game will make this change—which provides better control over the screen refresh process. This method does all of the drawing to the applet window by first drawing graphics to the back buffer. This buffer is then copied to the applet window during the paint() event.

The identity transform is the **starting point** of a vector-based transform that allows vector-based shapes to be rotated and moved around in the game. First, you start at the *identity* and then move the shape and rotate it from there. If you don't start off with the identity before manipulating a shape, then it will be moved with the previous shape rather than on its own.

```
/*****************************************************
 * applet update event to redraw the screen
 *****************************************************/
public void update(Graphics g) {
    //start off transforms at identity
    g2d.setTransform(identity);

    //erase the background
    g2d.setPaint(Color.BLACK);
    g2d.fillRect(0, 0, getSize().width, getSize().height);

    //print some status information
    g2d.setColor(Color.WHITE);
    g2d.drawString("Ship: " + Math.round(ship.getX()) + "," +
        Math.round(ship.getY()) , 5, 10);
    g2d.drawString("Move angle: " + Math.round(
        ship.getMoveAngle())+90, 5, 25);
    g2d.drawString("Face angle: " +  Math.round(
        ship.getFaceAngle()), 5, 40);

    //draw the game graphics
    drawShip();
    drawBullets();
    drawAsteroids();

    //repaint the applet window
    paint(g);
}
```

Drawing the Player's Ship

The drawShip() method is called by the update() event to draw the player's ship onto the back buffer at the correct X and Y location. Before drawing, the identity transform is set so that the ship's local coordinate system is used, rather than the previous vector's coordinates. Remember, a transform affects an object's X and Y position. The identity is the starting point (0,0).

When the ship is first drawn, it is actually centered at the origin, with the shape of the ship being drawn from –6 to +6 in the X and Y axes. So the ship is about 12 pixels square in size. If you don't draw a vector around the origin, then rotation will not work at all, because rotations occur at the origin—or rather, at the identity location.

```
/*****************************************************
 * drawShip called by applet update event
 *****************************************************/
public void drawShip() {
    //draw the ship
    g2d.setTransform(identity);
    g2d.translate(ship.getX(), ship.getY());
    g2d.rotate(Math.toRadians(ship.getFaceAngle()));
    g2d.setColor(Color.ORANGE);
    g2d.fill(ship.getShape());

    //draw bounding rectangle around ship
    if (showBounds) {
        g2d.setTransform(identity);
        g2d.setColor(Color.BLUE);
        g2d.draw(ship.getBounds());
    }
}
```

Drawing the Bullets

The drawBullets() method goes through the array of bullets and draws any bullets that need to be drawn. This only occurs if a bullet is alive using the isAlive() method. Then the bullet is transformed to its position on the screen, and the shape is drawn (which is a tiny rectangle).

```
/*****************************************************
 * drawBullets called by applet update event
 *****************************************************/
public void drawBullets() {
    for (int n = 0; n < BULLETS; n++) {
        if (bullet[n].isAlive()) {
            //draw the bullet
            g2d.setTransform(identity);
            g2d.translate(bullet[n].getX(), bullet[n].getY());
            g2d.setColor(Color.MAGENTA);
            g2d.draw(bullet[n].getShape());
        }
    }
}
```

Drawing the Asteroids

The drawAsteroids() method draws all of the asteroids in the ast[] array, depending on whether they are *alive* or not. When the player fires a bullet and it hits an asteroid, that asteroid's *alive* variable is set to false, so the asteroid is no longer drawn to the screen—and it is also ignored by the bullets after that. An interesting option in this method will draw the bounding rectangle around the asteroids if you have toggled bounding on by pressing the B key.

```
/*****************************************************
 * drawAsteroids called by applet update event
 *****************************************************/
public void drawAsteroids() {
    for (int n = 0; n < ASTEROIDS; n++) {
        if (ast[n].isAlive()) {
            //draw the asteroid
            g2d.setTransform(identity);
            g2d.translate(ast[n].getX(), ast[n].getY());
            g2d.rotate(Math.toRadians(ast[n].getMoveAngle()));
            g2d.setColor(Color.DARK_GRAY);
            g2d.fill(ast[n].getShape());

            //draw bounding rectangle
            if (showBounds) {
                g2d.setTransform(identity);
                g2d.setColor(Color.BLUE);
                g2d.draw(ast[n].getBounds());
            }
        }
    }
}
```

Screen Refresh

The paint() event occurs when the applet window needs to be refreshed. This method is called by the update() method and simply serves the purpose of drawing the back buffer to the applet window.

```
/*****************************************************
 * applet window repaint event--draw the back buffer
 *****************************************************/
public void paint(Graphics g) {
    g.drawImage(backbuffer, 0, 0, this);
}
```

Thread Events and the Game Loop

There are three thread events that are part of a program when you implement the Runnable interface in a Java applet. Runnable tells Java that your applet will support more than one thread. A thread is sort of a mini program that can run on its own. You create a new thread in the start() event, and then destroy that thread in the stop() event to keep things running smoothly.

The most interesting thread event is called run(). This event method contains the code for the game loop, which is a while loop that sort of powers the game and keeps it running at a consistent frame rate. This event calls the gameUpdate() method, which processes the current frame of the game by moving objects around on the screen, testing for collisions, and so on.

```
/*****************************************************
 * thread start event - start the game loop running
 *****************************************************/
public void start() {
    gameloop = new Thread(this);
    gameloop.start();
}
/*****************************************************
 * thread run event (game loop)
 *****************************************************/
public void run() {
    //acquire the current thread
    Thread t = Thread.currentThread();
    //keep going as long as the thread is alive
    while (t == gameloop) {
        try {
            //update the game loop
            gameUpdate();
            //shoot for 50 fps
            Thread.sleep(20);
        }
        catch(InterruptedException e) {
            e.printStackTrace();
        }
        repaint();
    }
}
```

```
/***************************************************
 * thread stop event
 ***************************************************/
public void stop() {
    gameloop = null;
}
```

Game Loop Update

The gameUpdate() method is called by the game loop thread when it's time to process the game for the next applet window refresh. The game loop is timed to hit around 50 frames per second (fps), and the window refresh occurs after gameUpdate is run. Normally the game loop will run as fast as possible and only the screen refresh will be tied to a specific frame rate, but in this first game, that difference is not important.

```
/***************************************************
 * move and animate the objects in the game
 ***************************************************/
private void gameUpdate() {
    updateShip();
    updateBullets();
    updateAsteroids();
    checkCollisions();
}
```

Updating the Ship

The updateShip() method updates the ship's X and Y position using the velocity variables. This method also "warps" the ship around when it crosses an edge of the screen (in which case the shape is moved to the opposite side of the screen). This is a technique used in many classic arcade games.

```
/***************************************************
 * Update the ship position based on velocity
 ***************************************************/
public void updateShip() {
    //update ship's X position, wrap around left/right
    ship.incX(ship.getVelX());
    if (ship.getX() < -10)
        ship.setX(getSize().width + 10);
    else if (ship.getX() > getSize().width + 10)
        ship.setX(-10);
    //update ship's Y position, wrap around top/bottom
    ship.incY(ship.getVelY());
```

```
        if (ship.getY() < -10)
            ship.setY(getSize().height + 10);
        else if (ship.getY() > getSize().height + 10)
            ship.setY(-10);
    }
```

Updating the Bullets

The updateBullets() method updates the X and Y position for each bullet that is currently alive using the velocity variables. When a bullet hits the edge of the screen, it is disabled.

```
/*****************************************************
 * Update the bullets based on velocity
 *****************************************************/
public void updateBullets() {
    //move the bullets
    for (int n = 0; n < BULLETS; n++) {
        if (bullet[n].isAlive()) {
            //update bullet's x position
            bullet[n].incX(bullet[n].getVelX());
            //bullet disappears at left/right edge
            if (bullet[n].getX() < 0 ||
                bullet[n].getX() > getSize().width)
            {
                bullet[n].setAlive(false);
            }
            //update bullet's y position
            bullet[n].incY(bullet[n].getVelY());
            //bullet disappears at top/bottom edge
            if (bullet[n].getY() < 0 ||
                bullet[n].getY() > getSize().height)
            {
                bullet[n].setAlive(false);
            }
        }
    }
}
```

Updating the Asteroids

The updateAsteroids() method updates the X and Y position of each asteroid that is currently alive based on the velocity variables. These X and Y values and velocities are all set to random values when the game starts up. The asteroids are warped around the edges of the screen. One interesting thing about the asteroids that differs from the ship and bullets is that the asteroids are rotated by a random number of degrees each frame, causing them to spin on the screen. This is a pretty nice effect that adds to the quality of the game.

```
/********************************************************
 * Update the asteroids based on velocity
 ********************************************************/
public void updateAsteroids() {
    //move and rotate the asteroids
    for (int n = 0; n < ASTEROIDS; n++) {
        if (ast[n].isAlive()) {
            //update the asteroid's X value
            ast[n].incX(ast[n].getVelX());
            if (ast[n].getX() < -20)
                ast[n].setX(getSize().width + 20);
            else if (ast[n].getX() > getSize().width + 20)
                ast[n].setX(-20);

            //update the asteroid's Y value
            ast[n].incY(ast[n].getVelY());
            if (ast[n].getY() < -20)
                ast[n].setY(getSize().height + 20);
            else if (ast[n].getY() > getSize().height + 20)
                ast[n].setY(-20);

            //update the asteroid's rotation
            ast[n].incMoveAngle(ast[n].getRotationVelocity());
            if (ast[n].getMoveAngle() < 0)
                ast[n].setMoveAngle(360 - ast[n].getRotationVelocity());
            else if (ast[n].getMoveAngle() > 360)
                ast[n].setMoveAngle(ast[n].getRotationVelocity());
        }
    }
}
```

Testing for Collisions

We haven't discussed collision detection yet, but I think you will get the hang of it here because this checkCollisions() method is straightforward. First, there is a loop that goes through the asteroid array (ast[]). Inside this loop, if an asteroid is alive, it is tested for collisions with any active bullets, then it is tested for a collision with the ship. If a collision occurs, then an explosion sound effect is played, and the asteroid is disabled. If it collided with a bullet, the bullet is also disabled. When the player's ship is hit, it is reset at the center of the screen with zero velocity. A collision occurs when one shape overlaps another shape, which is why we use the intersects() and contains() methods to determine when a collision occurs. Specifically, contains() is used to see if the bullet has hit an asteroid, while intersects() is used to see if an asteroid has hit the ship.

The key to the collision code here is a method in the Shape object called contains() that accepts a Rectangle or a Point and returns true if there is an overlap. This method makes it possible to perform bounding rectangle collision detection with just a few lines of code because the shapes already have built-in getBounds() methods available.

```
/*****************************************************
 * Test asteroids for collisions with ship or bullets
 *****************************************************/
public void checkCollisions() {
    //check for ship and bullet collisions with asteroids
    for (int m = 0; m<ASTEROIDS; m++) {
        if (ast[m].isAlive()) {
            //check for bullet collisions
            for (int n = 0; n < BULLETS; n++) {
                if (bullet[n].isAlive()) {

                    //perform the collision test
                    if (ast[m].getBounds().contains(
                            bullet[n].getX(), bullet[n].getY()))
                    {
                        bullet[n].setAlive(false);
                        ast[m].setAlive(false);
                        explode.play();
                        continue;
                    }
                }
            }
        }

        //check for ship collision
        if (ast[m].getBounds().intersects(ship.getBounds())) {
            ast[m].setAlive(false);
            explode.play();
            ship.setX(320);
            ship.setY(240);
            ship.setFaceAngle(0);
            ship.setVelX(0);
            ship.setVelY(0);
```

```
                continue;
            }
        }
    }
}
```

Keyboard Events

This game only uses the keyPressed() event to detect key presses, while keyReleased() and keyTyped() are ignored (although they must be in the source code listing because of the KeyListener interface). The most important parts of this method are found in the code following the thrust and fire keys, which are mapped to the Up arrow and Ctrl keys (the Enter key and spacebar can also be used to fire). When the Up arrow is pressed, this adds thrust to the ship, causing it to move.

definition

An *algorithm* is a mathematical expression that causes one of the variables in the expression to change in a consistent way. A movement algorithm causes, for instance, the x variable on an x - y coordinate plane to change so that it consistently increases in value, moving whatever object it represents horizontally across the screen.

An advanced movement algorithm is used to move the objects in the game, which is covered in the next section. Moving the ship must look as realistic as possible—so you can apply thrust to the ship, rotate to a new direction, then apply thrust, and that new angle of movement is added to the current velocity values. The result is a very realistic zero-gravity motion for the ship. Some programmers like to use a mass/acceleration algorithm to move a space ship. That is a good method, where the mass (or weight) of the ship affects how fast it can move. I have simulated this effect using a velocity algorithm instead, which, again, is covered in the next section.

```
/****************************************************
 * key listener events
 ****************************************************/
public void keyReleased(KeyEvent k) { }
public void keyTyped(KeyEvent k) { }
public void keyPressed(KeyEvent k) {
    int keyCode = k.getKeyCode();

    switch (keyCode) {
```

```java
case KeyEvent.VK_LEFT:
    //left arrow rotates ship left 5 degrees
    ship.incFaceAngle(-5);
    if (ship.getFaceAngle() < 0) ship.setFaceAngle(360-5);
    break;

case KeyEvent.VK_RIGHT:
    //right arrow rotates ship right 5 degrees
    ship.incFaceAngle(5);
    if (ship.getFaceAngle() > 360) ship.setFaceAngle(5);
    break;

case KeyEvent.VK_UP:
    //up arrow adds thrust to ship (1/10 normal speed)
    ship.setMoveAngle(ship.getFaceAngle() - 90);
    ship.incVelX(calcAngleMoveX(ship.getMoveAngle()) * 0.1);
    ship.incVelY(calcAngleMoveY(ship.getMoveAngle()) * 0.1);
    break;

//Ctrl, Enter, or Space can be used to fire weapon
case KeyEvent.VK_CONTROL:
case KeyEvent.VK_ENTER:
case KeyEvent.VK_SPACE:
    //fire a bullet
    currentBullet++;
    if (currentBullet > BULLETS - 1) currentBullet = 0;
    bullet[currentBullet].setAlive(true);
    //point bullet in same direction ship is facing
    bullet[currentBullet].setX(ship.getX());
    bullet[currentBullet].setY(ship.getY());
    bullet[currentBullet].setMoveAngle(ship.getFaceAngle() - 90);
    //fire bullet at angle of the ship
    double angle = bullet[currentBullet].getMoveAngle();
    double svx = ship.getVelX();
    double svy = ship.getVelY();
    bullet[currentBullet].setVelX(svx + calcAngleMoveX(angle) * 2);
    bullet[currentBullet].setVelY(svy + calcAngleMoveY(angle) * 2);
    //play shoot sound
    shoot.play();
    break;
```

```
        case KeyEvent.VK_B:
            //toggle bounding rectangles
            showBounds = !showBounds;
            break;
    }
}
```

Calculating Realistic Motion

The most fascinating part of this game is how the movement of the player's ship, the bullets, and the asteroids are all controlled by two methods that return floating-point values for the X and Y update for the object.

definition

Velocity is a rate of change of position calculated in pixels per second.

The calcAngleMoveX() method uses cosine to calculate the update value for X, returned as a double. The calcAngleMoveY() method uses sine to calculate the update value for Y, also returned as a double. These small methods accept a single parameter (the angle that a game object is facing) and return an estimated X and Y update value in pixels based on that angle. I can't stress enough how wonderful these two methods are! In the past, I have relied mainly on the brute force (and imprecise) method to move game objects (usually called *sprites*) on the screen. I would set the velocityX to 1 and velocityY to 0 to cause an object to move to the right. Or, I would set velocityX to 0 and velocityY to –1 to cause the game object to move up on the screen. These velocity variables, along with an object's X and Y values, would cause the object to move around on the screen in a certain way.

I have written many games that used this type of movement code. Invariably, these games include a lot of switch statements to account for each of the directions that an object might be facing. For instance, if a space ship sprite has eight directions of travel, then I would write a switch statement that considered the case for each direction (0 to 7, where 0 is north and 4 is south), and then update the X and Y values based on the ship's direction.

No longer! These wonderful methods now calculate the velocity for X and Y based on an object's orientation as an angle (from 0 to 360). Not only does this result in a more realistic game, but the source code is actually cleaner and shorter! As far as realism goes, this code supports every angle from 0 to 359 (where a circle is comprised of 360 degrees). You can point the space ship in this game at an angle of 1, then fire a weapon, and that bullet will travel just slightly off from due north.

The biggest difference between this new method of sprite movement from my previous game is that I previously used integers, but now I am using floating-point variables (doubles). This allows the velocityX and velocityY variables to reflect any of the 360 degrees of movement. For an angle of 45 degrees, velocityX is set to 1 pixel, while velocityY is set to 0. The cardinal directions (north, south, east, and west) are similarly predictable. But when dealing with an angle such as 17 degrees, the velocity variables will be set to some very unusual numbers. For instance, velocityX might be set to something like 0.01, while velocityY is set to something like 1.57. These numbers don't equate to actual pixel-level movements on the screen in a single frame, but when you consider that the game is running at 50 fps or more, then these values add up, and the ship or other game object is moved over time in the correct direction. Since the vector transform method expects floating-point values for X and Y, these velocity values work just fine with the part of the program that draws things on the screen. It is fascinating to watch, and we will be using this technique throughout the book.

Now, without further ado, here are the velocity calculation methods in all their simplistic glory:

```
/******************************************************
 * calculate X movement value based on direction angle
 ******************************************************/
public double calcAngleMoveX(double angle) {
    return (double) (Math.cos(angle * Math.PI / 180));
}


/******************************************************
 * calculate Y movement value based on direction angle
 ******************************************************/
public double calcAngleMoveY(double angle) {
    return (double) (Math.sin(angle * Math.PI / 180));
}
}
```

What You Have Learned

This chapter threw a lot of new concepts your way, without fully explaining all of them, but with the goal of giving you an opportunity to examine a nearly complete game and see how it was created from start to finish. This Asteroids-style game will be enhanced in subsequent chapters into an exciting arcade-style game with a scrolling background. Specifically, you learned

- How to use the Graphics2D class.
- How to use a thread as a game loop.

- How to draw vector graphics to make game objects.
- How to move an object based on its velocity.
- How to test for collisions between game objects.

Review Questions

The following questions will help you to determine how well you have learned the subjects discussed in this chapter. The answers are provided in Appendix A, "Chapter Quiz Answers."

1. What is the name of the method that calculates the velocity for X?
2. What is the base class from which Ship, Asteroid, and Bullet are inherited?
3. What classic Atari game inspired the game developed in this chapter?
4. What type of collision testing does this game use?
5. What method of the Shape class does this game use for collision testing?
6. What geometric shape class does the Ship and Asteroid classes use?
7. What geometric shape class does the Bullet class use?
8. Which applet event actually draws the screen?
9. What is the name of the interface class used to add threading support to the game?
10. What math function does calcAngleMoveX use to calculate the X velocity?

On Your Own

Although this game will be enhanced in future chapters, you will learn a lot by making changes to the source code to add some of your own ideas to the game right now. Use the following exercises to test your grasp of the material covered in this chapter.

1. If you apply a lot of thrust to the ship so that it is moving very fast across the screen, and then rotate around backwards and fire a bullet, that bullet will seem to stand still or move very slowly. This is because the bullet is based on the ship's velocity. This isn't very realistic. Modify the weapon firing code in the keyPressed event method to fire bullets at a fixed rate regardless of the ship's velocity.

2. The ship tends to rotate rather slowly when you press the Left or Right arrow keys, making it difficult to hit asteroids that are closing in on the ship from all directions. The rotation angle is adjusted by 5 degrees each time the keys are pressed. Modify the game so that the ship rotates much more quickly without changing this 5-degree value. In other words, you want it to rotate by the same value, but do these rotations more quickly.

PART II

JAVA 2-D GAME PROGRAMMING

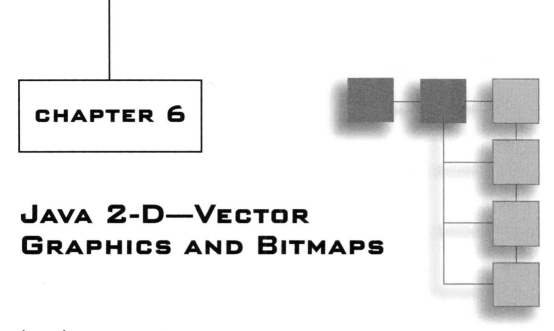

CHAPTER 6

JAVA 2-D—VECTOR GRAPHICS AND BITMAPS

The previous chapter really pushed the limits as far as the amount of information covered without thorough explanations beforehand. I wanted to immerse you in the source code for a game right up front before fully explaining all of the concepts to give you a feel for what is involved in creating a real game. The *Asteroids* clone was not a great game, and not even very good looking, but it was functional, if a bit nostalgic. Java has a robust and feature-rich set of classes for working with 2-D vector graphics and bitmaps, making it possible to draw rectangles, polygons, and other shapes very easily. Here are the key topics in this chapter:

Here are some of the questions that will be answered in this chapter:

- Drawing and manipulating vector graphics
- Using the AffineTransform class
- Applying the translation, rotation, and scaling of shapes
- Loading and drawing bitmap images
- Applying transformations to bitmap images

Programming Vector Graphics

You have already been exposed to a significant number of features in the Graphics2D class and other classes in java.awt (the abstract window toolkit), such as the Rectangle and Polygon classes. We will get into timing, the game loop, threads, and take a look at that Runnable interface in the next chapter. Although I'm eager to get into timing already, we'll stick with the basics for now and focus on graphics programming.

The core of Java's 2-D graphics engine is the `Graphics2D` class. This class is incredibly versatile for working with vector graphics and bitmapped graphics. For instance, `Graphics2D` has 10 different methods for drawing images in a variety of ways! In my opinion, this is somewhat of an overkill just to draw images on the screen. But Java is arguably known more for its versatility and convenience than for its raw speed. This class knows how to draw rectangles and many other shapes. But it can do a lot more than just draw—it can also move, rotate, and scale the shapes!

Working with Shapes

Let's write a short program to demonstrate. The RandomShapes program is shown in Figure 6.1, and the source code listing follows.

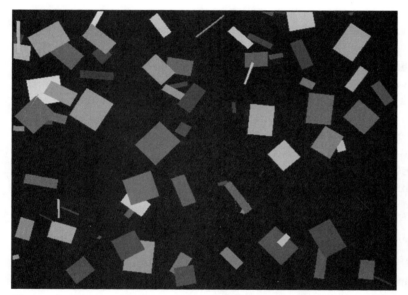

Figure 6.1 The RandomShapes program demonstrates the `Graphics2D` class.

```
/*************************************************************
 * Beginning Java 5 Game Programming
 * by Jonathan S. Harbour
 * RandomShapes program
 *************************************************************/

import java.awt.*;
import java.applet.*;
import java.awt.geom.*;
import java.util.*;
```

```java
public class RandomShapes extends Applet {
    //here's the shape used for drawing
    private Shape shape;

    //applet init event
    public void init() {
        shape = new Rectangle2D.Double(-1.0, -1.0, 1.0, 1.0);
    }

    //applet paint event
    public void paint(Graphics g) {
        //create an instance of Graphics2D
        Graphics2D g2d = (Graphics2D)g;

        //save the identity transform
        AffineTransform identity = new AffineTransform();

        //create a random number generator
        Random rand = new Random();

        //save the window width/height
        int width = getSize().width;
        int height = getSize().height;

        //fill the background with black
        g2d.setColor(Color.BLACK);
        g2d.fillRect(0, 0, width, height);

        for (int n = 0; n < 300; n++) {
            //reset Graphics2D to the identity transform
            g2d.setTransform(identity);

            //move, rotate, and scale the shape randomly
            g2d.translate(rand.nextInt() % width, rand.nextInt() % height);
            g2d.rotate(Math.toRadians(360 * rand.nextDouble()));
            g2d.scale(60 * rand.nextDouble(), 60 * rand.nextDouble());

            //draw the shape with a random color
            g2d.setColor(new Color(rand.nextInt()));
            g2d.fill(shape);
        }
    }
}
```

This program used the Graphics2D class to translate, rotate, and scale a Shape object randomly, which results in the screen being filled with random rectangles of varying sizes and orientations. This simple program illustrates the base concept behind the *Asteroids*-style game from the previous chapter—that Java provides the toolset for manipulating 2-D graphics, and it's up to you how you will use these versatile tools.

The RandomShapes program defines a Shape object (called *shape*) and then uses that basic object to create a Rectangle2D like so:

```
shape = new Rectangle2D.Double(-1.0, -1.0, 1.0, 1.0);
```

This works, even though the shape object was originally created as a Shape because Rectangle2D is derived from the Shape class. In other words, Rectangle2D inherits from Shape. This makes it possible to use the Graphics2D method fill to draw a filled rectangle, even though it was defined originally as a basic Shape. For each class, such as Rectangle, there is a floating-point version, such as Rectangle2D. Classes like Rectangle utilize integer values, while Rectangle2D uses floats and doubles. You can also use the Point and Polygon classes in similar fashion.

Working with Polygons

The Polygon class is a bit different than Point and Rectangle because it allows you to define the shape yourself using X and Y value pairs. You can construct a polygon with just a single point or a polygon with four points to duplicate the Point and Rectangle classes yourself. Or you can define custom polygons, such as the asteroids and ship in the previous chapter. The asteroid shape (shown in Figure 6.2) was defined like this:

```
private int[] astx = {-20,-13, 0,20,22, 20, 12,  2,-10,-22,-16};
private int[] asty = { 20, 23,17,20,16,-20,-22,-14,-17,-20, -5};
```

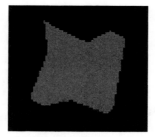

Figure 6.2 The asteroid shape.

These two arrays define the X and Y points for the polygon. We call a point a *vertex*, and the plural form is *vertices*. When you are creating a polygon in this manner, keep in mind that the X and Y arrays must pair up, since every X must go with a Y value to make a vertex.

When you're ready to draw a shape, whether it is a rectangle, a polygon, or something else, you have two choices. You can use the fill() method to draw the shape with a filled-in color. Or you can use the draw() method to draw the outline or border of the shape in the current color. The color is set with the setColor() method beforehand. Sometimes it can be confusing when you are trying to define the shape of a polygon using the two arrays of X and Y points, so you may want to design the polygon on paper or in a graphics editor first. Figure 6.3 shows the design of a five-sided star-shaped polygon.

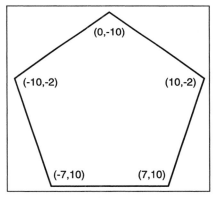

Figure 6.3 This five-sided polygon will be modeled in the RandomPolygons program.

Seeing a diagram of the image can really help, especially when you have a complex polygon in the works. Here are the arrays for defining this polygon. Note how the points directly correspond to the values in the figure.

```
private int[] xpoints = {  0,-10, -7,  7, 10 };
private int[] ypoints = {-10, -2, 10, 10, -2 };
```

Let's write a program to demonstrate how to create and draw polygons. The RandomPolygons program will use the five-sided star polygon with random rotation and scaling. The output of the program is shown in Figure 6.4.

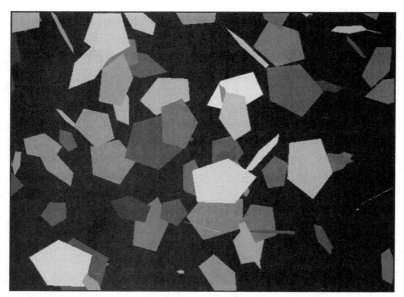

Figure 6.4 The RandomPolygons program draws star-shaped polygons.

```
/**********************************************************
 * Beginning Java 5 Game Programming
 * by Jonathan S. Harbour
 * RandomPolygons program
 **********************************************************/

import java.awt.*;
import java.applet.*;
import java.util.*;
import java.awt.geom.*;

public class RandomPolygons extends Applet {
    private int[] xpoints = {  0,-10, -7,  7, 10 };
    private int[] ypoints = {-10, -2, 10, 10, -2 };

    //here's the shape used for drawing
    private Polygon poly;

    //applet init event
    public void init() {
        poly = new Polygon(xpoints, ypoints, xpoints.length);
    }
```

```
//applet paint event
public void paint(Graphics g) {
    //create an instance of Graphics2D
    Graphics2D g2d = (Graphics2D) g;

    //save the identity transform
    AffineTransform identity = new AffineTransform();

    //create a random number generator
    Random rand = new Random();

    //save the window width/height
    int width = getSize().width;
    int height = getSize().height;

    //fill the background with black
    g2d.setColor(Color.BLACK);
    g2d.fillRect(0, 0, width, height);

    for (int n = 0; n < 300; n++) {
        //reset Graphics2D to the identity transform
        g2d.setTransform(identity);

        //move, rotate, and scale the shape randomly
        g2d.translate(rand.nextInt() % width, rand.nextInt() % height);
        g2d.rotate(Math.toRadians(360 * rand.nextDouble()));
        g2d.scale(5 * rand.nextDouble(), 5 * rand.nextDouble());

        //draw the shape with a random color
        g2d.setColor(new Color(rand.nextInt()));
        g2d.fill(poly);
    }
}
}
```

Rotating and Scaling Shapes

The preceding programs have used vector rotation to rotate rectangles and polygons by a random value. Now I want to give you a little more direct exposure to this feature by writing a program that rotates a single polygon on the screen using the arrow keys and, alternately, the mouse buttons. The scale factor is set to a fixed value of 20, which you can change if you want. Figure 6.5 shows the output of the RotatePolygon program.

Figure 6.5 The RotatePolygon
program rotates a star-shaped polygon.

There are a couple of notable differences between this program and the last one. This program just draws a single shape, so there is no need to set the identity transform before drawing. This program implements the KeyListener and MouseListener interfaces, which means that the program must use all of the methods defined in these interface classes, even if you don't plan to use them. It's an odd quirk that is inherent to how interface classes work because they are abstract.

```
/***********************************************************
 * Beginning Java 5 Game Programming
 * by Jonathan S. Harbour
 * RotatePolygon program
 ***********************************************************/
import java.awt.*;
import java.awt.event.*;
import java.applet.*;
import java.util.*;
import java.awt.geom.*;

public class RotatePolygon extends Applet implements KeyListener, MouseListener {
    private int[] xpoints = {  0,-10, -7,  7, 10 };
    private int[] ypoints = {-10, -2, 10, 10, -2 };

    //here's the shape used for drawing
    private Polygon poly;

    //polygon rotation variable
    int rotation = 0;

    //applet init event
    public void init() {
        //create the polygon
        poly = new Polygon(xpoints, ypoints, xpoints.length);
```

```
        //initialize the listeners
        addKeyListener(this);
        addMouseListener(this);
    }


    //applet paint event
    public void paint(Graphics g) {
        //create an instance of Graphics2D
        Graphics2D g2d = (Graphics2D) g;

        //save the identity transform
        AffineTransform identity = new AffineTransform();

        //save the window width/height
        int width = getSize().width;
        int height = getSize().height;

        //fill the background with black
        g2d.setColor(Color.BLACK);
        g2d.fillRect(0, 0, width, height);

        //move, rotate, and scale the shape randomly
        g2d.translate(width / 2, height / 2);
        g2d.scale(20, 20);
        g2d.rotate(Math.toRadians(rotation));

        //draw the shape with a random color
        g2d.setColor(Color.RED);
        g2d.fill(poly);
        g2d.setColor(Color.BLUE);
        g2d.draw(poly);
    }


    //handle keyboard events
    public void keyReleased(KeyEvent k) { }
    public void keyTyped(KeyEvent k) { }
    public void keyPressed(KeyEvent k) {
        switch (k.getKeyCode()) {
        case KeyEvent.VK_LEFT:
            rotation--;
            if (rotation < 0) rotation = 359;
            repaint();
```

```
            break;
        case KeyEvent.VK_RIGHT:
            rotation++;
            if (rotation > 360) rotation = 0;
            repaint();
            break;
        }
    }

    //handle mouse events
    public void mouseEntered(MouseEvent m) { }
    public void mouseExited(MouseEvent m) { }
    public void mouseReleased(MouseEvent m) { }
    public void mouseClicked(MouseEvent m) { }
    public void mousePressed(MouseEvent m) {
        switch(m.getButton()) {
        case MouseEvent.BUTTON1:
            rotation--;
            if (rotation < 0) rotation = 359;
            repaint();
            break;
        case MouseEvent.BUTTON3:
            rotation++;
            if (rotation > 360) rotation = 0;
            repaint();
            break;
        }
    }
}
```

Programming Bitmapped Graphics

I mentioned before that there are 10 methods for drawing bitmap images in Java. Actually, six of those methods are found in the base Graphics class, while the remaining four are found in Graphics2D. I think you will find the four Graphics2D methods more useful, so we won't spend any time working with the legacy versions.

The most amazing thing about Java is how the Graphics2D class' matrix math transforms work equally well with vectors *and* images. What this means is that you will be able to translate, rotate, and scale bitmap images just as easily as you have seen vector graphics being manipulated on screen. This awesome functionality will translate well into the subsequent chapters on sprite and animation programming. The real difference when working with images is that you will need to create a separate `AffineTransform` object to manipulate the `Image` object, rather than going directly through `Graphics2D`.

tip

When you are working on a game that uses bitmap files, you need to copy the files to the correct location or else the program won't run. The correct location for bitmap files is inside the classes directory in your project directory.

You can use the `getImage()` method to load a bitmap file stored in many different formats, with the most common being .png (portable network graphics) and .bmp (Windows bitmap).

Loading and Drawing Images

Let's write a program that demonstrates how to load and draw a bitmap image. We can use the `getImage()` method to load an image file, and then use `drawImage()` to draw it onto the applet window. Figure 6.6 shows the output from the DrawImage program. This high-quality castle image was rendered by Reiner Prokein using Caligari Truespace. He offers a large number of royalty-free game artwork, such as this castle, at his Web site, www.reinerstileset.de (a German site with an English translation).

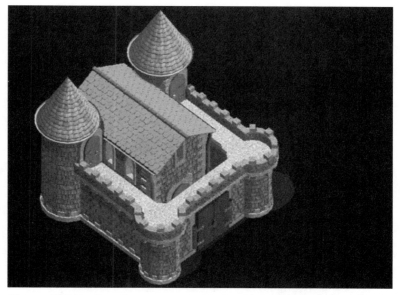

Figure 6.6 The DrawImage program loads a bitmap file and draws it.

```java
/****************************************************************
 * Beginning Java 5 Game Programming
 * by Jonathan S. Harbour
 * DrawImage program
 ****************************************************************/

package drawimage;
import java.awt.*;
import java.applet.*;
import java.net.*;

public class DrawImage extends Applet {
    //image variable
    private Image image;

    private URL getURL(String filename) {
        URL url = null;
        try {
            url = this.getClass().getResource(filename);
        }
        catch (Exception e) { }
        return url;
    }

    //applet init event
    public void init() {
        image = getImage(getURL("castle.png"));
    }

    //applet paint event
    public void paint(Graphics g) {
        //create an instance of Graphics2D
        Graphics2D g2d = (Graphics2D) g;

        //fill the background with black
        g2d.setColor(Color.BLACK);
        g2d.fillRect(0, 0, getSize().width, getSize().height);

        //draw the image
        g2d.drawImage(image, 0, 0, this);
    }
}
```

Applying Transforms to Images

Now I'll demonstrate how to apply a transformation to a simple bitmap image. This will make our sprite code in the upcoming chapters really fun because the sprite images will be manipulated with these transformations as well. Since this code is similar to the code for manipulating vectors, it should be familiar to you by now. The only difference when working with an image is that you must define a separate AffineTransform object for manipulating the Image object because the Graphics2D transforms are designed to work only with vectors. Figure 6.7 shows the output of the RandomImages program, showing a space ship image being moved, rotated, and scaled.

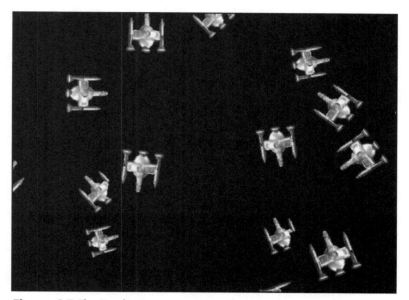

Figure 6.7 The RandomImages program draws images at random locations, with random rotation and scaling.

```
/*************************************************************
 * Beginning Java 5 Game Programming
 * by Jonathan S. Harbour
 * RandomImages program
 *************************************************************/
import java.awt.*;
import java.applet.*;
import java.util.*;
import java.awt.geom.*;
import java.net.*;
```

```java
public class RandomImages extends Applet {
    //image variable
    private Image image;

    //identity transformation
    AffineTransform identity = new AffineTransform();

    private URL getURL(String filename) {
        URL url = null;
        try {
            url = this.getClass().getResource(filename);
        }
        catch (Exception e) { }
        return url;
    }

    //applet init event
    public void init() {
        image = getImage(getURL("spaceship.png"));
    }

    //applet paint event
    public void paint(Graphics g) {
        //create an instance of Graphics2D
        Graphics2D g2d = (Graphics2D) g;

        //working transform object
        AffineTransform trans = new AffineTransform();

        //random number generator
        Random rand = new Random();

        //applet window width/height
        int width = getSize().width;
        int height = getSize().height;

        //fill the background with black
        g2d.setColor(Color.BLACK);
        g2d.fillRect(0, 0, getSize().width, getSize().height);
```

```
        //draw the image multiple times
        for (int n = 0; n < 50; n++) {
            trans.setTransform(identity);
            //move, rotate, scale the image randomly
            trans.translate(rand.nextInt()%width, rand.nextInt()%height);
            trans.rotate(Math.toRadians(360 * rand.nextDouble()));
            double scale = rand.nextDouble()+1;
            trans.scale(scale, scale);

            //draw the image
            g2d.drawImage(image, trans, this);
        }
    }
}
```

What You Have Learned

This chapter provides a bridge from the material you were immersed into in the previous chapter to the new concepts you will learn in the next chapter covering the basics of sprite programming. You will soon be animating game objects on the screen and working on a sprite handler class. Specifically, you learned

- How to use the Graphics2D class to manipulate vector graphics.
- How to translate, rotate, and scale vector shapes.
- How to draw bitmap images.
- How to translate, rotate, and scale bitmap images.

Review Questions

The following questions will help you to determine how well you have learned the subjects discussed in this chapter. The answers are provided in Appendix A, "Chapter Quiz Answers."

1. What is the primary class we've been using to manipulate vector graphics in this chapter?

2. Where is a good source of free game art on the Web that was recommended in this chapter?

3. What Graphics2D method is used to draw an image?

4. Which Java class contains the getImage() method?

5. What class makes it possible to perform translation, rotation, and scaling of shapes and images?

6. Which `Graphics2D` method draws a polygon?

7. Which transform method moves a shape or image to a new location?

8. What method initializes the keyboard listener interface?

9. What method in the `Random` class returns a double-precision floating-point value?

10. Which `KeyListener` event detects key presses?

On Your Own

Although this game will be enhanced in future chapters, you will learn a lot by making changes to the source code to add some of your own ideas to the game right now. Use the following exercises to test your grasp of the material covered in this chapter.

1. There are many example programs in this chapter that could be modified and experimented upon. Let's tweak the RandomImages program. Modify the program so that it loads and draws two different images randomly instead of just a single image.

2. Modify the RotatePolygon program so that it will rotate based on mouse movement instead of button clicks. You will need to implement the `MouseMotionListener` interface (and events) and call the `addMouseMotionListener` method to gain access to the `mouseMoved` event. In this event, you can track mouse movement and rotate the polygon accordingly.

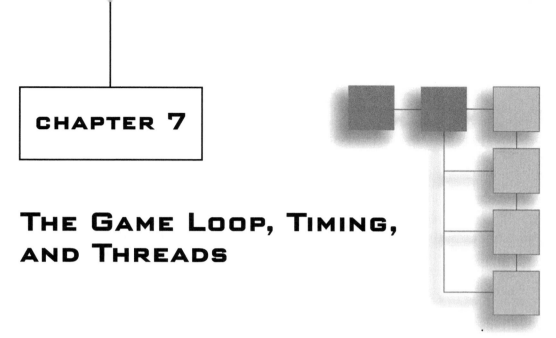

CHAPTER 7

THE GAME LOOP, TIMING, AND THREADS

You have learned how to use the Graphics2D class to program graphics using vector shapes and bitmap images, and you have even seen a nearly complete game written from scratch. You have learned how to load and play sound files, MIDI music files, and how to program the keyboard and mouse. By all accounts, you have the tools to create many different games already. But there are some tricks of the trade, secrets of the craft, that will help you to make your games stand out in the crowd and impress. This chapter discusses the game loop and its vital importance to a smooth-running game. You will learn about threads and timing, and will take the *Asteroids*-style game created in Chapter 5 into completely new territory, as it is modified extensively in the following pages.

Here are the specific topics you will learn about:

- Overriding default applet methods
- Using timing methods
- Starting and stopping a thread
- Using a thread for the game loop
- Building the *Galactic War* game

The Potency of a Game Loop

The key to creating a game loop to facilitate the needs of a high-speed game is Java's multi-threading capability. Threads are such an integral part of Java that it makes a special thread available to your program just for this purpose. This special thread is called Runnable, an interface class. However, it's entirely possible to write a Java game without threads by just using a simple game loop. I'll show you how to do this first, and then we'll take a look at threads as an even better form of game loop.

tip

An *interface class* is an abstract class with properties and methods that are defined but not implemented. A program that uses an interface class is said to consume it, and must implement all of the public methods in the interface. Typical examples include KeyListener and Runnable.

A Simple (Dead) Loop

The Runnable interface gives your program its own *awareness*. I realize this concept sounds a lot like artificial intelligence, but the term awareness is a good description of the Runnable interface. Before Runnable, your Java programs have been somewhat naive, capable of only processing during the screen refresh, and then only once. Let's take a look at an example. The SimpleLoop program is shown in Figure 7.1.

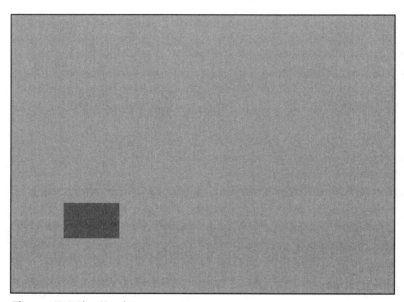

Figure 7.1 The SimpleLoop program.

```
/************************************************************
 * SimpleLoop program
 ************************************************************/
import java.awt.*;
import java.applet.*;
import java.util.*;
```

```
public class SimpleLoop extends Applet {
    Random rand = new Random();
    public void init() {
        //nothing to init this time
    }

    public void paint(Graphics g) {
        Graphics2D g2d = (Graphics2D) g;

        //create a random rectangle
        int w = rand.nextInt(100);
        int h = rand.nextInt(100);
        int x = rand.nextInt(getSize().width - w);
        int y = rand.nextInt(getSize().height - h);
        Rectangle rect = new Rectangle(x,y,w,h);

        //generate a random color
        int red = rand.nextInt(256);
        int green = rand.nextInt(256);
        int blue = rand.nextInt(256);
        g2d.setColor(new Color(red,green,blue));

        //draw the rectangle
        g2d.fill(rect);
    }
}
```

tip

The Random class is located in the java.awt.util class along with many other utility classes that provide commonly needed tools to your program. To use Random in your program, you must include this class with the following import statement:

```
import java.awt.util.*;
```

This simple program just creates a random rectangle and draws it on the screen during the applet's paint() event. This program has no loop whatsoever, so it cannot process anything in real time—not space ships, asteroids, jumping Italian plumbers, yellow dot-eaters, or female spelunkers packing dual Berettas. The only thing this program can do is draw a single rectangle.

Adding Some Interaction

There are some ways you can make the program a little more interactive. You could, for instance, draw a new rectangle every time the user hits a key or clicks the mouse. The only problem with these listener interfaces is that you have to implement all of them or none of them. That reminds me of Yoda's famous saying, "Do, or do not. There is no 'try.'" An interface class is an all or nothing proposition that tends to junk up your source code, not to mention that it takes a lot of work to type in all of those interface event methods every time! But there's no real workaround for the unused event methods.

note

I've been thinking about a way to use all of these interface classes (such as `Runnable` and the input listeners) by tucking them away into a class outside of the main program. This support class would provide my main program with real *events* when things happen, such as key presses, mouse movement, and other events. Perhaps this is the birth of an idea that will become some sort of game engine?

Let's modify the SimpleLoop program to make it possible to draw multiple rectangles based on user input. We'll automate this soon with an actual loop, but I want you to see this progression first.

tip

The `interface` classes `KeyListener` and `MouseListener` are found in the `java.awt.event` class. To use the events defined in these interfaces in your program, you must include this class with the following `import` statement:

```
import java.awt.event.*;
```

I'm just going to show you the changes to the program rather than the entire code listing because only a few things have been added to the SimpleLoop program. First, up at the top of the program with the `import` statements, make sure the following `import` statement is included. This is usually added automatically by JBuilder.

```
import java.awt.event.*;
```

Next, modify the main program class definition so that it implements the `KeyListener` and `MouseListener` interfaces.

```
public class SimpleLoop extends Applet implements KeyListener, MouseListener {
```

Next, add two lines of code to the `init()` event to get the key and mouse listeners working:

```
public void init() {
    addKeyListener(this);
    addMouseListener(this);
}
```

Next, add the key and mouse event methods. Most of them are not used, but must be defined anyway. The only two that are being used is `keyPressed()` and `mousePressed()`, and they both simply make a call to `repaint()`.

```
//handle keyboard events
public void keyReleased(KeyEvent k) { }
public void keyTyped(KeyEvent k) { }
public void keyPressed(KeyEvent k) {
    repaint();
}

//handle mouse events
public void mouseEntered(MouseEvent m) { }
public void mouseExited(MouseEvent m) { }
public void mouseReleased(MouseEvent m) { }
public void mouseClicked(MouseEvent m) { }
public void mousePressed(MouseEvent m) {
    repaint();
}
```

Now if you run this program, you'll see output that looks like Figure 7.2. What's this? The program still does the same thing—it just draws a single rectangle. Well, that is somewhat true and somewhat false. Try holding down a key or mouse button. See what happens? The program draws many rectangles very quickly. Even though it may appear to be filling the applet window with rectangles, it is simply drawing one rectangle at a time and refreshing the window very fast so that it appears to be filling. As soon as you release the key or button, you will see just one rectangle remaining.

Figure 7.2 Drawing many rectangles using key and mouse input.

Overriding Some Default Applet Behaviors

There is a serious problem with this program because it was supposed to just *add* a new rectangle every time the user presses a key or mouse button, not *redraw* the entire applet window—with a single rectangle left over. There is definitely something odd going on because this program *should have* worked as expected.

Well, it turns out that Java has been screwing with the screen without permission. Or rather, by *default*. The Applet class, which is the basis for the SimpleLoop program (recall that it *extends Applet*), provides many default event methods that do certain things for you. You don't even need to implement paint() if you don't want to, and the Applet base class will provide it for your program. Granted, nothing will be drawn on the window as a result, but the compiler won't give you an error. This differs from an interface class (such as KeyListener) that *mandates* that you must implement all of its abstract methods. So it's pretty obvious by this difference in functionality that Applet is not an interface class, but a fully-functioning class.

What happens then when you implement an Applet class method like init() or paint()? These methods are essentially empty inside the Applet class. Oh, they exist and are not abstract, but they don't *do anything*. The Applet class defines these methods in such a way that you can *override* them in your applet. For instance, in the SimpleLoop program, SimpleLoop is actually the name of the class, and it inherits from Applet. Therefore, SimpleLoop has the opportunity to override any of the methods in Applet that it wants to, including init() and paint().

However, there's another method that we haven't used yet called update(). A-ha! No, I wasn't holding out on you because you've actually used this method before—in the game project back in Chapter 5, "Creating Your First Java Game." The update() method actually *does* do something as coded in the Applet class—it calls repaint() to refresh the applet window. (Light bulb moment.)

Since the default update() method has been refreshing the screen for our programs, we have had absolutely no control over this process. That explains why only one rectangle was being drawn at a time in the SimpleLoop program—update() was refreshing the screen on its own. In a sense, your Java program is a *slave* to the master Applet class until you override the functionality by rewriting its methods. It's time to break the bonds of object-oriented slavery. Let's add the update() method to the program:

```
public void update(Graphics g) {
    paint(g);
}
```

As you can see, the update() method is bearing a single line of code, a call to the paint() method. This gives you complete control over the screen refresh because the default update() would not just repaint the screen, it would also *clear the screen*. Now you can run the SimpleLoop program and see a bunch of rectangles as originally expected, as shown in Figure 7.3.

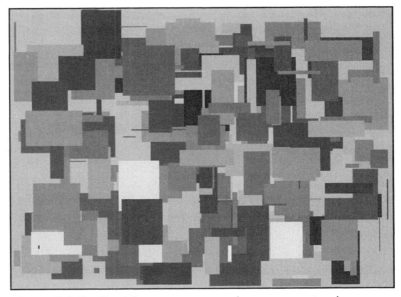

Figure 7.3 The SimpleLoop program now draws many rectangles.

I think this example makes it pretty clear that any serious game will need to override the update() method as well as paint(). But that doesn't really address the subject at hand—what about the loop? I've been calling this program "SimpleLoop" when no loop is even being used. Let's get to that now.

Feeling Loopy

There are quite a few Applet methods available that we haven't implemented yet, in addition to the standard methods you've seen so far. I'll go over the remaining key Applet methods at the end of this section to make you aware of them. For now, I'd like to introduce you to the next Applet method: start(). The start() method is invoked in your Java applet by the Web browser right after calling init(). So, you can use init() to get the game ready to go, and then use start() to get things moving.

Now you finally have an opportunity to add a real loop to this program. But just for kicks, what do you think would happen if you added a while() loop to the init() method? I tried it, so you should try it too. Doing this will lock up the applet, which will not even be displayed. Why? Because init() is called before the applet has even brought up the Web browser or applet viewer, so putting a loop here prevents the applet from drawing. However, this is not the case with the start() method, which is called after the applet has been initialized and is ready to go. The engine has been started and is just waiting for you to press the accelerator at this point. Let's add the start() method to our SimpleLoop program:

```
public void start() {
    while (true) {
        repaint();
    }
}
```

Now go ahead and run the program. Whoa, check it out in Figure 7.4! This program now screams, with thousands of rectangles being drawn every second, literally filling the window instantly. Now *that's* what I call a combustion-powered game loop! By adding this magical new method, start(), you're able to give the program a whole new dimension of functionality. It's sort of like a supercharger or turbocharger.

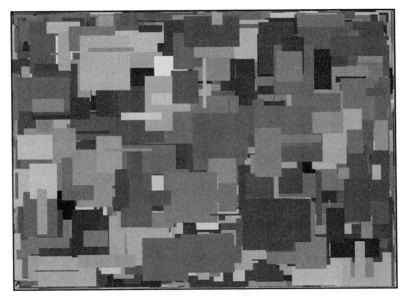

Figure 7.4 The SimpleLoop program, equipped with a real loop, now runs with potent speed.

You can build on this game loop, too. The call to repaint the window is only the last step in a game. First, you move your game objects around on the screen, perform collision testing, and so forth. You can perform all of these steps in the start() event and then call repaint() at the very end. Here is a suggestion (not actual code):

```
public void start() {
    //the game loop
    while (true) {
        //move the game objects
        updateObjects();

        //perform collision testing
        testCollisions();

        //redraw the window
        repaint();
    }
}
```

Recovering Long-Lost Applet Methods

Let's take a look at some more helpful methods in the Applet class that will be useful.

The showStatus() method is used to print some text in the bottom status bar of the browser window or applet viewer program:

```
showStatus(String msg)
```

The isActive() method determines if the applet is active, which is marked just before the start() event method is called:

```
boolean isActive()
```

The start() method is called after init() and is often used to resume the applet after the user has browsed away from the applet page and then returned.

```
void start()
```

The stop() method is called by the Web browser when the Web page changes, signifying that the applet is about to be destroyed.

```
void stop()
```

The destroy() method is called by the browser when the applet is about to be destroyed (removed from memory).

```
void destroy()
```

Stepping Up to Threads

You *can* build an entire game using a game loop within the start() method, as shown previously, and this is a perfectly legitimate way to build your game. I am even tempted to use this method myself for the "new and improved" *Asteroids*-style game (which we'll be upgrading later in this chapter).

We use the Runnable interface class to add threading support to a game. This interface has a single event method called run() that represents the thread's functionality. We can create this run() method in a game and that will act like the game loop. The thread just calls run() once, so you must add a while loop to this method. However, this while will be much different than the one you saw in the start() method earlier. This time, the while loop is running inside a thread that is separate from the main program. By implementing Runnable, a game becomes multi-threaded. In that sense, it will support multiple processors or processor cores! For instance, if you have a dual-core Athlon 64 or a Pentium D, you will be able to see the applet running in a thread that is separate from the Web browser or applet viewer program.

Starting and Stopping the Thread

To get a thread running in an applet, you have to create an instance of the Thread class, and then start it running using the applet's start() event. First, let's create the thread object:

```
Thread thread;
```

Next, create the thread in the start() event method:

```
public void start() {
    thread = new Thread(this);
    thread.start();
}
```

Then you can write the code for the thread's loop in the run() event method (part of Runnable). We'll take a look at what goes inside run() in a moment. First, let's take a look at the stop() event. This method is provided by the Applet class and can be overridden. It has no functionality by default. This is a convenient place to kill the thread, so let's do that:

```
public void stop() {
    thread = null;
}
```

The ThreadedLoop Program

Let's take a look at the entire ThreadedLoop project, and then I'll explain the loop for the thread inside the run() method.

```
/*****************************************************
 * ThreadedLoop program
 *****************************************************/

import java.awt.*;
import java.lang.*;
import java.applet.*;
import java.util.*;

public class ThreadedLoop extends Applet implements Runnable {
    //random number generator
    Random rand = new Random();

    //the main thread
    Thread thread;

    //count the number of rectangles drawn
    long count = 0;
```

```
//applet init event
public void init() {
    //not needed this time
}

//applet start event
public void start() {
    thread = new Thread(this);
    thread.start();
}

//thread run event
public void run() {
    long start = System.currentTimeMillis();

    //acquire the current thread
    Thread current = Thread.currentThread();

    //here's the new game loop
    while (current == thread) {
        try {
            Thread.sleep(0);
        }
        catch(InterruptedException e) {
            e.printStackTrace();
        }

        //draw something
        repaint();

        //figure out how fast it's running
        if (start + 1000 < System.currentTimeMillis()) {
            start = System.currentTimeMillis();
            showStatus("Rectangles per second: " + count);
            count = 0;
        }
    }
}

//applet stop event
public void stop() {
    thread = null;
}
```

```
//applet update event
public void update(Graphics g) {
    paint(g);
}

//applet paint event
public void paint(Graphics g) {
    Graphics2D g2d = (Graphics2D) g;

    //create a random rectangle
    int w = rand.nextInt(100);
    int h = rand.nextInt(100);
    int x = rand.nextInt(getSize().width - w);
    int y = rand.nextInt(getSize().height - h);
    Rectangle rect = new Rectangle(x,y,w,h);

    //generate a random color
    int red = rand.nextInt(256);
    int green = rand.nextInt(256);
    int blue = rand.nextInt(256);
    g2d.setColor(new Color(red,green,blue));

    //draw the rectangle
    g2d.fill(rect);

    //add another to the counter
    count++;
    }
}
```

Now let's examine this run() event that is called by the Runnable interface. There's a lot going on in this method. First, a variable called start gets the current time in milliseconds (System.currentTimeMillis()). This value is used to pause once per second to print out the total number of rectangles that have been drawn (see Figure 7.5).

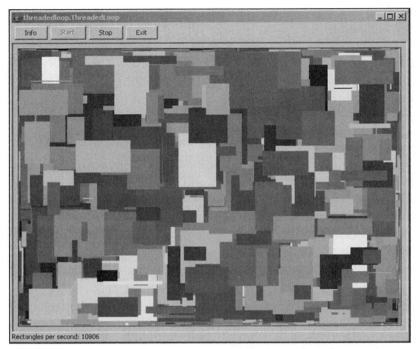

Figure 7.5 The ThreadedLoop program displays the number of rectangles drawn every second.

Next, a local variable is set to the current thread, and then a `while` loop is created.

```
Thread current = Thread.currentThread();
```

This local thread makes sure that our loop only processes thread events intended for the game loop because you can use multiple threads in a program.

```
while (current == thread)
```

The core of the `thread` loop includes a call to `Thread.sleep(0)`, which is a placeholder for slowing the game down to a consistent frame rate. Right now it's running as fast as possible because the `sleep()` method is being passed a 0. This single method call requires an error handler because it throws an `InterruptedException` if the thread is ever interrupted by another thread. This is an advanced subject that doesn't concern us. If the thread is interrupted, it's not a big deal—we'll just ignore any such error that might crop up.

```
try {
    Thread.sleep(0);
}
catch(InterruptedException e) {
    e.printStackTrace();
}
```

After this call to sleep, which will be used eventually to slow the game down to a consistent frame rate, then we can actually go ahead and do something productive by calling various game-related methods to update objects on the screen, perform collision testing, game logic to interact with enemies, and so on. In the block of code that follows, you can see some timing code inside an if statement. This code prints out the number of rectangles that have been drawn by the paint() event during the past 1000 milliseconds (which equals 1 second).

```
//draw something
repaint();

//figure out how fast it's running
if (start + 1000 < System.currentTimeMillis()) {
    start = System.currentTimeMillis();
    showStatus("Rectangles per second: " + count);
    count = 0;
}
```

The single call to repaint() actually makes this program *do something*; all of the rest of the code helps this method call to do its job effectively. Here inside the run() event, which houses the new threaded game loop, I've used one of the new Applet methods. The showStatus() method prints out a String to the status bar at the bottom of the Web browser or applet viewer.

Examining Multi-Threading

Aside from the sample game in Chapter 5, this program might have been your first exposure to multi-threaded programming. Java makes the process very easy compared to other languages. I've used a thread library called pthread to add thread support in my C++ programs in Linux and Windows, and it's not very easy to use at all compared to Java's built-in support for threads. We will continue to use threads in every subsequent chapter, so you will have had a lot of exposure to this subject by the time you complete the book.

note

Game Programming All In One, Third Edition, which will be released in mid-2006, covers the pthread library and many other cross-platform game programming subjects, and is based around the Allegro library and the C++ language.

Building the *Galactic War* Game

Chapter 5, "Creating Your First Java Game," gave you an example of a semi-complete *Asteroids*-style game to give you a feel for what would be covered in the upcoming chapters. You have now learned enough about basic graphics and bitmap images to greatly enhance the game. That original game featured a class called BaseVectorShape, which contained all of the properties needed to manipulate game objects on the screen (the asteroids, bullets, and ship). Now, in this chapter, I'm going to make some changes, starting with a re-naming of BaseVectorShape to BaseGameEntity. I will show you a new class called VectorEntity, which inherits from BaseGameEntity and provides a new property, a Shape object, that made it possible to draw basic rectangles and polygons for the game.

By upgrading the space ship to an image and doing away with the vector ship (which was little more than a filled triangle), the game is really starting to look more like a real game. Despite the nostalgia many of us feel for vectors, there is no substitute for bitmapped graphics. But one of the goals I set out to achieve for this game is to add the ability to use an image instead of a shape, while still retaining the existing transformation features (most importantly, real-time rotation).

Due to this new bitmapped graphics support, it's time to launch this game project by giving it a new name. Instead of *Asteroids*, I have called this project *Galactic War*, and the Java project will be referred to as such from now on. You will be able to open up the project from Chapter 5 and continue using it, or you can just copy the .java files from the old project to the new project. Here are the source code files you will want to import into the new GalacticWar project in JBuilder:

- BaseVectorShape.java
- Asteroid.java
- Bullet.java
- Ship.java
- SoundClip.java
- MidiSequence.java

Note that I did not include the main source code file, Asteroids.java. There are a few changes needed to add image support to the game, so I will just give you the complete source code listing for the main code file, which is now called GalacticWar.java. The complete GalacticWar project is shown in Figure 7.6.

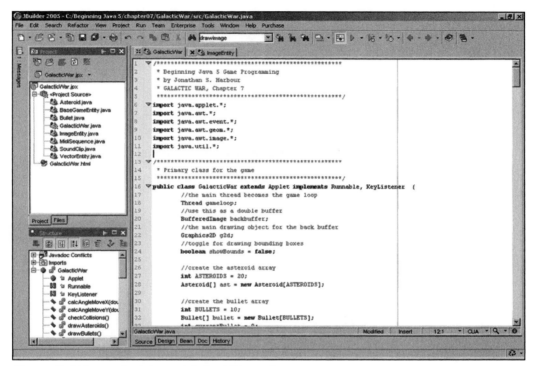

Figure 7.6 The newly christened GalacticWar project.

Changing the Base Class

The BaseVectorShape class needs to be renamed to BaseGameEntity. You can rename the class filename directly in the JBuilder project window and then rename the class in the code window. Rename the class from BaseVectorShape to BaseGameEntity in the class definition, and also rename the class constructor.

I'll be the first one to admit that this class might have been so named from the start. But writing code is a dynamic process, and it's hard to foresee what changes you are likely to make to code in the future. This code is changing with every new chapter. It is not based around an existing game or game engine, so you are seeing changes being made to this game from one step to the next!

Here is the code for this class with the renamed class shown in bold.

```java
public class BaseGameEntity extends Object {
    //variables
    protected boolean alive;
    protected double x,y;
    protected double velX, velY;
    protected double moveAngle, faceAngle;

    //accessor methods
    public boolean isAlive() { return alive; }
    public double getX() { return x; }
    public double getY() { return y; }
    public double getVelX() { return velX; }
    public double getVelY() { return velY; }
    public double getMoveAngle() { return moveAngle; }
    public double getFaceAngle() { return faceAngle; }

    //mutator methods
    public void setAlive(boolean alive) { this.alive = alive; }
    public void setX(double x) { this.x = x; }
    public void incX(double i) { this.x += i; }
    public void setY(double y) { this.y = y; }
    public void incY(double i) { this.y += i; }
    public void setVelX(double velX) { this.velX = velX; }
    public void incVelX(double i) { this.velX += i; }
    public void setVelY(double velY) { this.velY = velY; }
    public void incVelY(double i) { this.velY += i; }
    public void setFaceAngle(double angle) { this.faceAngle = angle; }
    public void incFaceAngle(double i) { this.faceAngle += i; }
    public void setMoveAngle(double angle) { this.moveAngle = angle; }
    public void incMoveAngle(double i) { this.moveAngle += i; }

    //default constructor
    public BaseGameEntity() {
        setAlive(false);
        setX(0.0);
        setY(0.0);
        setVelX(0.0);
        setVelY(0.0);
        setMoveAngle(0.0);
        setFaceAngle(0.0);
    }
}
```

Generalizing the Vector Classes

In the Asteroids project in Chapter 5, "Creating Your First Java Game," there were several classes to handle the ship, asteroids, and bullets in the game. Now we're going to generalize these three classes and make them more general-purpose, since a lot of code is shared among these classes. The Ship class will be replaced entirely with a new class called ImageEntity (covered next). Let me show you what we're going to do with the Asteroid and Bullet classes.

Add a new class to your project and call it VectorEntity. This class is very simple, as the following code suggests. Note that this class inherits from BaseGameEntity now!

```
/***********************************************************
 * Base vector shape class for game entities
 ***********************************************************/
import java.awt.*;

public class VectorEntity extends BaseGameEntity {
    //variables
    private Shape shape;

    //accessor methods
    public Shape getShape() { return shape; }

    //mutator methods
    public void setShape(Shape shape) { this.shape = shape; }

    //default constructor
    VectorEntity() {
        setShape(null);
    }
}
```

The New Asteroid Class

The Asteroid class will be modified now to use VectorEntity as a base class. This frees up a lot of code that was previously duplicated in Asteroid and the other classes. The Asteroid class inherits from VectorEntity, which in turn inherits from BaseGameEntity. You can open up the Asteroid.java file that you copied over from the project in Chapter 5, or you can just add this as new class to the Galactic War project.

```
/*********************************************************
 * Asteroid class derives from BaseVectorShape
 *********************************************************/
import java.awt.*;

public class Asteroid extends VectorEntity {
    //define the asteroid polygon shape
    private int[] astx = {-20,-13, 0,20,22, 20, 12,  2,-10,-22,-16};
    private int[] asty = { 20, 23,17,20,16,-20,-22,-14,-17,-20, -5};

    //rotation speed
    protected double rotVel;
    public double getRotationVelocity() { return rotVel; }
    public void setRotationVelocity(double v) { rotVel = v; }

    //bounding rectangle
    public Rectangle getBounds() {
        Rectangle r;
        r = new Rectangle((int)getX() - 20, (int) getY() - 20, 40, 40);
        return r;
    }

    //default constructor
    Asteroid() {
        setShape(new Polygon(astx, asty, astx.length));
        setAlive(true);
        setRotationVelocity(0.0);
    }
}
```

The New Bullet Class

Much of the code in the previous Bullet class has now been moved to VectorEntity as well, so we can just rewrite this class and give it the specific information relevant to a bullet object (most notably, that the getBounds() method returns a Rectangle that is one pixel wide and one pixel high).

```
/*********************************************************
 * Bullet class derives from BaseVectorShape
 *********************************************************/
import java.awt.*;

public class Bullet extends VectorEntity {
```

```
    //bounding rectangle
    public Rectangle getBounds() {
        Rectangle r;
        r = new Rectangle((int)getX(), (int) getY(), 1, 1);
        return r;
    }

    Bullet() {
        //create the bullet shape
        setShape(new Rectangle(0, 0, 1, 1));
        setAlive(false);
    }
}
```

The ImageEntity Class

Now that the vector-based classes are updated and ready to go, let's focus our attention on the Ship class. As a matter of fact, the Ship class no longer exists in the new Galactic War project. So if you copied this class over from the project in Chapter 5, go ahead an delete it. We're upgrading this class to *raster graphics*, using bitmap images instead of vectors!

The ImageEntity class gives us the ability to use a bitmap image for the objects in the game instead of just vector-based shapes (such as the asteroid polygon). It's never a good idea to completely upgrade a game with some new technique, which is why some of the objects in the game are still vectors. I recommend making small, incremental changes, play-testing the game after each major change to ensure it still runs. There's nothing more frustrating than spending two hours making dramatic changes to a source code file only to find the changes have completely broken the program so that it will either not compile or it is full of bugs.

The ImageEntity class also inherits from the BaseGameEntity class, so it is related to VectorEntity. With the availability of this new class, the old Ship class is no longer needed. The new ship object in the main source code file will be instantiated from ImageEntity directly! This is the best reason to encapsulate a game entity, when you can duplicate it with a reusable class, which is now possible with ImageEntity. This class is awesome! It encapsulates all of the functionality we need to load and draw bitmap images, while still retaining the ability to rotate and move them on the screen!

tip

In the near future, the VectorEntity, Asteroid, and Bullet classes will all go away—replaced by ImageEntity when we upgrade these shapes to bitmaps.

```
/********************************************************
 * Base game image class for bitmapped game entities
 ********************************************************/
import java.awt.*;
import java.awt.Graphics2D;
import java.awt.geom.*;
import java.applet.*;
import java.net.*;

public class ImageEntity extends BaseGameEntity {
    //variables
    private Image image;
    private Applet applet;
    private AffineTransform at;
    private Graphics2D g2d;

    //default constructor
    ImageEntity(Applet a) {
        applet = a;
        setImage(null);
        setAlive(true);
    }

    //sets and returns the entity's image object
    public Image getImage() { return image; }
    public void setImage(Image image) { this.image = image; }

    //returns the width and height of the entity
    public int width() {
        return getImage().getWidth(applet);
    }
    public int height() {
        return getImage().getHeight(applet);
    }

    //returns the center of the entity in pixels
    public double getCenterX() {
        return getX() + width() / 2;
    }
    public double getCenterY() {
        return getY() + height() / 2;
    }
```

```
    //set reference to the drawing object
    public void setGraphics(Graphics2D g) {
        g2d = g;
    }

     private URL getURL(String filename) {
        URL url = null;
        try {
            url = this.getClass().getResource(filename);
        }
        catch (Exception e) { }
        return url;
     }

    //load an image file
    public void load(String filename) {
        setImage(applet.getImage(getURL(filename)));
        while(getImage().getWidth(applet) <= 0);
        double x = applet.getSize().width/2  - width()/2;
        double y = applet.getSize().height/2 - height()/2;
        at = AffineTransform.getTranslateInstance(x, y);
    }

    //move and rotate the entity
    public void transform() {
        at.setToIdentity();
        at.translate((int)getX() + width()/2, (int)getY() + height()/2);
        at.rotate(Math.toRadians(getFaceAngle()));
        at.translate(-width()/2, -height()/2);
    }

    //draw the entity
    public void draw() {
        g2d.drawImage(getImage(), at, applet);
    }

    //bounding rectangle
    public Rectangle getBounds() {
        return new Rectangle((int)getX(),(int)getY(),width(),height());
    }
}
```

The Main Source Code File: GalacticWar.java

The actual gameplay hasn't changed much in this new revision. Figure 7.7 shows the game with a new bitmap image being used for the player's space ship. However, we have upgraded the core classes significantly in this update, which will be very useful in the next chapter, where ImageEntity will see a lot more use. I'll introduce you to a sprite class, too!

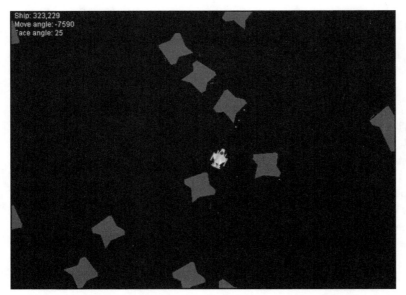

Figure 7.7 The player's space ship is now a bitmap image rather than a polygon.

The new `ImageEntity` class even provides a new version of the `getBounds()` method used to perform collision testing. You can still toggle the bounding rectangles by pressing the B key. The rectangle around the player's ship is shown in Figure 7.8. The collision code is a little too strict for a truly enjoyable game because the bounding rectangles are slightly too big. We'll correct this by fine-tuning the collision code in the next two chapters.

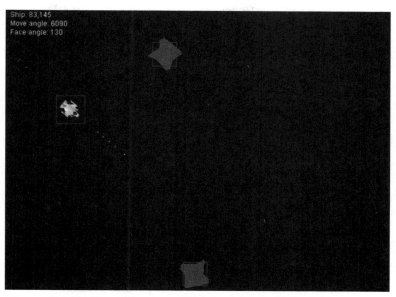

Figure 7.8 The bounding rectangles are used for collision testing.

I am not one who enjoys wasting space, so I have given much thought to the matter and decided to provide the entire source code listing for the game, which is now contained in GalacticWar.java. The majority of the code remains unchanged from the Asteroids.java file back in Chapter 5, so you may just open that file and modify it as indicated. I have highlighted in bold all of the lines of code that have changed.

If the source code for a particular method has not changed at all, I simply comment out the code and insert the statement //no changes needed; so keep an eye out for this comment, and then re-use that code from the Chapter 5 project. It is a beautiful testament to object-oriented programming that so few changes are needed to this source code file!

```
/*****************************************************
* GALACTIC WAR, Chapter 7
 *****************************************************/
import java.applet.*;
import java.awt.*;
import java.awt.event.*;
import java.awt.geom.*;
import java.awt.image.*;
import java.util.*;


/*****************************************************
 * Primary class for the game
 *****************************************************/
```

```java
public class GalacticWar extends Applet implements Runnable, KeyListener  {
        //the main thread becomes the game loop
        Thread gameloop;
        //use this as a double buffer
        BufferedImage backbuffer;
        //the main drawing object for the back buffer
        Graphics2D g2d;
        //toggle for drawing bounding boxes
        boolean showBounds = false;

        //create the asteroid array
        int ASTEROIDS = 20;
        Asteroid[] ast = new Asteroid[ASTEROIDS];

        //create the bullet array
        int BULLETS = 10;
        Bullet[] bullet = new Bullet[BULLETS];
        int currentBullet = 0;

        //the player's ship
        ImageEntity ship = new ImageEntity(this);

        //create the identity transform
        AffineTransform identity = new AffineTransform();

        //create a random number generator
        Random rand = new Random();

        //load sound effects
        SoundClip shoot;
        SoundClip explode;

        /*****************************************************
         * applet init event
         *****************************************************/
        public void init() {
            //create the back buffer for smooth graphics
            backbuffer = new BufferedImage(640, 480, BufferedImage.TYPE_INT_RGB);
            g2d = backbuffer.createGraphics();
```

```java
        //set up the ship
        ship.setX(320);
        ship.setY(240);
        ship.load("spaceship1.png");
        ship.setGraphics(g2d);

        //set up the bullets
        for (int n = 0; n<BULLETS; n++) {
            bullet[n] = new Bullet();
        }

        //set up the asteroids
        for (int n = 0; n<ASTEROIDS; n++) {
            ast[n] = new Asteroid();
            ast[n].setRotationVelocity(rand.nextInt(3)+1);
            ast[n].setX((double)rand.nextInt(600)+20);
            ast[n].setY((double)rand.nextInt(440)+20);
            ast[n].setMoveAngle(rand.nextInt(360));
            double ang = ast[n].getMoveAngle() - 90;
            ast[n].setVelX(calcAngleMoveX(ang));
            ast[n].setVelY(calcAngleMoveY(ang));
        }

        //load sound files
        shoot = new SoundClip("shoot.wav");
        explode = new SoundClip("explode.wav");

        //start the user input listener
        addKeyListener(this);
    }

    /*****************************************************
     * applet update event to redraw the screen
     *****************************************************/
    public void update(Graphics g) {
        //NO CHANGES HERE
    }

    /*****************************************************
     * drawShip called by applet update event
     *****************************************************/
    public void drawShip() {
```

```
    //transform and draw the ship
    ship.transform();
    ship.draw();

      //draw bounding rectangle around ship
      if (showBounds) {
          g2d.setTransform(identity);
          g2d.setColor(Color.BLUE);
          g2d.draw(ship.getBounds());
      }

}
```

There are no changes beyond this point. Please double-check the source code listing in your new Galactic War project to ensure that all of the methods following this point are included (from the project in Chapter 5).

```
/****************************************************
 * drawBullets called by applet update event
 ****************************************************/
public void drawBullets() {
    //NO CHANGES HERE
}


/****************************************************
 * drawAsteroids called by applet update event
 ****************************************************/
public void drawAsteroids() {
    //NO CHANGES HERE
}


/****************************************************
 * applet window repaint event--draw the back buffer
 ****************************************************/
public void paint(Graphics g) {
    //NO CHANGES HERE
}


/****************************************************
 * thread start event - start the game loop running
 ****************************************************/
public void start() {
    //NO CHANGES HERE
}
```

```
/****************************************************
 * thread run event (game loop)
 ****************************************************/
public void run() {
    //NO CHANGES HERE
}
/****************************************************
 * thread stop event
 ****************************************************/
public void stop() {
    //NO CHANGES HERE
}


/****************************************************
 * move and animate the objects in the game
 ****************************************************/
private void gameUpdate() {
    //NO CHANGES HERE
}


/****************************************************
 * Update the ship position based on velocity
 ****************************************************/
public void updateShip() {
    //NO CHANGES HERE
}


/****************************************************
 * Update the bullets based on velocity
 ****************************************************/
public void updateBullets() {
    //NO CHANGES HERE
}


/****************************************************
 * Update the asteroids based on velocity
 ****************************************************/
public void updateAsteroids() {
    //NO CHANGES HERE
}
```

```
/****************************************************
 * Test asteroids for collisions with ship or bullets
 ****************************************************/
public void checkCollisions() {
    //NO CHANGES HERE
}


/****************************************************
 * key listener events
 ****************************************************/
public void keyReleased(KeyEvent k) { }
public void keyTyped(KeyEvent k) { }
public void keyPressed(KeyEvent k) {
    //NO CHANGES HERE
}


/****************************************************
 * calculate X movement value based on direction angle
 ****************************************************/
public double calcAngleMoveX(double angle) {
    //NO CHANGES HERE
}


/****************************************************
 * calculate Y movement value based on direction angle
 ****************************************************/
public double calcAngleMoveY(double angle) {
    //NO CHANGES HERE
}
}
```

What You Have Learned

This was a heavyweight chapter that covered some very difficult subjects. But the idea is to get up the most difficult part of a hill so you can reach the peak, and then head on down the other side. That is what this chapter represents, the last few steps up to the peak. You have now learned the most difficult and challenging aspects of writing a Java game at this point, and you are now ready to start heading down the hill at a more leisurely pace in the upcoming chapters. This chapter explained

- How to create a high-performance threaded game loop.
- How to override default applet methods.
- How to manipulate a bitmap image with transformations.

Review Questions

The following questions will help you to determine how well you have learned the subjects discussed in this chapter.

1. What is the name of the game that was created in this chapter from a previous project?
2. What is the name of the base class used to create game objects?
3. What is the name of the class that handles vector-based graphics?
4. What is the new class that was created in this chapter to handle bitmap images?
5. Which method do we use to load a bitmap image in an applet?
6. What is the name of the method that returns the directory containing the applet (or HTML container) file?
7. What is the name of the method that returns the entire URL string including the applet (or HTML container) file?
8. What class do you use to store a bitmap image?
9. Which `Graphics2D` method is used to draw a bitmap image?
10. What is the name of the custom method that calculates the X velocity based on the angle that an object is facing?

On Your Own

The following exercises will test your comprehension of the topics covered in this chapter by making some important changes to the projects.

1. The ThreadedLoop program runs at break-neck speed with no delay. Modify the thread delay value to see if you can slow down the number of rectangles being drawn to just 1,000 rectangles per second.

2. Soon we will be upgrading the bullets and asteroids in the game to bitmap images. See if you can accomplish this task on your own ahead of time using the new ImageEntity class to replace the bullets with small bitmap images.

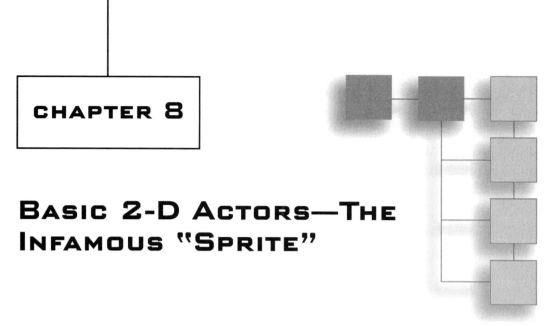

CHAPTER 8

BASIC 2-D ACTORS—THE INFAMOUS "SPRITE"

U p to this point you have learned about a lot of Java classes that are useful for making a game, particularly the Graphics2D class. The previous two chapters provided the groundwork for this chapter by showing you how to tap into the Graphics2D class to draw vectors and bitmaps. At this point, the source code for even a simple bitmap-based game will tend to be too complicated and too difficult to manage without a better way to handle the objects in a game. What you need at this point is a new class that knows how to work with game objects—something known as an *actor* or a *sprite*. The goal of this chapter is to develop a way to handle the game objects moving around on the screen and to enhance the *Galactic War* game with some significant new gameplay features.

Here are the specific topics you will learn about:

- Loading and drawing images
- Drawing opaque and transparent images
- Creating a Sprite class
- Learning about collision testing

Drawing (More) Images

You learned some of the basics of how to load and draw a bitmap in Chapter 7, "The Game Loop, Timing, and Threads," so you are at least familiar with the Image class and the getImage() method. Java is very versatile when it comes to loading and drawing bitmap images on the screen. In the last chapter, I showed you how to pass the Applet class to the ImageEntity class in order to load a bitmap file, as well as to report on the applet's width and height, among other things. By passing `this` to the `ImageEntity`'s constructor, you were able to pass a reference to the current `Applet` object to the `ImageEntity`, and then gain access to all of the functionality of the `Applet` inside the `ImageEntity` class.

Now, it might be easier to load a bitmap image first and then construct an `ImageEntity` by passing an `Image` object to it, but that's a messy way to write code. In general, you want your classes to be as self-reliant as possible. Since I never plan to write a Java game as a standalone application, and I plan to run my Java games in a Web browser, I am not concerned with this reliance on the `Applet` object in my other classes. However, what if you don't need anything from the `Applet` except for the `getImage()` method? There is a better way.

Bitmap File Loader—Revisited

The Abstract Windowing Toolkit, known as AWT, provides a class called `Toolkit` that knows how to load a bitmap file. It's smart enough to look in the current URL path where the applet is located (something that you must pass to the `getImage()` method). You can use `Toolkit` in your own custom `Sprite` class, or you can instantiate a global `Toolkit` object and then use it throughout the game; there are many options. Let's take a look at how this class works:

```
Toolkit tk = Toolkit.getDefaultToolkit();
Image ship = tk.getImage("star_destroyer.png");
```

First, I created a `Toolkit` object by returning the object passed back from `Toolkit.getDefaultToolkit()`. This method returns a `Toolkit` object that represents the state of the Java program or applet. You can then use this `Toolkit` object's `getImage()` method to load a bitmap file. Since we want our applets to be Java archive (JAR) friendly, so that the programs will run on the Web as efficiently as possible, I will use the `getURL()` method that was introduced back in Chapter 4, "Sound Effects and Music."

```
Image ship = tk.getImage(getURL("star_destroyer.png"));
```

Although the Toolkit provides an alternate way to load files, `ImageEntity` (our key image-handling class) still uses a reference to the main Applet class to determine such things as the applet's width and height. You can use the `Applet.getImage()` method or the `Toolkit.getImage()` method to load an image since they are essentially the same. The real convenient thing about `Toolkit` is that it gives you a way to load images without relying on a reference to `Applet`.

Opaque Images

Let's start with what you have already learned up to this point: how to load and draw a bitmap without any transparency. At this point it doesn't matter whether you use the `Applet` or the `Toolkit` to load a bitmap file because the end result will be the same. I leave it to you to decide which method you prefer, and I will use them both interchangeably.

Let's write a short program to serve as a basis for discussing this topic. The output from the BitmapTest program is shown in Figure 8.1. I have highlighted the key portions of code in bold in the listing that follows.

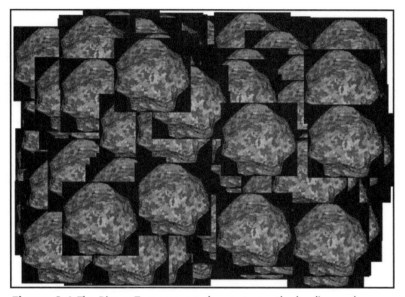

Figure 8.1 The BitmapTest program demonstrates the loading and drawing of opaque images.

```
/*****************************************************
* BitmapTest program
*****************************************************/

import java.awt.*;
import java.applet.*;
import java.util.*;
import java.net.*;

public class BitmapTest extends Applet implements Runnable {
    int screenWidth = 640;
    int screenHeight = 480;
    Image image;
    Thread gameloop;
    Random rand = new Random();
```

```java
    private URL getURL(String filename) {
        URL url = null;
        try {
            url = this.getClass().getResource(filename);
        }
        catch (Exception e) { }
        return url;
    }

    public void init() {
        Toolkit tk = Toolkit.getDefaultToolkit();
        image = tk.getImage(getURL("asteroid1.png"));
    }

    public void start() {
        gameloop = new Thread(this);
        gameloop.start();
    }

    public void stop() {
        gameloop = null;
    }

    public void run() {
        Thread t = Thread.currentThread();
        while (t == gameloop) {
            try {
                Thread.sleep(20);
            }
            catch (InterruptedException e) {
                e.printStackTrace();
            }
            repaint();
        }
    }

    public void update(Graphics g) {
        paint(g);
    }
```

```
public void paint(Graphics g) {
    Graphics2D g2d = (Graphics2D) g;
    int width = screenWidth - image.getWidth(this) - 1;
    int height = screenHeight - image.getHeight(this) - 1;
    g2d.drawImage(image, rand.nextInt(width), rand.nextInt(height), this);
}
}
```

This short program loads the bitmap image shown in Figure 8.2. In many programming languages and graphics libraries, you must specify a transparent pixel color to be used for transparency. In the example shown here, the black region around the edges of the asteroid would be considered the "tranparent zone" of the image. This transparent color is black in the example shown here (with an RGB value of 0,0,0), but other colors can be used for the transparent color too—the color pink (255,0,255) is often used for the transparent color because it stands out so well.

Figure 8.2 This opaque bitmap image contains no transparency information.

However, Java uses a more advanced method to handle transparency, as the next section explains.

Transparent Images

Java is a smart language that handles a lot of things for the programmer automatically, including the drawing of transparent images. This really makes life easier for a Java game programmer because many game libraries use a transparent pixel for transparency instead of a mask layer. So instead of dealing with transparency in code, it's handled in the source artwork. If you supply Java with a transparent bitmap file, it will draw that image transparently.

Most Java programs use the PNG (Portable Network Graphics) format because it offers decent compression and transparency information without sacrificing image quality. You will need to use a graphics editor, such as Paint Shop Pro, to convert images from whatever source format they are in (most likely, the BMP format) to the PNG format, along with the mask layer that makes transparency possible.

Figure 8.3 shows the asteroid image loaded into Paint Shop Pro with a new transparency layer. The checkerboard background behind the asteroid image itself represents the transparent region.

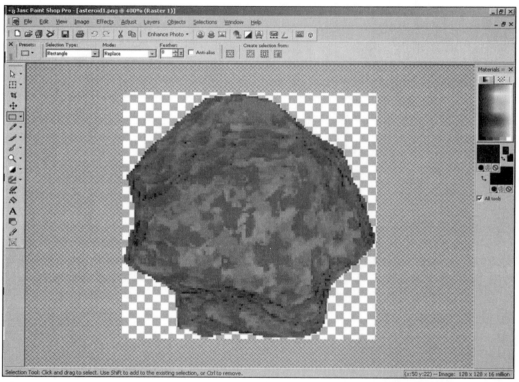

Figure 8.3 The asteroid image has been given a transparent mask layer in Paint Shop Pro.

Let's take the same program you just typed in for the BitmapTest and run it again. Only this time, it will load up a new version of the asteroid1.png file that has been edited to support transparency. Figure 8.4 shows the output from the TransparentTest program. The source code has not changed, but the PNG file has, which accounts for the difference!

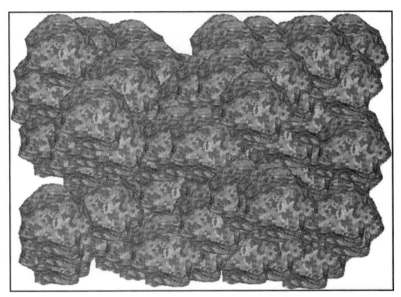

Figure 8.4 The TransparentTest program demonstrates how to draw a transparent bitmap.

Working Some Masking Magic

Let's take a look at how you actually create a masked PNG image. I'm using Paint Shop Pro because it's my favorite graphics editor. If you want to use this program, you can download the trial version from www.jasc.com. Since Corel recently acquired the company that created Paint Shop Pro, the link may be forwarded to www.corel.com. I've used Corel Painter, and I am not surprised that they acquired Paint Shop Pro because Painter is a dreadful graphics editor. I just hope Corel doesn't change my favorite editor too dramatically in the future!

Let's take a look at an asteroid image (see Figure 8.5).

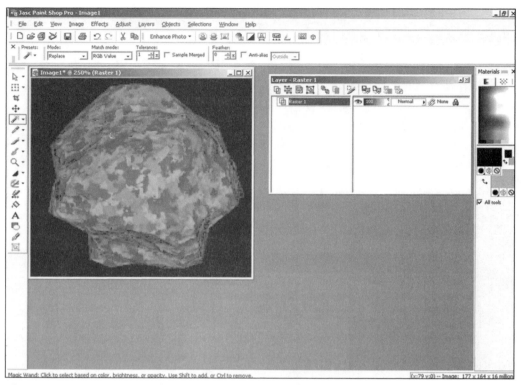

Figure 8.5 A 3-D rendition of a clumpy asteroid (courtesy of Edgar Ibarra).

In order to add a transparency layer to an image you need to locate the Magic Wand tool available in most graphics editors. After selecting the tool with your mouse, click somewhere in the black region (or on any pixel that isn't part of the game object). This should locate the edges of the game object and highlight everything around it (see Figure 8.6).

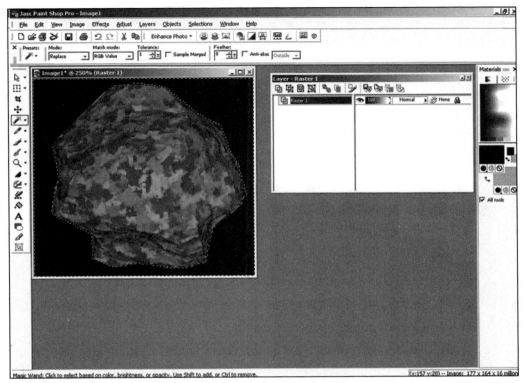

Figure 8.6 The outer edge of the asteroid image has been selected with the Magic Wand tool.

Now that you have a selection available, you need to invert it because this selection will actually exclude the image. In Paint Shop Pro, click on the Selections menu and choose Invert (see Figure 8.7). The result of the inverted selection is shown in Figure 8.8.

tip

If you have a complex image and would like to exclude many portions of it in order to select the boundary of the real image, you can hold down the Shift key while clicking with the Magic Wand tool inside portions of the image to add new selections.

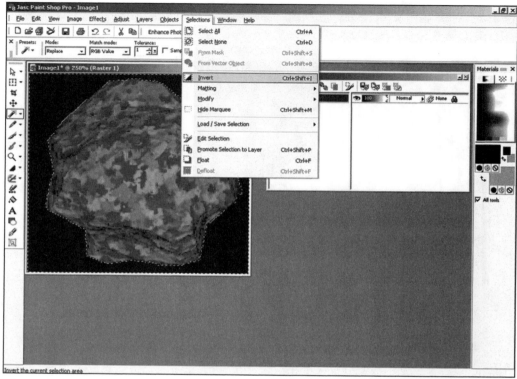

Figure 8.7 Preparing to invert the selection.

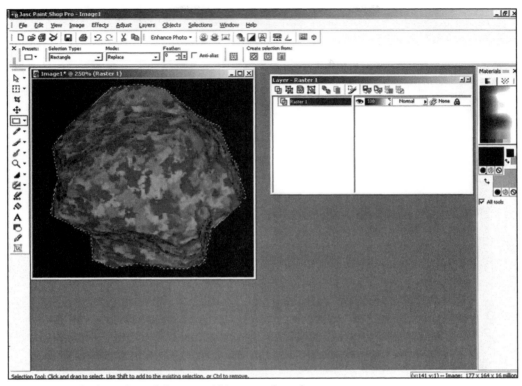

Figure 8.8 The boundary of the asteroid is now selected.

The next step is to create a new mask layer in the image to represent the transparent portion. You can tell Paint Shop Pro to generate a mask based on the selection you've made in the image. To do this, open the Layers menu, select New Mask Layer, and then Show Selection, as shown in Figure 8.9.

tip

Although I am basing this tutorial on the excellent graphic editor, Paint Shop Pro, most professional graphic editors support layers and provide similar features to those found in PSP. The GIMP, for instance, is a freeware graphic editor with comparable features, and is available on many platforms (Windows, Linux, etc). Download The GIMP (GNU Image Manipulation Program) from www.gimp.org.

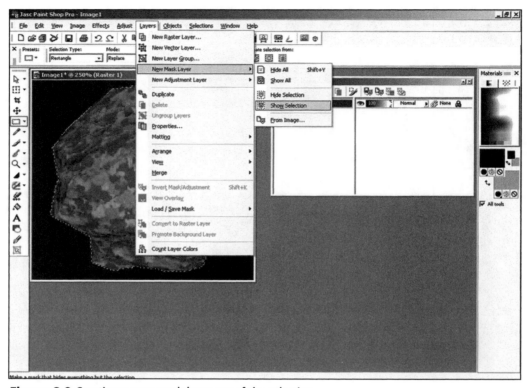

Figure 8.9 Creating a new mask layer out of the selection.

The transparency has been created based on the masked selection in Figure 8.10. The result looks very nice; this asteroid is ready for prime time!

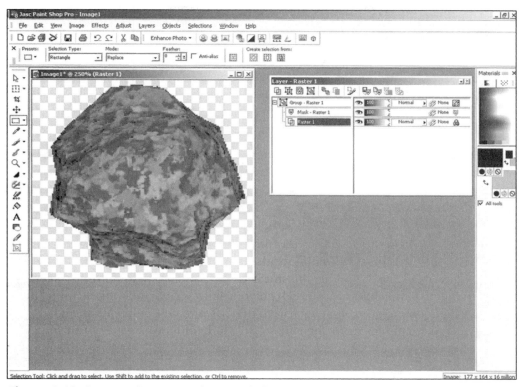

Figure 8.10 The asteroid image now has a masked transparency layer.

Using Sprites

A sprite usually represents an animated graphic image that moves around in a game and is involved with other images. The difference between a regular image and a sprite is often that a sprite will encapsulate the image data as well as the methods needed to manipulate it. Since ImageEntity can already load and draw itself, a new Sprite class will simply extend ImageEntity and add some new properties.

I would like to build a pair of classes to simplify creating sprites for use in a game. We will create the Sprite class next, and then add a new AnimatedSprite class in the next chapter, which will cover sprite animation. The new Sprite class that I'm going to show you here might be described as a *heavy class*. What I mean by "heavy" is that this is not a simple, abstract class. Instead, it is tied closely to the Applet and Graphics2D objects in our main program. You would not be able to use this Sprite class on its own in a Java application (a standalone program) because it relies on the presence of the main applet to function. Now, don't get me wrong, it's entirely possible to write a Java game that runs as a standalone program, since Java programs are not *required* to run in a Web browser. However, that is the direction I have chosen to take in this book. As a result, the Sprite class has been designed to work well in this environment.

For instance, a sprite cannot draw itself without the use of the Applet and Graphics2D objects in a main program. Although the Sprite class could use methods like getGraphics() to pull information from the main applet, our games are using a double buffer, which is accessed through a global Graphics2D object in conjunction with a BufferedImage object.

In previous chapters, you have seen the evolution of basic vector graphics classes to the current BaseGameEntity and ImageEntity classes used to draw images. The BaseGameEntity class handles all of the position, velocity, rotation, and other logistical properties, while ImageEntity makes use of them by providing methods such as transform() and draw(). I want to simplify the Sprite class so it doesn't expose all of these properties and methods but provides a simpler means to load and draw images. This simplification will be especially helpful in the next chapter because animation tends to complicate things.

To further simplify things, I want to build a Sprite class that uses *position* and *velocity* rather than individual X and Y values for these properties (as implemented in BaseGameEntity). Therefore, the Sprite class will not inherit from ImageEntity; it will *use* this class internally instead.

I also want the accessor methods to resemble simple properties, while the mutator methods will be in the usual "set" format. For instance, I want the Sprite class to have a position() method that returns the position of the Sprite object; but it will use a setPosition() method to change the X and Y values. For instance, I want to be able to access a sprite's position and velocity by writing code like this:

```
sprite.position().X()
sprite.position().Y()
```

On top of all these desires, I also do not want to be concerned with numeric data types! I don't want to typecast integers, floats, and doubles! So, this Sprite class will need to deal with the differences in the data types automatically and not complain about it! These are minor semantic issues, but they tend to seriously clean up the code. For example, some of the *update* methods in the *Galactic War* game can be taken out of the main code file and internalized in the Sprite class. These are some significant demands in the design of the Sprite class, but I think the result will be solid! First, let's take a look at a support class that will make it possible.

tip

An *accessor method* is a method that returns a private variable in a class. A *mutator method* is a method that changes a private variable in a class.

The Point2D Class

The Point2D class is a helper class with the sole job of storing and providing X and Y values in a variety of numerical formats. There is a Java library that also contains a Point2D class, but it was unsuitable for our purposes here. However, there should be no conflict because that class is contained within a package.

```
/*********************************************************
* Point2D Class
 *********************************************************/
class Point2D extends Object {
    private double x, y;

    //int constructor
    Point2D(int x, int y) {
        setX(x);
        setY(y);
    }
    //float constructor
    Point2D(float x, float y) {
        setX(x);
        setY(y);
    }
    //double constructor
    Point2D(double x, double y) {
        setX(x);
        setY(y);
    }

    //X property
    double X() { return x; }
    public void setX(double x) { this.x = x; }
    public void setX(float x) { this.x = (double) x; }
    public void setX(int x) { this.x = (double) x; }

    //Y property
    double Y() { return y; }
    public void setY(double y) { this.y = y; }
    public void setY(float y) { this.y = (double) y; }
    public void setY(int y) { this.y = (double) y; }
}
```

The Sprite Class

Following is the source code for the new Sprite class. This class includes a *ton* of features! In fact, it's so loaded with great stuff that you probably won't even know what to do with it all at this point. I am not a big fan of inheritance, preferring to build core functionality into each class I use (for one thing, too much inheritance slows down code).

Collision Testing

The Sprite class includes several methods for detecting collisions with other sprites, and it also provides tests for collision with Rectangle and Point2D objects as a convenience. Remember that I wanted this Sprite class to be intuitive and not cause the compiler to complain about silly things like data type conversions? Well, the same is true of the collision testing code.

There are three versions of the collidesWith() method in the Sprite class, providing support for three different parameters:

- Rectangle
- Sprite
- Point2D

This should cover just about any game object that you would like to test for a collision. Since these methods are built into the Sprite class, you can call them with a single parameter, and the internal data in the sprite itself is used for the second parameter that would normally be passed to a collision routine.

Sprite Class Source Code

This new Sprite class meets all of the design goals I set out to achieve with it, and it will be demonstrated in the new version of *Galactic War* later in this chapter. This class does not inherit from anything other than the base Object, although it uses an ImageEntity internally for access to that class' excellent support for image loading and drawing.

```
/*********************************************************
 * Sprite class
 *********************************************************/
import java.awt.*;
import java.applet.*;

public class Sprite extends Object {
    private ImageEntity entity;
    protected Point2D pos;
    protected Point2D vel;
    protected double rotRate;
    protected int currentState;
```

```
//constructor
Sprite(Applet a, Graphics2D g2d) {
    entity = new ImageEntity(a);
    entity.setGraphics(g2d);
    entity.setAlive(false);
    pos = new Point2D(0, 0);
    vel = new Point2D(0, 0);
    rotRate = 0.0;
    currentState = 0;
}

//load bitmap file
public void load(String filename) {
    entity.load(filename);
}

//perform affine transformations
public void transform() {
    entity.setX(pos.X());
    entity.setY(pos.Y());
    entity.transform();
}

//draw the image
public void draw() {
    entity.g2d.drawImage(entity.getImage(),entity.at,entity.applet);
}

//draw bounding rectangle around sprite
public void drawBounds(Color c) {
    entity.g2d.setColor(c);
    entity.g2d.draw(getBounds());
}

//update the position based on velocity
public void updatePosition() {
    pos.setX(pos.X() + vel.X());
    pos.setY(pos.Y() + vel.Y());
}
```

```java
//methods related to automatic rotation factor
public double rotationRate() { return rotRate; }
public void setRotationRate(double rate) { rotRate = rate; }
public void updateRotation() {
    setFaceAngle(faceAngle() + rotRate);
    if (faceAngle() < 0)
        setFaceAngle(360 - rotRate);
    else if (faceAngle() > 360)
        setFaceAngle(rotRate);
}

//generic sprite state variable (alive, dead, collided, etc)
public int state() { return currentState; }
public void setState(int state) { currentState = state; }

//returns a bounding rectangle
public Rectangle getBounds() { return entity.getBounds(); }

//sprite position
public Point2D position() { return pos; }
public void setPosition(Point2D pos) { this.pos = pos; }

//sprite movement velocity
public Point2D velocity() { return vel; }
public void setVelocity(Point2D vel) { this.vel = vel; }

//returns the center of the sprite as a Point2D
public Point2D center() {
    return(new Point2D(entity.getCenterX(),entity.getCenterY()));
}

//generic variable for selectively using sprites
public boolean alive() { return entity.isAlive(); }
public void setAlive(boolean alive) { entity.setAlive(alive); }

//face angle indicates which direction sprite is facing
public double faceAngle() { return entity.getFaceAngle(); }
public void setFaceAngle(double angle) {
    entity.setFaceAngle(angle);
}
public void setFaceAngle(float angle) {
    entity.setFaceAngle((double) angle);
}
```

```
    public void setFaceAngle(int angle) {
        entity.setFaceAngle((double) angle);
    }

    //move angle indicates direction sprite is moving
    public double moveAngle() { return entity.getMoveAngle(); }
    public void setMoveAngle(double angle) {
        entity.setMoveAngle(angle);
    }
    public void setMoveAngle(float angle) {
        entity.setMoveAngle((double) angle);
    }
    public void setMoveAngle(int angle) {
        entity.setMoveAngle((double) angle);
    }

    //returns the source image width/height
    public int imageWidth() { return entity.width(); }
    public int imageHeight() { return entity.height(); }

    //check for collision with a rectangular shape
    public boolean collidesWith(Rectangle rect) {
        return (rect.intersects(getBounds()));
    }
    //check for collision with another sprite
    public boolean collidesWith(Sprite sprite) {
        return (getBounds().intersects(sprite.getBounds()));
    }
    //check for collision with a point
    public boolean collidesWith(Point2D point) {
        return (getBounds().contains(point.X(), point.Y()));
    }
}
```

tip

Animation is a feature missing from the Sprite class at this point because we'll be going over that
subject in the next chapter.

Enhancing *Galactic War*

I am very excited about the new capabilities we now have available with the new `Sprite` class! The *Galactic War* game has so much potential that I'm eager to implement, but the game has been somewhat hobbled up to this point due to its being limited—first by vectors, then by simple bitmaps. Now that we have this useful new `Sprite` class available with some serious functionality built into it, the game will really start to resemble what I am envisioning for it.

The first thing I want to do is enlarge the applet window to 800 x 600. I realize that 640 x 480 provides better support for users of low-end PCs; but the truth of the matter is, most users run their PCs at 1024 x 768, while a similarly large percentage use 1280 x 960 or 1280 x 1024. Only a tiny minority of PC users run the system at the lower resolutions. 800 x 600 will give the game more breathing room due to the large size of the asteroids.

As you can see in Figure 8.11, the game has been completely converted to bitmapped graphics, doing away finally with the vestiges of its vector graphics ancestry.

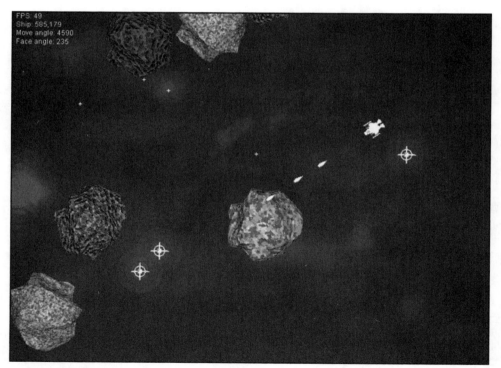

Figure 8.11 The new version of *Galactic War*.

The New *Galactic War* Bitmaps

There are a lot of high-quality bitmaps in the game now, giving it a sharp, catchy appearance. The first and most significant change to the game is that it now uses a background bitmap instead of a blank, black background. The bluespace.png background image was created by Reiner Prokein and is shown in Figure 8.12. This is one of the few backgrounds you can find in Reiner's Tileset collection at www.reinerstileset.de (most of his work involves tiles and sprites).

Figure 8.12 The background image used in *Galactic War*.

There are five different types of asteroids of the large variety in this iteration of *Galactic War*. These gigantic rocks will be blasted into smaller pieces in later iterations of the game; at this point, shooting one of them simply causes it to disappear. I wanted to use very large starting asteroids to make the game more interesting by breaking them up into many smaller rocks.

The asteroids shown in Figure 8.13 were rendered by a talented 3-D artist by the name of Edgar Ibarra, who actually created these asteroid models for a project I was working on several years ago. I have converted the asteroid bitmaps to the PNG format using Paint Shop Pro, as well as applied a transparency mask in the process, as discussed earlier in this chapter.

Figure 8.13 The five unique asteroids featured in the game.

The space ship has also been upgraded significantly from the version presented in the previous chapter. I based the space ship on a design by Reiner Prokein and significantly modified it to give it a more distinct look with a pseudo–3-D appearance (note the four guns, top and bottom). The ship sprite is shown in Figure 8.14. This is a great-looking ship, if I do say so myself. I'd like to add a small fire animation coming out of the engine nozzles when you press the Up arrow key to apply thrust (future enhancement!).

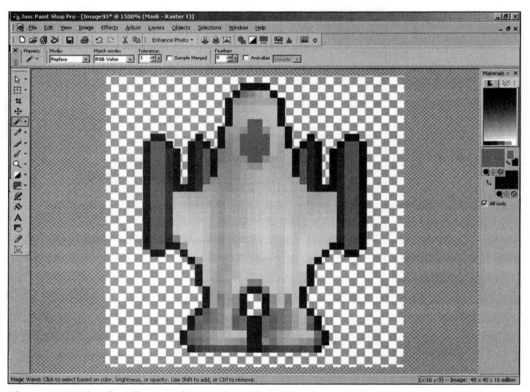

Figure 8.14 The player's space ship used in *Galactic War*.

The New and Improved Source Code

There's a *lot* of source code here for the new version of the game. This is necessary because the game is now taking shape with a lot of functionality, and it has room for new features in upcoming chapters. Future chapters will actually involve additions and changes to the monumental work done in *this* chapter, which is now a new foundational version of the game.

The first thing I'd like to point out is that *Galactic War* is no longer using the VectorShape class, so you can remove it from the project. I have made no changes to BaseGameEntity or ImageEntity, so those can remain in the project (ImageEntity is used by the Sprite class internally). You can see the current state of the project by looking at its list of files in Figure 8.15. Here are the files now present in the project:

- BaseGameEntity.java
- GalacticWar.java
- ImageEntity.java
- MidiSequence.java
- Point2D.java
- SoundClip.java
- Sprite.java

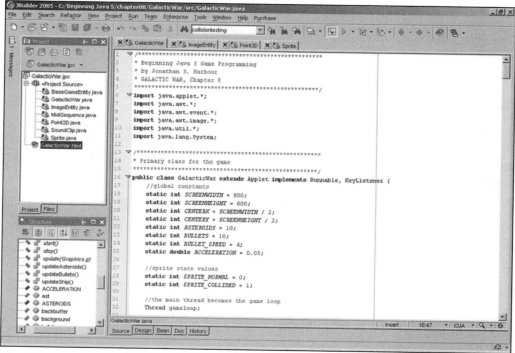

Figure 8.15 The GalacticWar project loaded up in JBuilder 2005.

The first code listing here includes the main class definition for *GalacticWar* along with the global variables. I have highlighted key changes to the game in bold text.

```
/****************************************************
* GALACTIC WAR, Chapter 8
****************************************************/
import java.applet.*;
import java.awt.*;
import java.awt.event.*;
import java.awt.image.*;
import java.util.*;
import java.lang.System;


/****************************************************
* Primary class for the game
****************************************************/
public class GalacticWar extends Applet implements Runnable, KeyListener {
    //global constants
```

```
static int SCREENWIDTH = 800;
static int SCREENHEIGHT = 600;
static int CENTERX = SCREENWIDTH / 2;
static int CENTERY = SCREENHEIGHT / 2;
static int ASTEROIDS = 10;
static int BULLETS = 10;
static int BULLET_SPEED = 4;
static double ACCELERATION = 0.05;

//sprite state values
static int SPRITE_NORMAL = 0;
static int SPRITE_COLLIDED = 1;

//the main thread becomes the game loop
Thread gameloop;

//double buffer objects
BufferedImage backbuffer;
Graphics2D g2d;

//various toggles
boolean showBounds = true;
boolean collisionTesting = true;

//define the game objects
ImageEntity background;
Sprite ship;
Sprite[] ast = new Sprite[ASTEROIDS];
Sprite[] bullet = new Sprite[BULLETS];
int currentBullet = 0;

//create a random number generator
Random rand = new Random();

//define the sound effects objects
SoundClip shoot;
SoundClip explode;

//simple way to handle multiple keypresses
boolean keyDown, keyUp, keyLeft, keyRight, keyFire;
```

```
//frame rate counter
int frameCount = 0, frameRate = 0;
long startTime = System.currentTimeMillis();
```

The showBounds and collisionTesting variables are used to draw some helpful information on the screen, which is invaluable while developing a complex game. Figure 8.16 shows the game with bounding boxes and collision testing turned on. When a collision occurs, the bounding boxes of the two objects are drawn in red instead of blue. You can turn off collision testing altogether, if needed for testing.

This brings up an important point about the current state of the game. There are a lot of new features in the game, and it pretty much looks the way it will when finished—except for a scrolling background and a few other tidbits. The game really doesn't take any action at this point based on a collision. Instead, collisions are detected and that status information is made available to the game through the sprite's state property (which is generic enough for use however you see fit). We'll revisit the process of responding to collisions in the next chapter.

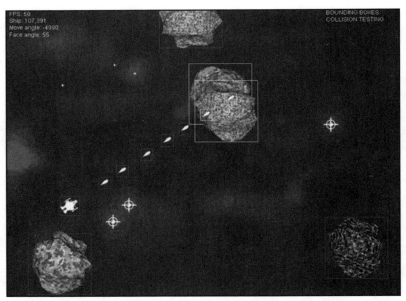

Figure 8.16 Bounding boxes and collisions are toggled with the B and C keys.

Next up is the init() event method of the applet.

```java
/*****************************************************
 * applet init event
 *****************************************************/
public void init() {
    //create the back buffer for smooth graphics
    backbuffer = new BufferedImage(SCREENWIDTH, SCREENHEIGHT,
        BufferedImage.TYPE_INT_RGB);
    g2d = backbuffer.createGraphics();

    //load the background image
    background = new ImageEntity(this);
    background.load("bluespace.png");

    //set up the ship
    ship = new Sprite(this, g2d);
    ship.load("spaceship.png");
    ship.setPosition(new Point2D(CENTERX, CENTERY));
    ship.setAlive(true);

    //set up the bullets
    for (int n = 0; n<BULLETS; n++) {
        bullet[n] = new Sprite(this, g2d);
        bullet[n].load("plasmashot.png");
    }

    //set up the asteroids
    for (int n = 0; n<ASTEROIDS; n++) {
        ast[n] = new Sprite(this, g2d);
        ast[n].setAlive(true);
        //load the asteroid image
        int i = rand.nextInt(5)+1;
        ast[n].load("asteroid" + i + ".png");
        //set to a random position on the screen
        int x = rand.nextInt(SCREENWIDTH);
        int y = rand.nextInt(SCREENHEIGHT);
        ast[n].setPosition(new Point2D(x, y));
        //set rotation angles to a random value
        ast[n].setFaceAngle(rand.nextInt(360));
        ast[n].setMoveAngle(rand.nextInt(360));
        ast[n].setRotationRate(rand.nextDouble());
        //set velocity based on movement direction
```

```
        double ang = ast[n].moveAngle() - 90;
        double velx = calcAngleMoveX(ang);
        double vely =  calcAngleMoveY(ang);
        ast[n].setVelocity(new Point2D(velx, vely));
    }

    //start the user input listener
    addKeyListener(this);
}
```

The next section of code is the main game update portion of the game, including the applet update() event, the paint() event, and three methods to draw the game objects: drawShip(), drawBullets(), and drawAsteroids().

```
/*******************************************************
 * applet update event to redraw the screen
 *******************************************************/
public void update(Graphics g) {
    //calculate frame rate
    frameCount++;
    if (System.currentTimeMillis() > startTime + 1000) {
        startTime = System.currentTimeMillis();
        frameRate = frameCount;
        frameCount = 0;
    }

    //draw the background
    g2d.drawImage(background.getImage(),0,0,SCREENWIDTH-1,SCREENHEIGHT-1,this);

    //draw the game graphics
    drawAsteroids();
    drawShip();
    drawBullets();

    //print status information on the screen
    g2d.setColor(Color.WHITE);
    g2d.drawString("FPS: " + frameRate, 5, 10);
    long x = Math.round(ship.position().X());
    long y = Math.round(ship.position().Y());
    g2d.drawString("Ship: " + x + "," + y , 5, 25);
    g2d.drawString("Move angle: " + Math.round(
        ship.moveAngle())+90, 5, 40);
    g2d.drawString("Face angle: " +  Math.round(
        ship.faceAngle()), 5, 55);
```

```
    if (showBounds) {
        g2d.setColor(Color.GREEN);
        g2d.drawString("BOUNDING BOXES", SCREENWIDTH-150, 10);
    }
    if (collisionTesting) {
        g2d.setColor(Color.GREEN);
        g2d.drawString("COLLISION TESTING", SCREENWIDTH-150, 25);
    }

    //repaint the applet window
    paint(g);
}

/*****************************************************
 * drawShip called by applet update event
 *****************************************************/
public void drawShip() {
    // set the transform for the image
    ship.transform();
    ship.draw();
    if (showBounds) {
        if (ship.state() == SPRITE_COLLIDED)
            ship.drawBounds(Color.RED);
        else
            ship.drawBounds(Color.BLUE);
    }
}

/*****************************************************
 * drawBullets called by applet update event
 *****************************************************/
public void drawBullets() {
    for (int n = 0; n < BULLETS; n++) {
        if (bullet[n].alive()) {
            //draw the bullet
            bullet[n].transform();
            bullet[n].draw();
            if (showBounds) {
                if (bullet[n].state() == SPRITE_COLLIDED)
                    bullet[n].drawBounds(Color.RED);
                else
                    bullet[n].drawBounds(Color.BLUE);
```

```
                    }
                }
            }
        }


        /*****************************************************
         * drawAsteroids called by applet update event
         *****************************************************/
        public void drawAsteroids() {
            for (int n = 0; n < ASTEROIDS; n++) {
                if (ast[n].alive()) {
                    //draw the asteroid
                    ast[n].transform();
                    ast[n].draw();
                    if (showBounds) {
                        if (ast[n].state() == SPRITE_COLLIDED)
                            ast[n].drawBounds(Color.RED);
                        else
                            ast[n].drawBounds(Color.BLUE);
                    }
                }
            }
        }


        /*****************************************************
         * applet window repaint event--draw the back buffer
         *****************************************************/
        public void paint(Graphics g) {
            g.drawImage(backbuffer, 0, 0, this);
        }
```

The next section of code updates the game via the *gameloop* thread, which calls gameUpdate().
This method, in turn, calls methods to process user input, update the ship, bullets, and
asteroids, and perform collision testing.

```
        /*****************************************************
         * thread start event - start the game loop running
         *****************************************************/
        public void start() {
            gameloop = new Thread(this);
            gameloop.start();
        }
```

```
/*****************************************************
 * thread run event (game loop)
 *****************************************************/
public void run() {
    //acquire the current thread
    Thread t = Thread.currentThread();
    //keep going as long as the thread is alive
    while (t == gameloop) {
        try {
            Thread.sleep(20);
        }
        catch(InterruptedException e) {
            e.printStackTrace();
        }
        //update the game loop
        gameUpdate();
        repaint();
    }
}
/*****************************************************
 * thread stop event
 *****************************************************/
public void stop() {
    gameloop = null;
}


/*****************************************************
 * move and animate the objects in the game
 *****************************************************/
private void gameUpdate() {
    checkInput();
    updateShip();
    updateBullets();
    updateAsteroids();
    if (collisionTesting) checkCollisions();
}


/*****************************************************
 * Update the ship position based on velocity
 *****************************************************/
public void updateShip() {
```

```java
        ship.updatePosition();
        double newx = ship.position().X();
        double newy = ship.position().Y();

        //wrap around left/right
        if (ship.position().X() < -10)
            newx = SCREENWIDTH + 10;
        else if (ship.position().X() > SCREENWIDTH + 10)
            newx = -10;

        //wrap around top/bottom
        if (ship.position().Y() < -10)
            newy = SCREENHEIGHT + 10;
        else if (ship.position().Y() > SCREENHEIGHT + 10)
            newy = -10;

        ship.setPosition(new Point2D(newx, newy));
        ship.setState(SPRITE_NORMAL);
    }


    /*****************************************************
     * Update the bullets based on velocity
     *****************************************************/
    public void updateBullets() {
        //move the bullets
        for (int n = 0; n < BULLETS; n++) {
            if (bullet[n].alive()) {

                //update bullet's x position
                bullet[n].updatePosition();

                //bullet disappears at left/right edge
                if (bullet[n].position().X() < 0 ||
                    bullet[n].position().X() > SCREENWIDTH)
                {
                    bullet[n].setAlive(false);
                }

                //update bullet's y position
                bullet[n].updatePosition();
```

```
                    //bullet disappears at top/bottom edge
                    if (bullet[n].position().Y() < 0 ||
                        bullet[n].position().Y() > SCREENHEIGHT)
                    {
                        bullet[n].setAlive(false);
                    }

                    bullet[n].setState(SPRITE_NORMAL);                }
        }
    }


    /*******************************************************
     * Update the asteroids based on velocity
     *******************************************************/
    public void updateAsteroids() {
        //move and rotate the asteroids
        for (int n = 0; n < ASTEROIDS; n++) {
            if (ast[n].alive()) {
                //update the asteroid's position and rotation
                ast[n].updatePosition();
                ast[n].updateRotation();

                int w = ast[n].imageWidth()-1;
                int h = ast[n].imageHeight()-1;
                double newx = ast[n].position().X();
                double newy = ast[n].position().Y();

                //wrap the asteroid around the screen edges
                if (ast[n].position().X() < -w)
                    newx = SCREENWIDTH + w;
                else if (ast[n].position().X() > SCREENWIDTH + w)
                    newx = -w;
                if (ast[n].position().Y() < -h)
                    newy = SCREENHEIGHT + h;
                else if (ast[n].position().Y() > SCREENHEIGHT + h)
                    newy = -h;

                ast[n].setPosition(new Point2D(newx,newy));
                ast[n].setState(SPRITE_NORMAL);
            }
        }
    }
```

```java
/*******************************************************
 * Test asteroids for collisions with ship or bullets
 ******************************************************/
public void checkCollisions() {
    //check for collision between asteroids and bullets
    for (int m = 0; m<ASTEROIDS; m++) {
        if (ast[m].alive()) {
            //iterate through the bullets
            for (int n = 0; n < BULLETS; n++) {
                if (bullet[n].alive()) {
                    //collision?
                    if (ast[m].collidesWith(bullet[n])) {
                        bullet[n].setState(SPRITE_COLLIDED);
                        ast[m].setState(SPRITE_COLLIDED);
                        explode.play();
                    }
                }
            }
        }
    }

    //check for collision asteroids and ship
    for (int m = 0; m<ASTEROIDS; m++) {
        if (ast[m].alive()) {
            if (ship.collidesWith(ast[m])) {
                ast[m].setState(SPRITE_COLLIDED);
                ship.setState(SPRITE_COLLIDED);
                explode.play();
            }
        }
    }
}
```

The next section of code processes keyboard input. The game has progressed to the point where the simplistic keyboard input from earlier chapters was insufficient, so I've added support to the game for multiple key presses now. This works through the use of several global variables: keyLeft, keyRight, and so on. These booleans are set to true during the keyPressed() event and set to false during the keyReleased() event method. This provides support for multiple keys at the same time in a given frame of the game loop. There is a practical limit to the number of keys you will be able to press at a time, but this code makes the game fluid-looking, and the input is smoother than the jerky input in the last chapter.

```
/*****************************************************
 * process keys that have been pressed
 *****************************************************/
public void checkInput() {
    if (keyLeft) {
        //left arrow rotates ship left 5 degrees
        ship.setFaceAngle(ship.faceAngle() - 5);
        if (ship.faceAngle() < 0) ship.setFaceAngle(360 - 5);
    }
    else if (keyRight) {
        //right arrow rotates ship right 5 degrees
        ship.setFaceAngle(ship.faceAngle() + 5);
        if (ship.faceAngle() > 360) ship.setFaceAngle(5);
    }
    if (keyUp) {
        //up arrow applies thrust to ship
        applyThrust();
    }
}

/*****************************************************
 * key listener events
 *****************************************************/
public void keyTyped(KeyEvent k) { }
public void keyPressed(KeyEvent k) {
    switch (k.getKeyCode()) {
    case KeyEvent.VK_LEFT:
        keyLeft = true;
        break;
    case KeyEvent.VK_RIGHT:
        keyRight = true;
        break;
    case KeyEvent.VK_UP:
        keyUp = true;
        break;
    case KeyEvent.VK_CONTROL:
        keyFire = true;
        break;
    case KeyEvent.VK_B:
        //toggle bounding rectangles
        showBounds = !showBounds;
        break;
```

```
        case KeyEvent.VK_C:
            //toggle collision testing
            collisionTesting = !collisionTesting;
            break;
        }
    }
    public void keyReleased(KeyEvent k) {
        switch (k.getKeyCode()) {
        case KeyEvent.VK_LEFT:
            keyLeft = false;
            break;
        case KeyEvent.VK_RIGHT:
            keyRight = false;
            break;
        case KeyEvent.VK_UP:
            keyUp = false;
            break;
        case KeyEvent.VK_CONTROL:
            keyFire = false;
            fireBullet();
            break;
        }
    }

    public void applyThrust() {
        //up arrow adds thrust to ship (1/10 normal speed)
        ship.setMoveAngle(ship.faceAngle() - 90);

        //calculate the X and Y velocity based on angle
        double velx = ship.velocity().X();
        velx += calcAngleMoveX(ship.moveAngle()) * ACCELERATION;
        double vely = ship.velocity().Y();
        vely += calcAngleMoveY(ship.moveAngle()) * ACCELERATION;
        ship.setVelocity(new Point2D(velx, vely));
    }
    public void fireBullet() {
        //fire a bullet
        currentBullet++;
        if (currentBullet > BULLETS - 1) currentBullet = 0;
        bullet[currentBullet].setAlive(true);
```

```
//set bullet's starting point
int w = bullet[currentBullet].imageWidth();
int h = bullet[currentBullet].imageHeight();
double x = ship.center().X() - w/2;
double y = ship.center().Y() - h/2;
bullet[currentBullet].setPosition(new Point2D(x,y));

//point bullet in same direction ship is facing
bullet[currentBullet].setFaceAngle(ship.faceAngle());
bullet[currentBullet].setMoveAngle(ship.faceAngle() - 90);

//fire bullet at angle of the ship
double angle = bullet[currentBullet].moveAngle();
double svx = calcAngleMoveX(angle) * BULLET_SPEED;
double svy = calcAngleMoveY(angle) * BULLET_SPEED;
bullet[currentBullet].setVelocity(new Point2D(svx, svy));

//play shoot sound
shoot.play();
}
```

The last section of code concludes the main code listing for this new version of *Galactic War*, implementing the now-familiar calcAngleMoveX() and calcAngleMoveY() methods.

```
/******************************************************
 * Angular motion for X and Y is calculated
 ******************************************************/
public double calcAngleMoveX(double angle) {
    double movex = Math.cos(angle * Math.PI / 180);
    return movex;
}
public double calcAngleMoveY(double angle) {
    double movey = Math.sin(angle * Math.PI / 180);
    return movey;
}
}
```

What You Have Learned

This significant chapter produced a monumental new version of *Galactic War* that is a foundation for the chapters to come. The final vestiges of the game's vector-based roots have been discarded, and the game is now fully implemented with bitmaps. In this chapter, you learned

- How to create a new, powerful Sprite class.
- How to implement a sprite state to report events such as collisions.
- How to detect multiple key presses.
- How to write reusable methods and classes.
- How to create transparent PNG files.
- How to load and draw transparent images.

Review Questions

The following questions will help you to determine how well you have learned the subjects discussed in this chapter.

1. What is the name of the support class created in this chapter to help the Sprite class manage position and velocity?

2. During which keyboard event should you disable a key press variable, when detecting multiple key presses with global variables?

3. What are the three types of parameters you can pass to the collidesWith() method?

4. What Java class provides an alternate method for loading images that is not tied to the applet?

5. Which Java package do you need to import to use the Graphics2D class?

6. What numeric data type does the Point2D class (created in this chapter) use for internal storage of the X and Y values?

7. What data types can the Point2D class work with at the constructor level?

8. Which sprite property determines the angle at which the sprite will move?

9. Which sprite property determines at which angle an image is pointed, regardless of movement direction?

10. What is the transparency layer in a PNG file called?

On Your Own

The following exercise will challenge your comprehension of the material presented in this chapter.

1. The *Galactic War* game is in a transition at this point, after having been upgraded significantly from vector-based graphics. At present, it does not perform any action due to collisions other than to report that a collision has occurred. We want to separate the *collision testing* code from the *collision response* code. Add a method that is called from gameUpdate() that displays the position (x,y) of any object that has collided with another object, for debugging purposes. You can do this by looking at a sprite's state property.

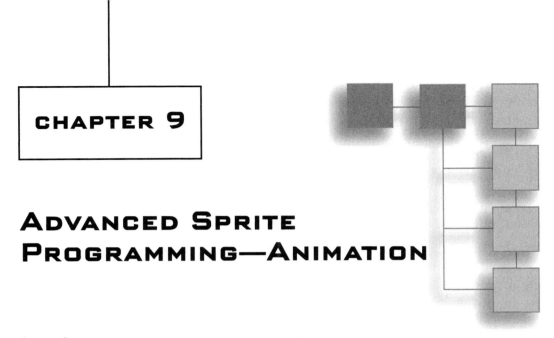

CHAPTER 9

ADVANCED SPRITE PROGRAMMING—ANIMATION

This chapter adds a significant new feature to your set of Java game programming tools—the ability to load and play animation and apply that knowledge to an enhanced new sprite class. You will learn about the different ways to store a sprite animation, how to access a single frame in an animation strip, and you will see a new class called AnimatedSprite with some serious new functionality that greatly extends the base Sprite class.

Here are the specific topics you will learn about:

- Sprite animation techniques
- Drawing individual sprite frames
- Keeping track of animation frames
- Encapsulating sprite animation in a class
- Enhancing the *Galactic War* game

Sprite Animation

Over the years I have seen many different techniques for sprite animation. Of the many algorithms and implementations I've studied, I believe there are two essential ways to animate a graphic object on the screen.

Animation Techniques

First, there is the *sequence* method. This type of animation involves loading a bitmap image for each frame of the animation in sequence, and then animating them on the screen by drawing each image in order. This technique tends to take a long time to load all of the animation frames, especially in a large game with many sprites. There is also the system overhead required to maintain so many images in memory, even if they are small. Figure 9.1 shows an example.

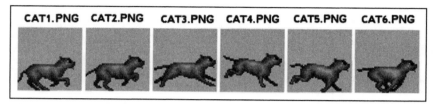

Figure 9.1 An animation sequence with frames stored in individual bitmap files.

Drawing an animation sequence is somewhat of a challenge when loading individual frames because of the logistics of it. How should you store the images, in an array or a linked list? I've seen some implementations using both methods, and neither is very friendly, so to speak, because the code is so unpleasant.

The second sprite animation technique is the *tiled* method. This type of animation involves storing an entire animation sequence inside a single bitmap file, also known as an *animation strip*. Inside this bitmap file are the many frames of the animation laid out in a single row or with many columns and rows. Figure 9.2 shows an animation strip on a single row, while Figure 9.3 shows a larger animation with many columns and rows.

Figure 9.2 An animation strip with a single row.

Figure 9.3 An animation strip with four columns and two rows.

Drawing Individual Frames

The key to drawing a single frame from an animation sequence stored in a tiled bitmap is to figure out where each frame is located *algorithmically*. It's impossible to manually code the X and Y position for each frame in the image; the very thought of it gives me hives. Not only would it take hours to jot down the X,Y position of every frame, but the bitmap file could easily be modified, thus rendering the manually calculated points irrelevant. This is computer science, after all, so there is an algorithm for almost everything.

You can calculate the column (that is, the number of frames *across*) by dividing the frame number by the number of columns and multiplying that by the height of each frame.

```
frameY = (frameNumber / columns) * height;
```

This will give you the correct row down into the image where your desired frame is located, but it will not provide you with the actual *column*, or X value. For that, you need a similar, but somewhat different, solution:

```
frameX = (frameNumber % columns) * width;
```

As you might have noticed, this looks almost exactly like the formula for calculating frameY. The only difference is that we're multiplying by width, and using the *modulus* character instead of the *division* character. Modulus returns the *remainder* of a division, rather than the answer itself. If you want the Y value, you look at the division *answer*; if you want the X value, you look at the division *remainder*.

Here is a complete method that draws a single frame out of an animation sequence. There are a lot of parameters in this method! Fortunately, they are all clearly labeled with descriptive names. It's obvious that we pass it the source Image, the destination Graphics2D object (which does the real drawing), the destination location (X and Y), the number of columns across, the frame number you want to draw, and then the width and height of a single frame. What you get in return is the desired animation frame on the destination surface (which can be your back buffer or the applet window).

```
public void drawFrame(Image source, Graphics2D dest,
    int destX, int destY, int cols, int frame, int width, int height)
{
    int frameX = (frame % cols) * width;
    int frameY = (frame / cols) * height;
    dest.drawImage(source, destX, destY, destX+width, destY+height,
        frameX, frameY, frameX+width, frameY+height, this);
}
```

Keeping Track of Animation Frames

Acquiring the desired animation frame is just the first step toward building an animated sprite in Java. After you have figured out how to grab a single frame, you must then decide what to do with it! For instance, how do you tell your program which frame to draw, and how does the program update the current frame each time through the game loop?

I've found that the easiest way to do this is with a simple update method that increments the animation frame and then tests it against the bounds of the animation sequence. For instance,

```
currentFrame += animationDirection;
if (currentFrame > totalFrames-1) {
    currentFrame = 0;
}
else if (currentFrame < 0) {
    currentFrame = totalFrames-1;
}
```

Take a close look at what's going on in the code above. First, the current frame is incremented by an arbitrary value stored in a variable called animationDirection. This will always be either –1 or 1 to animate forward or backward. Then, the next line checks the upper boundary (totalFrames-1) and loops back to 0 if the boundary is crossed. Similarly, the lower boundary is checked, setting currentFrame to the upper boundary value if necessary. The end result is that three variables are needed:

- currentFrame
- totalFrames
- animationDirection

You would want to call this update code from the thread's run() event method. But, speaking of the thread, that does bring up an important issue—timing. Obviously, you don't want every sprite in the game to animate at exactly the same rate! Some sprites will move very slowly, while others will have fast animations. This is really an issue of fine-tuning the gameplay, but you must have some sort of mechanism in place for implementing timing for each animated sprite *separately*.

You can accomplish this by adding a couple more variables to the mix. First, you will need to increment a counter each time through the game loop. If that counter reaches a certain threshold value, then you reset the counter and go through the process of updating the animation frame as before. Let's use variables called frameCount and frameDelay. The frame delay is usually a smaller value than you would expect—such as 5 to 10, but usually not much more. A delay of 10 in a game loop running at 50 fps means that the object only animates at 5 fps, which is very slow indeed. I often use values of 1 to 5 for the frame delay. Here is the updated animation code with a delay in place:

```
frameCount++;
if (frameCount > frameDelay) {
    frameCount=0;
    currentFrame += animationDirection;
    if (currentFrame > totalFrames-1) {
        currentFrame = 0;
    }
    else if (currentFrame < 0) {
        currentFrame = totalFrames-1;
    }
}
```

Testing Sprite Animation

I'd like to go through a complete example with you so these concepts will feel more real to you, and so that you can see the dramatic result when a sprite is animated. The AnimationTest program loads a massive 64-frame animation sequence (shown in Figure 9.4) and animates it on the screen while moving the sprite around at the same time. Since we are sticking to the subject of animation in this chapter, the program doesn't attempt to do any transforms, such as rotation. But can you imagine the result of an animated sprite that can *also* be rotated?

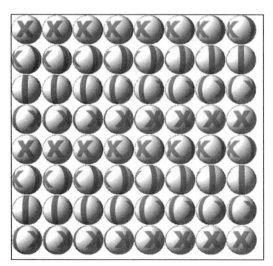

Figure 9.4 An animated ball with 64 frames.

The output from the program is shown in Figure 9.5. Following is the code listing for the AnimationTest program. I have highlighted key portions of code (that are new to this chapter) in bold text.

224   Chapter 9 ■ Advanced Sprite Programming—Animation

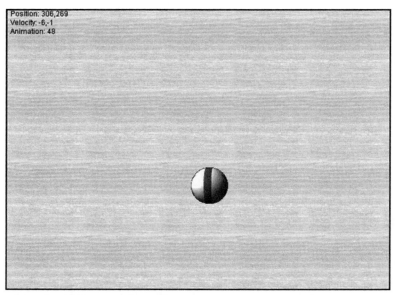

Figure 9.5 The AnimationTest program.

```
/****************************************************
* AnimationTest program
****************************************************/
import java.awt.*;
import java.applet.*;
import java.util.*;
import java.awt.image.*;

public class AnimationTest extends Applet  implements Runnable {
    static int SCREENWIDTH = 640;
    static int SCREENHEIGHT = 480;
    Thread gameloop;
    Random rand = new Random();

    //double buffer objects
    BufferedImage backbuffer;
    Graphics2D g2d;

    //background image
    Image background;
```

```java
//sprite variables
Image ball;
int ballX = 300, ballY = 200;
int speedX, speedY;

//animation variables
int currentFrame = 0;
int totalFrames = 64;
int animationDirection = 1;
int frameCount = 0;
int frameDelay = 5;

private URL getURL(String filename) {
    URL url = null;
    try {
        url = this.getClass().getResource(filename);
    }
    catch (Exception e) {}
    return url;
}

public void init() {
    Toolkit tk = Toolkit.getDefaultToolkit();

    //create the back buffer for smooth graphics
    backbuffer = new BufferedImage(SCREENWIDTH, SCREENHEIGHT,
        BufferedImage.TYPE_INT_RGB);
    g2d = backbuffer.createGraphics();

    //load the background image
    background = tk.getImage(getURL("woodgrain.png"));

    //load the ball animation strip
    ball = tk.getImage(getURL("xball.png"));

    speedX = rand.nextInt(6)+1;
    speedY = rand.nextInt(6)+1;
}

public void start() {
    gameloop = new Thread(this);
    gameloop.start();
}
```

```java
public void stop() {
    gameloop = null;
}

public void run() {
    Thread t = Thread.currentThread();
    while (t == gameloop) {
        try {
            Thread.sleep(20);
        }
        catch (InterruptedException e) {
            e.printStackTrace();
        }
        gameUpdate();
        repaint();
    }
}

public void gameUpdate() {
    //see if it's time to animate
    frameCount++;
    if (frameCount > frameDelay) {
        frameCount=0;
        //update the animation frame
        currentFrame += animationDirection;
        if (currentFrame > totalFrames - 1) {
            currentFrame = 0;
        }
        else if (currentFrame < 0) {
            currentFrame = totalFrames - 1;
        }
    }

    //update the ball position
    ballX += speedX;
    if ((ballX < 0) || (ballX > SCREENWIDTH - 64)) {
        speedX *= -1;
        ballX += speedX;
    }
    ballY += speedY;
    if ((ballY < 0) || (ballY > SCREENHEIGHT - 64)) {
        speedY *= -1;
```

```
                ballY += speedY;
            }
        }

    public void update(Graphics g) {
        //draw the background
        g2d.drawImage(background, 0, 0, SCREENWIDTH-1, SCREENHEIGHT-1, this);

        //draw the current frame of animation
        drawFrame(ball, g2d, ballX, ballY, 8, currentFrame, 64, 64);

        g2d.setColor(Color.BLACK);
        g2d.drawString("Position: " + ballX + "," + ballY, 5, 10);
        g2d.drawString("Velocity: " + speedX + "," + speedY, 5, 25);
        g2d.drawString("Animation: " + currentFrame, 5, 40);

        paint(g);
    }


    public void paint(Graphics g) {
        //draw the back buffer to the screen
        g.drawImage(backbuffer, 0, 0, this);
    }

    //draw a single frame of animation
    public void drawFrame(Image source, Graphics2D dest,
                          int x, int y, int cols, int frame,
                          int width, int height)
    {
        int fx = (frame % cols) * width;
        int fy = (frame / cols) * height;
        dest.drawImage(source, x, y, x+width, y+height,
                       fx, fy, fx+width, fy+height, this);
    }
}
```

Encapsulating Sprite Animation in a Class

There are some significant new pieces of code in the AnimationTest program that we'll definitely need for *Galactic War*. All of the properties can be *stuffed* (that's slang for "encapsulated" or "wrapped") into a class, and we can reuse that beautiful drawFrame() method as well. One really great thing about moving drawFrame() into a class is that most of the parameters can be eliminated, as they will be pulled out of the class internally. Setting up an animation will require a few steps up front when the game starts up, but after that, drawing an animated sprite will be an automatic process with just one or two method calls. I'll highlight the important code in bold.

```java
/*****************************************************
 * AnimatedSprite class
 *****************************************************/
import java.awt.*;
import java.applet.*;
import java.awt.image.*;
import java.net.*;

public class AnimatedSprite extends Sprite {
    //this image holds the large tiled bitmap
    private Image animimage;
    //temp image passed to parent draw method
    BufferedImage tempImage;
    Graphics2D tempSurface;
    //custom properties
    private int currFrame, totFrames;
    private int animDir;
    private int frCount, frDelay;
    private int frWidth, frHeight;
    private int cols;

    public AnimatedSprite(Applet applet, Graphics2D g2d) {
        super(applet, g2d);
        currFrame = 0;
        totFrames = 0;
        animDir = 1;
        frCount = 0;
        frDelay = 0;
        frWidth = 0;
        frHeight = 0;
        cols = 0;
    }

    private URL getURL(String filename) {
        URL url = null;
        try {
            url = this.getClass().getResource(filename);
        }
```

```
        catch (Exception e) {}
        return url;
}

public void load(String filename, int columns, int rows,
        int width, int height)
{
        //load the tiled animation bitmap
        Toolkit tk = Toolkit.getDefaultToolkit();
        animimage = tk.getImage(getURL(filename));
        setColumns(columns);
        setTotalFrames(columns * rows);
        setFrameWidth(width);
        setFrameHeight(height);

        //frame image is passed to parent class for drawing
        tempImage = new BufferedImage(width, height,
            BufferedImage.TYPE_INT_ARGB);
        tempSurface = tempImage.createGraphics();
        super.setImage(tempImage);
}

public int currentFrame() { return currFrame; }
public void setCurrentFrame(int frame) { currFrame = frame; }

public int frameWidth() { return frWidth; }
public void setFrameWidth(int width) { frWidth = width; }

public int frameHeight() { return frHeight; }
public void setFrameHeight(int height) { frHeight = height; }

public int totalFrames() { return totFrames; }
public void setTotalFrames(int total) { totFrames = total; }

public int animationDirection() { return animDir; }
public void setAnimationDirection(int dir) { animDir = dir; }

public int frameCount() { return frCount; }
public void setFrameCount(int count) { frCount = count; }

public int frameDelay() { return frDelay; }
public void setFrameDelay(int delay) { frDelay = delay; }
```

```
    public int columns() { return cols; }
    public void setColumns(int num) { cols = num; }

  public void updateAnimation() {
        frCount++;
        if (frameCount() > frameDelay()) {
            setFrameCount(0);
            //update the animation frame
            setCurrentFrame(currentFrame() + animationDirection());
            if (currentFrame() > totalFrames() - 1) {
                setCurrentFrame(0);
            }
            else if (currentFrame() < 0) {
                setCurrentFrame(totalFrames() - 1);
            }
        }
    }


  public void draw() {
        //calculate the current frame's X and Y position
        int frameX = (currentFrame() % columns()) * frameWidth();
        int frameY = (currentFrame() / columns()) * frameHeight();

        //copy the frame onto the temp image
        tempSurface.drawImage(animimage, 0, 0, frameWidth()-1,
            frameHeight()-1, frameX, frameY, frameX+frameWidth(),
            frameY+frameHeight(), applet());

        //pass the temp image on to the parent class and draw it
        super.setImage(tempImage);
        super.transform();
        super.draw();
    }
}
```

Testing the AnimatedSprite Class

I'm not going to list the complete source code for the AnimationClass example program, because it is essentially the same as the AnimationTest program, only it uses the new AnimatedSprite class. There is one difference, though: by inheriting from Sprite, the AnimatedSprite class allows you to rotate the animated sprites while they are drawing! This is due to the functionality provided by ImageEntity, a core support class for sprite drawing.

I will show you the key portion of the program that differs from the AnimationTest program (which was covered earlier in the chapter). Figure 9.6 shows the output of the program, which you can open up and run from the CD-ROM if you wish.

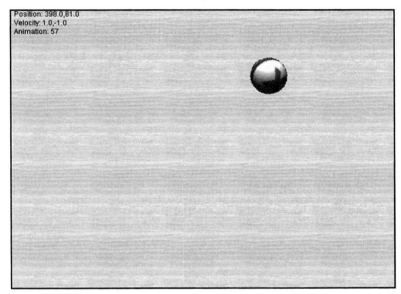

Position: 398.0,81.0
Velocity: 1.0,-1.0
Animation: 57

Figure 9.6 Testing the `AnimatedSprite` class.

Here is a list of all the classes used in the AnimationClass program. You can copy these files from the previous chapter. The new project is called AnimationClass.

- AnimatedSprite.java
- AnimationClass.java
- BaseGameEntity.java
- ImageEntity.java
- Point2D.java
- Sprite.java

Here is the source code for the `init()` event method in the AnimationClass program. The rest of the program is similar to AnimationTest so I won't repeat the code here. The important thing is that you understand how to load an animation using the `AnimatedSprite` class.

```
//sprite variables
AnimatedSprite ball;

public void init() {
    //create the back buffer for smooth graphics
    backbuffer = new BufferedImage(SCREENWIDTH, SCREENHEIGHT,
        BufferedImage.TYPE_INT_RGB);
    g2d = backbuffer.createGraphics();

    //load the background image
    Toolkit tk = Toolkit.getDefaultToolkit();
    background = tk.getImage(getURL("woodgrain.png"));

    //load the ball animation strip
    ball = new AnimatedSprite(this, g2d);
    ball.load("xball.png", 8, 8, 64, 64);
    ball.setPosition(new Point2D(300,200));
    ball.setFrameDelay(1);
    ball.setVelocity(new Point2D(1,1));
    ball.setRotationRate(1.0);
}
```

Enhancing *Galactic War*

We'll make a minor enhancement to *Galactic War* in this chapter by adding support for an animated explosion. In order to facilitate this, some new code must be written to handle the timing and state properties for each sprite. The goal in this chapter is to add a handler for responding to ship-asteroid collisions. When a collision occurs, the game should animate an explosion over the ship, and then put the ship into a temporary invulnerability mode so the player can get the heck out of the way before another collision occurs.

Responding to collisions in a civilized manner is the first step, then the next is the addition of timing to the response code. The new animated explosion in the game is a 16-frame sequence, which is shown in Figure 9.7.

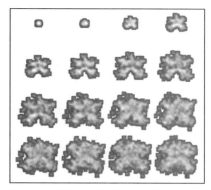

Figure 9.7 The 16-frame animated explosion (courtesy of Reiner Prokein).

When the explosion code is added to the game, the ship will literally blow up when it collides with an asteroid (see Figure 9.8).

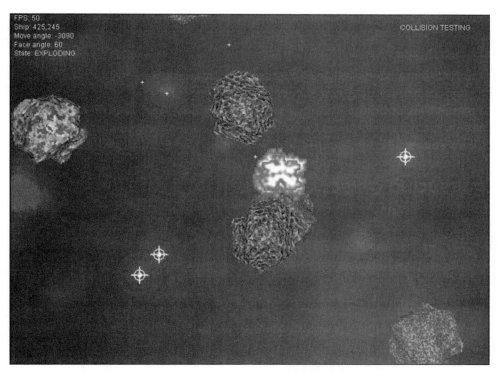

Figure 9.8 The new animated explosion is now part of the game.

Let's take a look at the changes required to update the game to support explosions. There's more involved here than just loading up the animation and drawing it because we have to account for timing and sprite state values. The first change is in the global section at the top of the class: note the changes in bold.

tip

The *static* keyword defines a variable that does not change.

```
public class GalacticWar extends Applet implements Runnable, KeyListener {
    //global constants
    static int SCREENWIDTH = 800;
    static int SCREENHEIGHT = 600;
    static int CENTERX = SCREENWIDTH / 2;
    static int CENTERY = SCREENHEIGHT / 2;
    static int ASTEROIDS = 10;
    static int BULLETS = 10;
    static int BULLET_SPEED = 4;
    static double ACCELERATION = 0.05;

    //sprite state values
    static int STATE_NORMAL = 0;
    static int STATE_COLLIDED = 1;
    static int STATE_EXPLODING = 2;

    //the main thread becomes the game loop
    Thread gameloop;

    //double buffer objects
    BufferedImage backbuffer;
    Graphics2D g2d;

    //various toggles
    boolean showBounds = true;
    boolean collisionTesting = true;
    long collisionTimer = 0;

    //define the game objects
    ImageEntity background;
    Sprite ship;
    Sprite[] ast = new Sprite[ASTEROIDS];
```

```
Sprite[] bullet = new Sprite[BULLETS];
int currentBullet = 0;
AnimatedSprite explosion;

//create a random number generator
Random rand = new Random();

//sound effects
SoundClip shoot;
SoundClip explode;

//simple way to handle multiple keypresses
boolean keyDown, keyUp, keyLeft, keyRight, keyFire;

//frame rate counters and other timing variables
int frameCount = 0, frameRate = 0;
long startTime = System.currentTimeMillis();
```

Make the following changes near the top of the init() event method to switch the background object from an Image to an ImageEntity.

```
public void init() {
    //create the back buffer for smooth graphics
    backbuffer = new BufferedImage(SCREENWIDTH, SCREENHEIGHT,
        BufferedImage.TYPE_INT_RGB);
    g2d = backbuffer.createGraphics();

    //load the background image
    background = new ImageEntity(this);
    background.load("bluespace.png");
```

Next, scroll down inside the init() event method a bit more until you have found the call to addKeyListener(this) and insert the following code in bold. This code loads a 16-frame explosion animation.

```
    //load the explosion
    explosion = new AnimatedSprite(this, g2d);
    explosion.load("explosion96x96x16.png", 4, 4, 96, 96);
    explosion.setFrameDelay(2);
    explosion.setAlive(false);

    //start the user input listener
    addKeyListener(this);
```

Next, go to the update() event and look for the line of code that draws the background and make the changes noted in bold. Then, a few lines further down, add the new line of code shown in bold.

```
//draw the background
g2d.drawImage(background.getImage(),0,0,SCREENWIDTH-1,SCREENHEIGHT-1,this);

//draw the game graphics
drawAsteroids();
drawShip();
drawBullets();
drawExplosions();
```

Now, while you're still in the update() method, scroll down a few lines to the part of the method that draws status information on the screen and add the following code to display the ship's current state.

```
if (ship.state()—STATE_NORMAL)
    g2d.drawString("State: NORMAL", 5, 70);
else if (ship.state()—STATE_COLLIDED)
    g2d.drawString("State: COLLIDED", 5, 70);
else if (ship.state()—STATE_EXPLODING)
    g2d.drawString("State: EXPLODING", 5, 70);
```

Now, scroll down past the three draw methods and add the following method after drawAsteroids(). This is just the first version of the explosion code, and it only draws a single animated explosion. Later, the game will need to support several explosions at a time.

```
public void drawExplosions() {
    //explosions don't need separate update method
    if (explosion.alive()) {
        explosion.updateAnimation();
        if (explosion.currentFrame() == explosion.totalFrames()-1) {
            explosion.setCurrentFrame(0);
            explosion.setAlive(false);
        }
        else {
            explosion.draw();
        }
    }
}
```

Next, scroll down a bit more to the gameUpdate() method. Modify it with the additional lines of code shown in bold.

```
***source start
    private void gameUpdate() {
        checkInput();
        updateShip();
        updateBullets();
        updateAsteroids();
        if (collisionTesting) {
            checkCollisions();
            handleShipCollisions();
            handleBulletCollisions();
            handleAsteroidCollisions();
        }
    }
```

Scroll down just past the checkCollisions() method and add the following new methods to the game. The two collision handler routines for asteroids and bullets are not implemented yet, as the goal is first to get a response for ship-asteroid collisions along with an animated explosion. The handleShipCollisions() method uses the ship sprite's state property extensively to monitor the current state of a collision, and it adds a 3-second delay after a collision has occurred so the player can get out of the way before collisions start to occur again.

```
    public void handleShipCollisions() {
        if (ship.state() == STATE_COLLIDED) {
            collisionTimer = System.currentTimeMillis();
            ship.setVelocity(new Point2D(0,0));
            ship.setState(STATE_EXPLODING);
            startExplosion(ship);
        }
        else if (ship.state() == STATE_EXPLODING) {
            if (collisionTimer + 3000 < System.currentTimeMillis()) {
                ship.setState(STATE_NORMAL);
            }
        }
    }


    public void startExplosion(Sprite sprite) {
        if (!explosion.alive()) {
            double x = sprite.position().X() -
                sprite.getBounds().width / 2;
            double y = sprite.position().Y() -
                sprite.getBounds().height / 2;
            explosion.setPosition(new Point2D(x, y));
```

```
            explosion.setCurrentFrame(0);
            explosion.setAlive(true);
        }
    }

    public void handleBulletCollisions() {
        for (int n = 0; n<BULLETS; n++) {
            if (bullet[n].state() == STATE_COLLIDED) {
                //nothing to do yet
            }
        }
    }

    public void handleAsteroidCollisions() {
        for (int n = 0; n<ASTEROIDS; n++) {
            if (ast[n].state() == STATE_COLLIDED) {
                //nothing to do yet
            }
        }
    }
```

What You Have Learned

This chapter tackled the difficult subject of sprite animation. Adding support for animation is not an easy undertaking, but this chapter provided you with the knowledge, and a new class called AnimatedSprite, that will make it possible for you to write your own games without reinventing the wheel every time you need to load an image and draw it. Here are the key topics you learned:

- How an animation is stored in a bitmap file
- How to load and draw an animation strip from a single bitmap file
- How to animate a sprite with timing
- How to put it all together into a reusable class

Review Questions

The following questions will help you to determine how well you have learned the subjects discussed in this chapter.

1. What is the name of the animation class created in this chapter?
2. Which class does the new animation class inherit from?
3. How many frames of animation were there in the animated ball sprite?

4. What do you call an animation that is stored inside many files?

5. What do you call an animation that is all stored in a single file?

6. Which sprite state constant should you look for when a collision has occurred?

7. What is the name of the normal sprite state constant?

8. Which sprite state constant gets set when a sprite is in the process of blowing up?

9. What is the name of the method developed for the AnimationTest program that draws a single frame in an animation strip?

10. What is the name of the new collision handler for the player's ship?

On Your Own

The following exercises will help you to determine how well you have understood the new material introduced in this chapter.

1. Add another explosion to *Galactic War* so that the asteroids blow up like the player's ship when they collide with the ship.

2. Add support for collisions between the asteroids and the bullets.

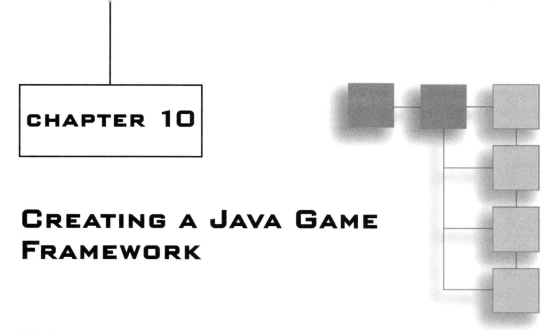

CHAPTER 10

CREATING A JAVA GAME FRAMEWORK

Y ou have learned all of the basics of 2D game programming in the previous nine chapters, and you have been upgrading the *Galactic War* game along the way to test the new topics discussed in each chapter. The source code for an applet-based game is becoming a bit tedious at this point. You've seen that there is a lot of code that does not change very much from one game to the next, now that you know how to write a typical game in Java. I don't want to enforce too much structure for your Java-based game projects, but I also think it will be helpful to add a little bit of organization to the code you've learned thus far. There are a lot of events and methods that must be called and monitored regularly and since this code doesn't change very often, it would clean up the main game's source code considerably by moving that reusable code into a separate class. This chapter shows you how to create a Java game framework. You will be able to write a game that extends a new Game class, and your game won't need to worry about the logistical details any longer. Instead, you will be able to focus on higher-level gameplay topics, like collision testing and game logic.

Here are the specific topics you will learn about:

- Event-driven game programming
- Creating a Java applet-based game engine
- Internalizing the sprite handler
- Adapting *Galactic War* to the new game engine

Adjusting to Event-Driven Programming

The biggest obstacle to the adoption of a game framework, or a game engine, is that you must give up direct (active) control of the game and accept an indirect (passive) programming methodology. Adapting *Galactic War* from a direct to a passive game was very challenging, and I would like to share my experience with you so that you will not have to go through the pains of developing your own game framework the hard way. I could have completed the game two or three times over in the time I've spent building the game engine in this chapter, but the end result is a powerful framework for creating additional games for delivery on the Web.

Exploring the Class Library

Let's take a look at the class library as it exists at this point, after the changes made in the previous chapter. Figure 10.1 shows a diagram of the four main classes we've developed so far. The diagram doesn't include the VectorEntity class any longer, since it is no longer being used. The sound classes are also excluded because I want to focus on graphics right now.

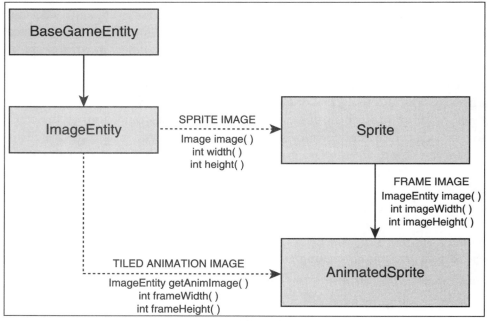

Figure 10.1 The four key Java classes developed so far for working with graphics.

First, BaseGameEntity contains the basic movement and orientation variables that are passed on to the ImageEntity class. This class adds the capability to move, rotate, and draw bitmap images, and it is the core class. From this point, a new class called Sprite was developed. Now, Sprite does not *inherit* from ImageEntity, but rather, it *uses* this core class to store its internal image used for drawing sprites. That is why the link from ImageEntity to Sprite is a dotted line. Next, we have AnimatedSprite, which is the core of the upcoming game framework due to its overall high-level animated sprite capabilities.

When you look at this diagram and resolve the connections in the reverse direction, you find that AnimatedSprite inherits from Sprite several key properties: an image and its width and height. AnimatedSprite also makes use of an ImageEntity to store its often large, tiled image containing frames of animation (per the previous chapter). The Sprite class likewise, looking backward, consumes an image and its width and height properties. You can use this diagram if you ever start to feel overwhelmed while perusing the *Galactic War* source code in these final chapters because the game is becoming *tighter*.

I use the word "tight" to describe the situation where the source code is not becoming *bloated*, as is often the case when a game becomes more advanced. Instead, *Galactic War* moved from a direct coding model to an indirect, passive model using a newly developed sprite-based game engine that is developed in this chapter. The source code listing for the game is about the same as it was in the previous chapter, but the game is about four times more complex!

Building the Game Class

The purpose of the game framework, or game engine if you prefer, is to encapsulate the *platform code* that the game is developed on. In this case, we're talking about a Java applet that runs in a Web browser. So, the goal of this chapter is to build a game engine that simplifies building games as Java applets.

The first step is to create a new class. I opened the *Galactic War* project from the last chapter and began modifying it. First, I created a new class called Game. Feel free to call this class anything you want. The Game class will need to extend the Applet class, like our programs have for the last nine chapters. This new class will also need to implement the key and mouse listener interfaces. It will also need to handle the game loop thread on its own, so the derived game will not need to be bothered with such details (or rather, logistics, since we're trying to manage the logistics of an applet).

Encapsulating a Standard Java Applet

Here are the main events that you're accustomed to seeing in a Java applet-based program up to this point. I'm including the mouse events because they are going to be part of the framework, even if we haven't used them very much.

```
public void init()
public void update(Graphics g)
public void paint(Graphics g)
public void start()
public void run()
public void stop()
public void keyTyped(KeyEvent k)
public void keyPressed(KeyEvent k)
public void keyReleased(KeyEvent k)
public void mousePressed(MouseEvent e)
public void mouseReleased(MouseEvent e)
public void mouseMoved(MouseEvent e)
public void mouseDragged(MouseEvent e)
public void mouseEntered(MouseEvent e)
public void mouseExited(MouseEvent e)
public void mouseClicked(MouseEvent e)
```

Even if you ignore the mouse listener events, there are a lot of raw events in this listing that every applet-based game must implement at a minimum. As for things like key events, we want to completely replace the stock events with a keyboard handler that supports multiple key presses and releases. Well, I experimented with quite a few different ways to do this, and I came up with a solution that is versatile but not totally internal to the Game class. The key events are passed on to the game, which can then use a few global boolean variables to keep track of keys needed by the game. The mouse events are parsed and several mouse properties are made available to provide your game with mouse button and movement information.

Custom Game Events

In place of the standard applet events, I want this class to send events to the game that are directly related to gameplay issues, like sprite collision and screen refresh. The most crucial methods in the Game class use the AnimatedSprite class. The Game class has the following features:

- Performs automatic double buffering
- Maintains a consistent frame rate
- Handles the input listeners
- Manages the game loop thread
- Maintains an internal linked list for sprites
- Performs an automatic frame rate calculation

- Automatically moves and draws all active sprites
- Performs collision testing on all active sprites
- Passes important events on to the game

That's a hefty list of goals for any sprite-based game engine. This framework allows you to build far more complex games than would be possible with the simple arrays we've been using in the previous chapters. The key to the sprite handler is the java.util.LinkedList class. By using a linked list containing AnimatedSprite objects, you can dynamically add and remove sprites without adversely affecting performance. I've managed to get several hundred sprites on the screen at once, with collision testing and all the rest, and the game still ran at a decent frame rate. Keep in mind, the target platform here is a Web browser! Any time you add some overhead to a system, you will inherently introduce some inefficiency. There's a trade off between simple speed and your desire to have an engaging, complex game with a lot of graphics on the screen . I like having the ability to add an explosion to the game at any point without having to worry about that explosion after it has finished animating itself. AnimatedSprite has a lot of properties and methods that make this possible (such as the lifetime and lifeage variables that the Game class uses to terminate a sprite when its lifespan is completed).

Here are the new events introduced in the sprite engine. These events are declared as abstract because the inheriting class must implement them. They do not contain any source code in the Game class, although Game does call them. This is what gives the sprite engine the ability to pass events on to the game while still handling all the real work behind the scenes.

```
void gameStartup()
void gameTimedUpdate()
void gameRefreshScreen()
void gameShutdown()
void gameKeyDown(int keyCode)
void gameKeyUp(int keyCode)
void gameMouseDown()
void gameMouseUp()
void gameMouseMove()
void spriteUpdate(AnimatedSprite sprite)
void spriteDraw(AnimatedSprite sprite)
void spriteDying(AnimatedSprite sprite)
void spriteCollision(AnimatedSprite spr1, AnimatedSprite spr2)
```

The Game Class Source Code

Here is the complete source code listing for the Game class, which I have been describing to you thus far. Much of this code should be familiar to you because we've used it extensively in previous chapters. I will highlight the *crucial code* in bold that is not directly related to the applet. While perusing the source code for the Game class, pay close attention to all bold lines of code, and then take note of the rest of the code. This should help you to grasp exactly what this class does.

```java
/****************************************************
 * Applet Game Framework class
 ****************************************************/

import java.applet.*;
import java.awt.*;
import java.awt.event.*;
import java.awt.image.*;
import java.lang.System;
import java.util.*;

abstract class Game extends Applet implements Runnable, KeyListener,
    MouseListener, MouseMotionListener {

    //the main game loop thread
    private Thread gameloop;

    //internal list of sprites
    private LinkedList _sprites;
    public LinkedList sprites() { return _sprites; }

    //screen and double buffer related variables
    private BufferedImage backbuffer;
    private Graphics2D g2d;
    private int screenWidth, screenHeight;

    //keep track of mouse position and buttons
    private Point2D mousePos = new Point2D(0,0);
    private boolean mouseButtons[] = new boolean[4];

    //frame rate counters and other timing variables
    private int _frameCount = 0;
    private int _frameRate = 0;
    private int desiredRate;
    private long startTime = System.currentTimeMillis();
```

```java
//local applet object
public Applet applet() { return this; }

//game pause state
private boolean _gamePaused = false;
public boolean gamePaused() { return _gamePaused; }
public void pauseGame() { _gamePaused = true; }
public void resumeGame() { _gamePaused = false; }

//declare the game event methods that sub-class must implement
abstract void gameStartup();
abstract void gameTimedUpdate();
abstract void gameRefreshScreen();
abstract void gameShutdown();
abstract void gameKeyDown(int keyCode);
abstract void gameKeyUp(int keyCode);
abstract void gameMouseDown();
abstract void gameMouseUp();
abstract void gameMouseMove();
abstract void spriteUpdate(AnimatedSprite sprite);
abstract void spriteDraw(AnimatedSprite sprite);
abstract void spriteDying(AnimatedSprite sprite);
abstract void spriteCollision(AnimatedSprite spr1, AnimatedSprite spr2);

/****************************************************
 * constructor
 ****************************************************/
public Game(int frameRate, int width, int height) {
    desiredRate = frameRate;
    screenWidth = width;
    screenHeight = height;
}

//return g2d object so sub-class can draw things
public Graphics2D graphics() { return g2d; }

//current frame rate
public int frameRate() { return _frameRate; }

//mouse buttons and movement
public boolean mouseButton(int btn) { return mouseButtons[btn]; }
public Point2D mousePosition() { return mousePos; }
```

```java
/*****************************************************
 * applet init event method
 *****************************************************/
public void init() {
    //create the back buffer and drawing surface
    backbuffer = new BufferedImage(screenWidth, screenHeight,
        BufferedImage.TYPE_INT_RGB);
    g2d = backbuffer.createGraphics();

    //create the internal sprite list
    _sprites = new LinkedList<AnimatedSprite>();

    //start the input listeners
    addKeyListener(this);
    addMouseListener(this);
    addMouseMotionListener(this);

    //this method implemented by sub-class
    gameStartup();
}


/*****************************************************
 * applet update event method
 *****************************************************/
public void update(Graphics g) {
    //calculate frame rate
    _frameCount++;
    if (System.currentTimeMillis() > startTime + 1000) {
        startTime = System.currentTimeMillis();
        _frameRate = _frameCount;
        _frameCount = 0;

        //once every second all dead sprites are deleted
        purgeSprites();
    }
    //this method implemented by sub-class
    gameRefreshScreen();

    //draw the internal list of sprites
    if (!gamePaused()) {
        drawSprites();
    }
```

```
        //redraw the screen
        paint(g);
}


/****************************************************
  * applet window paint event method
  ****************************************************/
 public void paint(Graphics g) {
        g.drawImage(backbuffer, 0, 0, this);
 }


 /****************************************************
  * thread start event - start the game loop running
  ****************************************************/
 public void start() {
        gameloop = new Thread(this);
        gameloop.start();
 }
 /****************************************************
  * thread run event (game loop)
  ****************************************************/
 public void run() {
        //acquire the current thread
        Thread t = Thread.currentThread();

        //process the main game loop thread
        while (t == gameloop) {
            try {
                //set a consistent frame rate
                Thread.sleep(1000 / desiredRate);
            }
            catch(InterruptedException e) {
                e.printStackTrace();
            }

            //update the internal list of sprites
            if (!gamePaused()) {
                updateSprites();
                testCollisions();
            }

            //allow main game to update if needed
            gameTimedUpdate();
```

```
            //refresh the screen
            repaint();
        }
    }


    /****************************************************
     * thread stop event
     ****************************************************/
    public void stop() {
        //kill the game loop
        gameloop = null;

        //this method implemented by sub-class
        gameShutdown();
    }


    /****************************************************
     * key listener events
     ****************************************************/
    public void keyTyped(KeyEvent k) { }
    public void keyPressed(KeyEvent k) {
        gameKeyDown(k.getKeyCode());
    }
    public void keyReleased(KeyEvent k) {
        gameKeyUp(k.getKeyCode());
    }


    /****************************************************
     * checkButtons stores the state of the mouse buttons
     ****************************************************/
    private void checkButtons(MouseEvent e) {
            switch(e.getButton()) {
            case MouseEvent.BUTTON1:
                mouseButtons[1] = true;
                mouseButtons[2] = false;
                mouseButtons[3] = false;
                break;
            case MouseEvent.BUTTON2:
                mouseButtons[1] = false;
                mouseButtons[2] = true;
                mouseButtons[3] = false;
                break;
```

```
            case MouseEvent.BUTTON3:
                mouseButtons[1] = false;
                mouseButtons[2] = false;
                mouseButtons[3] = true;
                break;
        }
}


/*****************************************************
 * mouse listener events
 *****************************************************/
public void mousePressed(MouseEvent e) {
    checkButtons(e);
    mousePos.setX(e.getX());
    mousePos.setY(e.getY());
    gameMouseDown();
}
public void mouseReleased(MouseEvent e) {
    checkButtons(e);
    mousePos.setX(e.getX());
    mousePos.setY(e.getY());
    gameMouseUp();
}
public void mouseMoved(MouseEvent e) {
    checkButtons(e);
    mousePos.setX(e.getX());
    mousePos.setY(e.getY());
    gameMouseMove();
}
public void mouseDragged(MouseEvent e) {
    checkButtons(e);
    mousePos.setX(e.getX());
    mousePos.setY(e.getY());
    gameMouseDown();
    gameMouseMove();
}
public void mouseEntered(MouseEvent e) {
    mousePos.setX(e.getX());
    mousePos.setY(e.getY());
    gameMouseMove();
}
```

```java
    public void mouseExited(MouseEvent e) {
        mousePos.setX(e.getX());
        mousePos.setY(e.getY());
        gameMouseMove();
    }
    //this event is not needed
    public void mouseClicked(MouseEvent e) { }


    /*****************************************************
     * X and Y velocity calculation functions
     *****************************************************/
    protected double calcAngleMoveX(double angle) {
        return (double)(Math.cos(angle * Math.PI / 180));
    }
    protected double calcAngleMoveY(double angle) {
        return (double) (Math.sin(angle * Math.PI / 180));
    }


    /*****************************************************
     * update the sprite list from the game loop thread
     *****************************************************/
    protected void updateSprites() {
        for (int n=0; n < _sprites.size(); n++) {
            AnimatedSprite spr = (AnimatedSprite) _sprites.get(n);
            if (spr.alive()) {
                spr.updatePosition();
                spr.updateRotation();
                spr.updateAnimation();
                spriteUpdate(spr);
                spr.updateLifetime();
                if (!spr.alive()) {
                    spriteDying(spr);
                }
            }
        }
    }


    /*****************************************************
     * perform collision testing of all active sprites
     *****************************************************/
    protected void testCollisions() {
      //iterate through the sprite list, test each sprite against
```

```
    //every other sprite in the list
    for (int first=0; first < _sprites.size(); first++) {

        //get the first sprite to test for collision
        AnimatedSprite spr1 = (AnimatedSprite) _sprites.get(first);
        if (spr1.alive()) {

            //look through all sprites again for collisions
            for (int second = 0; second < _sprites.size(); second++) {

                //make sure this isn't the same sprite
                if (first != second) {

                    //get the second sprite to test for collision
                    AnimatedSprite spr2 = (AnimatedSprite)
                        _sprites.get(second);
                    if (spr2.alive()) {
                        if (spr2.collidesWith(spr1)) {
                            spriteCollision(spr1, spr2);
                            break;
                        }
                        else
                            spr1.setCollided(false);
                    }
                }
            }
        }
    }
}


/*****************************************************
 * draw all active sprites in the sprite list
 * sprites lower in the list are drawn on top
 *****************************************************/
protected void drawSprites() {
    //draw sprites in reverse order (reverse priority)
    for (int n=0; n<_sprites.size(); n++) {
        AnimatedSprite spr = (AnimatedSprite) _sprites.get(n);
        if (spr.alive()) {
            spr.updateFrame();
            spr.transform();
            spr.draw();
```

```
                    spriteDraw(spr);
            }
        }
    }


    /*****************************************************
     * once every second during the frame update, this method
     * is called to remove all dead sprites from the linked list
     *****************************************************/
    private void purgeSprites() {
        for (int n=0; n < _sprites.size(); n++) {
            AnimatedSprite spr = (AnimatedSprite) _sprites.get(n);
            if (!spr.alive()) {
                _sprites.remove(n);
            }
        }
    }
}
```

Enhancing *Galactic War*

You will be surprised to learn that the source code for *Galactic War* has remained about the same lengthwise, even though the game is dramatically more complex with significant new gameplay features. It is truly only a few steps away from completion, and my goal in the next chapter will be to add more gameplay features (such as powerups). Just play the game for a few seconds, and you'll immediately see a need for powerups! This game is *hard*! If you can manage to keep from destroying some of the larger asteroids while working on the smaller ones, you might have a chance; but once you start letting bullets fly and asteroids begin to break into smaller pieces, you will have to be quick on the maneuvering to keep from becoming space dust (which I have just become—see Figure 10.2).

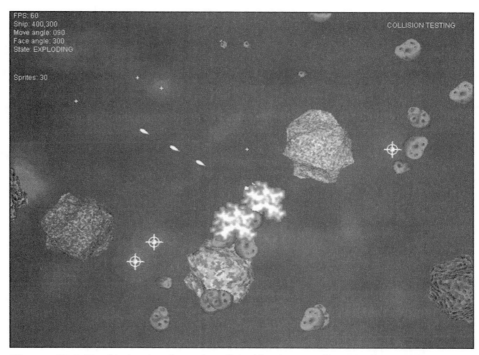

Figure 10.2 My ship has just been demolished by three medium-sized asteroids.

Exploring the New *Galactic War* Source Code

Rather than go over the source code solely from a functional point of view, I'm going to take you on a tour of the code along with screenshots of key aspects of the game that are impacted by specific sections of the source code. For a game this complex, 630 or so lines of code is surprising (not counting the support classes). I have highlighted all key lines of code in bold text so they will stand out. If you pay close attention to the bold lines of code, the code listings should make more sense to you.

Let's get started with the opening credits for the game, where all the initial variables and objects are defined. The most significant thing about this code is the short class definition! The GalacticWar class just extends Game—and that's it! Beyond that, the initialization of the game's graphics is all done here. The images defined and loaded at the beginning are used whenever a new sprite needs to be added to the internal sprite list.

```
/*******************************************************
* GALACTIC WAR, Chapter 10
*******************************************************/
import java.awt.*;
import java.util.*;
import java.lang.System;
import java.awt.event.*;

public class GalacticWar extends Game {
    //these must be static because they are passed to a constructor
    static int FRAMERATE = 60;
    static int SCREENWIDTH = 800;
    static int SCREENHEIGHT = 600;

    //misc global constants
    final int ASTEROIDS = 10;
    final int BULLET_SPEED = 4;
    final double ACCELERATION = 0.05;
    final double SHIPROTATION = 5.0;

    //sprite state values
    final int STATE_NORMAL = 0;
    final int STATE_COLLIDED = 1;
    final int STATE_EXPLODING = 2;

    //sprite types
    final int SPRITE_SHIP = 1;
    final int SPRITE_ASTEROID_BIG = 10;
    final int SPRITE_ASTEROID_MEDIUM = 11;
    final int SPRITE_ASTEROID_SMALL = 12;
    final int SPRITE_ASTEROID_TINY = 13;
    final int SPRITE_BULLET = 100;
    final int SPRITE_EXPLOSION = 200;

    //various toggles
    boolean showBounds = false;
    boolean collisionTesting = true;

    //define the images used in the game
    ImageEntity background;
    ImageEntity bulletImage;
    ImageEntity[] bigAsteroids = new ImageEntity[5];
    ImageEntity[] medAsteroids = new ImageEntity[2];
```

```
ImageEntity[] smlAsteroids = new ImageEntity[3];
ImageEntity[] tnyAsteroids = new ImageEntity[4];
ImageEntity[] explosions = new ImageEntity[2];
ImageEntity[] shipImage = new ImageEntity[2];

//create a random number generator
Random rand = new Random();

//used to make ship temporarily invulnerable
long collisionTimer = 0;

//some key input tracking variables
boolean keyLeft, keyRight, keyUp, keyFire, keyB, keyC;

/******************************************************
 * constructor
 ******************************************************/
public GalacticWar() {
    //call base Game class' constructor
    super(FRAMERATE, SCREENWIDTH, SCREENHEIGHT);
}

/******************************************************
 * gameStartup event passed by game engine
 ******************************************************/
void gameStartup() {
    //load the background image
    background = new ImageEntity(this);
    background.load("bluespace.png");

    //create the ship sprite--first in the sprite list
    shipImage[0] = new ImageEntity(this);
    shipImage[0].load("spaceship.png");
    shipImage[1] = new ImageEntity(this);
    shipImage[1].load("ship_thrust.png");

    AnimatedSprite ship = new AnimatedSprite(this, graphics());
    ship.setSpriteType(SPRITE_SHIP);
    ship.setImage(shipImage[0].getImage());
    ship.setFrameWidth(ship.imageWidth());
    ship.setFrameHeight(ship.imageHeight());
    ship.setPosition(new Point2D(SCREENWIDTH/2, SCREENHEIGHT/2));
    ship.setAlive(true);
```

```
            ship.setState(STATE_NORMAL);
            sprites().add(ship);

            //load the bullet sprite image
            bulletImage = new ImageEntity(this);
            bulletImage.load("plasmashot.png");

            //load the explosion sprite image
            explosions[0] = new ImageEntity(this);
            explosions[0].load("explosion.png");
            explosions[1] = new ImageEntity(this);
            explosions[1].load("explosion2.png");

            //load the big asteroid images (5 total)
            for (int n = 0; n<5; n++) {
                bigAsteroids[n] = new ImageEntity(this);
                String fn = "asteroid" + (n+1) + ".png";
                bigAsteroids[n].load(fn);
            }
            //load the medium asteroid images (2 total)
            for (int n = 0; n<2; n++) {
                medAsteroids[n] = new ImageEntity(this);
                String fn = "medium" + (n+1) + ".png";
                medAsteroids[n].load(fn);
            }
            //load the small asteroid images (3 total)
            for (int n = 0; n<3; n++) {
                smlAsteroids[n] = new ImageEntity(this);
                String fn = "small" + (n+1) + ".png";
                smlAsteroids[n].load(fn);
            }
            //load the tiny asteroid images (4 total)
            for (int n = 0; n<4; n++) {
                tnyAsteroids[n] = new ImageEntity(this);
                String fn = "tiny" + (n+1) + ".png";
                tnyAsteroids[n].load(fn);
            }

            //create the random asteroid sprites
            for (int n = 0; n<ASTEROIDS; n++) {
                createAsteroid();
            }
        }
```

Game Loop Update and Screen Refresh

Now let's take a look at some key events passed here from the Game class. Remember, these methods were defined as *abstract* in Game so that they would be implemented here in the derived source code file. The gameTimedUpdate() method is called from within the timed game loop thread. The gameRefreshScreen() method is called from the applet update() event. I'm not currently using gameShutdown(), but it is available if you need to clean house before the program ends.

Now let's take a look at Figure 10.3, which shows the game fairly early on in the run. The same toggles are still available in the game, including collision testing and bounding box display. There are four stages to destroying an asteroid:

- large, detailed asteroids
- medium asteroid chunks
- small asteroid pieces
- tiny asteroids

Don't let the tiny asteroids fool you—they will still damage your ship, and they can be destroyed by your guns. Speaking of damage, the game would be more fun if the ship's health were displayed somewhere on the screen—a good feature to add in the next chapter.

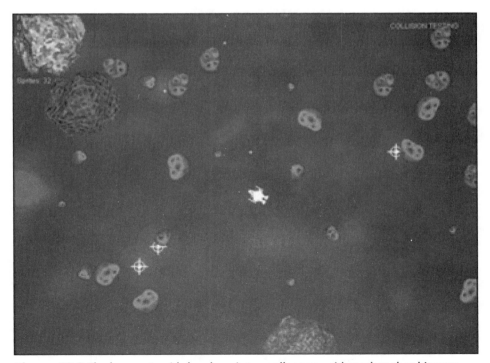

Figure 10.3 The large asteroids break up into smaller ones, either when they hit your ship or when you fire a plasma bolt.

```java
/*****************************************************
 * gameTimedUpdate event passed by game engine
 ****************************************************/
void gameTimedUpdate() {
    checkInput();
}


/*****************************************************
 * gameRefreshScreen event passed by game engine
 ****************************************************/
void gameRefreshScreen() {
    Graphics2D g2d = graphics();

    //the ship is always the first sprite in the linked list
    AnimatedSprite ship = (AnimatedSprite)sprites().get(0);

    //draw the background
    g2d.drawImage(background.getImage(),0,0,SCREENWIDTH-1,
        SCREENHEIGHT-1,this);

    //print status information on the screen
    g2d.setColor(Color.WHITE);
    g2d.drawString("FPS: " + frameRate(), 5, 10);
    long x = Math.round(ship.position().X());
    long y = Math.round(ship.position().Y());
    g2d.drawString("Ship: " + x + "," + y , 5, 25);
    g2d.drawString("Move angle: " +
        Math.round(ship.moveAngle())+90, 5, 40);
    g2d.drawString("Face angle: " +
        Math.round(ship.faceAngle()), 5, 55);
    if (ship.state()==STATE_NORMAL)
        g2d.drawString("State: NORMAL", 5, 70);
    else if (ship.state()==STATE_COLLIDED)
        g2d.drawString("State: COLLIDED", 5, 70);
    else if (ship.state()==STATE_EXPLODING)
        g2d.drawString("State: EXPLODING", 5, 70);

    //display the number of sprites currently in use
    g2d.drawString("Sprites: " + sprites().size(), 5, 120);

    if (showBounds) {
        g2d.setColor(Color.GREEN);
```

```
        g2d.drawString("BOUNDING BOXES", SCREENWIDTH-150, 10);
    }
    if (collisionTesting) {
        g2d.setColor(Color.GREEN);
        g2d.drawString("COLLISION TESTING", SCREENWIDTH-150, 25);
    }
}


/*******************************************************
 * gameShutdown event passed by game engine
 *******************************************************/
void gameShutdown() {
    //oh well, let the garbage collector have at it..
}
```

Updating and Drawing Sprites

Next, let's take a look at the spriteUpdate() and spriteDraw() events, which are passed on by the Game class. The spriteDying() event is also available here, but it's not currently being used in the game. You would use this event to keep a sprite alive if you want to keep it around by setting alive back to true.

The game engine processes all of the sprites in the linked list automatically (by the game loop thread). After each sprite is updated, control is sent to spriteUpdate() to give you a chance to fool around with the sprite if you need to (it is passed as a parameter). You can make any changes you want to the sprite, and those changes will be stored back in the linked list because you are working with an object reference—the actual object in the linked list, not just a copy.

This is truly where the sprite engine shows its power. You can fire as many weapons as you want, and they will strike an unknown number of sprites, which will each blow up in an animated explosion—and the linked list keeps track of all these details for you. All we really have to do is put together a new scratch sprite, give it an image from one of our global images, and then pop it off to the sprite list. This sprite will then automatically move around on the screen, rotate (if rotation is set), and animate (if frames exist). This new sprite will also be included in collision testing. The engine allows you to determine whether a collision "sticks" or not by giving you control at the key point where a collision has occurred, passing both sprites to your implementation of the spriteCollision() event.

When I was first developing the engine, I thought it would be too limiting to move all of the sprites into the list. I kept the ship outside the list for a while, and then realized that to truly make the internal sprite handler work the way it is supposed to, you really need to give it all of the sprites it needs to update, draw, and test for collision. When you get tired of a sprite, just set its alive property to false, and then the game engine will remove it from the list a few seconds later! Furthermore, as you learned in the previous chapter, you can make use of the features in AnimatedSprite for limiting the lifetime of a sprite. By setting the lifespan of a sprite, you can have it automatically terminate after a certain number of passes through the game loop. For instance, the "flaming plasma" projectiles fired from the ship are given a lifetime of 200 loops. The engine detects when the age is beyond the lifespan threshold, and then kills the sprite automagically!

Figure 10.4 shows the game after all of the large asteroids have been broken down into smaller ones. The game is truly crazy at this point, with close to a hundred small asteroids floating around your ship on various random trajectories! It's hard enough just to spin and shoot frantically, let alone move around. I even had to cheat to keep from getting blown up repeatedly! (I'll share the cheat with you at our next stop in this trip through the source code.)

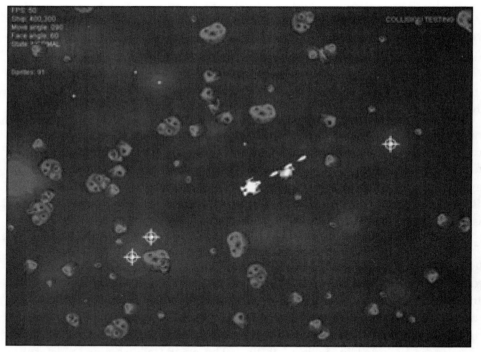

Figure 10.4 The ship is overwhelmed with asteroids and in need of some weapon upgrades!

```
/******************************************************
 * spriteUpdate event passed by game engine
 ******************************************************/
public void spriteUpdate(AnimatedSprite sprite) {
    switch(sprite.spriteType()) {
    case SPRITE_SHIP:
        warp(sprite);
        break;

    case SPRITE_BULLET:
        warp(sprite);
        break;

    case SPRITE_EXPLOSION:
        if (sprite.currentFrame() == sprite.totalFrames()-1) {
            sprite.setAlive(false);
        }
        break;

    case SPRITE_ASTEROID_BIG:
    case SPRITE_ASTEROID_MEDIUM:
    case SPRITE_ASTEROID_SMALL:
    case SPRITE_ASTEROID_TINY:
        warp(sprite);
        break;
    }
}


/******************************************************
 * spriteDraw event passed by game engine
 * called by the game class after each sprite is drawn
 * to give you a chance to manipulate the sprite
 ******************************************************/
public void spriteDraw(AnimatedSprite sprite) {
    if (showBounds) {
        if (sprite.collided())
            sprite.drawBounds(Color.RED);
        else
            sprite.drawBounds(Color.BLUE);
    }
}
```

```
/******************************************************
 * spriteDying event passed by game engine
 * called after a sprite's age reaches its lifespan
 * at which point it will be killed off, and then removed from
 * the linked list. you can cancel the purging process here.
 ******************************************************/
public void spriteDying(AnimatedSprite sprite) {
    //currently no need to revive any sprites
}
```

Handling Sprite Collisions

The most important event in the game is probably the spriteCollision() event, which is passed from the engine to your source code automatically. The engine goes through the list of active sprites (where the alive property is true) and tests each one for collision with all the other sprites in the list (except for the same one—we don't want to have objects blow themselves up for no reason!).

Take a look at Figure 10.5, which shows the ship firing several volleys of flaming plasma bolts toward asteroids. There are several bolts traveling away from the ship at various angles, and several explosions that are animating on the screen. Figure 10.5 shows sprite collision testing in progress. The engine, as implemented in the Game class, and inherited by GalacticWar, goes through the sprites and tests them all for collision—but that's all it does. Look at the sprite counter in this figure—132 sprites! This number includes the ship, bullets, asteroids, and explosions, and the number rises and falls dynamically with the gameplay. (The engine clears out unused sprites that have "died" once every second when the frame rate is calculated.)

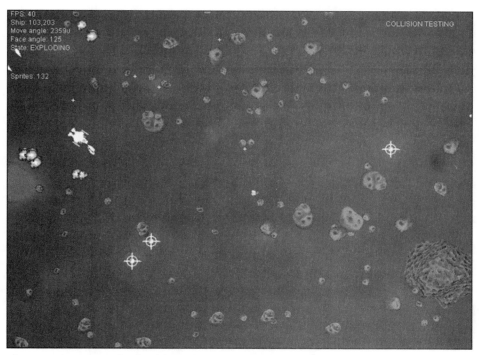

Figure 10.5 Projectiles fired from the ship eventually get passed through the spriteCollision() event when they collide with asteroids.

There is no more logic going on behind the scenes than the test for collision itself. The engine simply passes both sprites that have interacted to the spriteCollision() method. At this point, it's entirely up to you to decide what to do with the conflicting sprites. You can destroy them, have them bounce away from each other, or anything else. So all you have to do is figure out what kinds of sprites have been passed to you through the spriteCollision() event. You can do this with your own predefined constants (defined as a static int in Java). For example, I have defined SPRITE_EXPLOSION for all explosions. Yes, explosion sprites are tested for collision like everything else—but we simply ignore them, let them play out, and then disappear. The value of each constant is not important, as long as each one is different. Since I defined each of the four types of asteroids with a separate constant, I had to write a helper method called isAsteroid() to handle them all in the same way when they are passed through the event handlers.

Now, how about that cheat I promised? When I get into a tough spot in the game, I hold down the left or right arrow key to spin while hitting *both* fire buttons (the Ctrl keys). This launches twice as many volleys of plasma bolts, as Figure 10.6 shows.

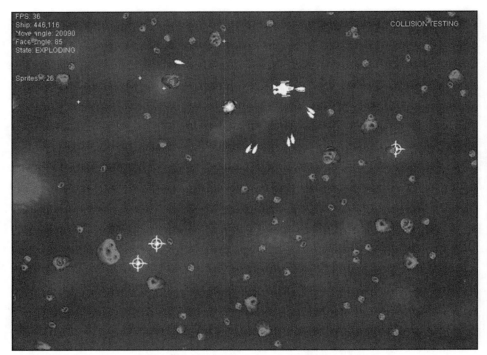

Figure 10.6 You can launch twice as many bolts using *both* Ctrl keys!

```
/****************************************************
 * spriteCollision event passed by game engine
 ****************************************************/
public void spriteCollision(AnimatedSprite spr1, AnimatedSprite spr2) {
    //jump out quickly if collisions are off
    if (!collisionTesting) return;

    //figure out what type of sprite has collided
    switch(spr1.spriteType()) {
    case SPRITE_BULLET:
        //did bullet hit an asteroid?
        if (isAsteroid(spr2.spriteType())) {
            spr1.setAlive(false);
            spr2.setAlive(false);
            breakAsteroid(spr2);
        }
        break;
    case SPRITE_SHIP:
        //did asteroid crash into the ship?
```

```
                if (isAsteroid(spr2.spriteType())) {
                    if (spr1.state() == STATE_NORMAL) {
                        collisionTimer = System.currentTimeMillis();
                        spr1.setVelocity(new Point2D(0, 0));
                        double x = spr1.position().X() - 10;
                        double y = spr1.position().Y() - 10;
                        startBigExplosion(new Point2D(x, y));
                        spr1.setState(STATE_EXPLODING);
                        spr2.setAlive(false);
                        breakAsteroid(spr2);
                    }
                    //make ship temporarily invulnerable
                    else if (spr1.state() == STATE_EXPLODING) {
                        if (collisionTimer + 3000 <
                            System.currentTimeMillis()) {
                            spr1.setState(STATE_NORMAL);
                        }
                    }
                }
            }
            break;
        }
    }
```

Keyboard and Mouse Events

The keyboard and mouse handlers are not always used, but you must still implement
them in your program. You might wonder then, How is this any better than just using the
listeners directly in the game's source code file? That's a good question! Basically, we want
to homogenize the events as much as possible. Note that the keyboard events pass nothing but the key scan code, and the mouse events pass nothing at all—you must access the
mouse information through the mousePos and mouseButtons variables (with their associated
accessor methods). Simply knowing about a keyboard or mouse event is enough; we don't
need all of the extra information that Java sends the program.

```
/****************************************************
 * gameKeyDown event passed by game engine
 ****************************************************/
public void gameKeyDown(int keyCode) {
    switch(keyCode) {
    case KeyEvent.VK_LEFT:
        keyLeft = true;
        break;
```

```
            case KeyEvent.VK_RIGHT:
                keyRight = true;
                break;
            case KeyEvent.VK_UP:
                keyUp = true;
                break;
            case KeyEvent.VK_CONTROL:
                keyFire = true;
                break;
            case KeyEvent.VK_B:
                //toggle bounding rectangles
                showBounds = !showBounds;
                break;
            case KeyEvent.VK_C:
                //toggle collision testing
                collisionTesting = !collisionTesting;
                break;
        }
    }


    /*****************************************************
     * gameKeyUp event passed by game engine
     *****************************************************/
    public void gameKeyUp(int keyCode) {
        switch(keyCode) {
        case KeyEvent.VK_LEFT:
            keyLeft = false;
            break;
        case KeyEvent.VK_RIGHT:
            keyRight = false;
            break;
        case KeyEvent.VK_UP:
            keyUp = false;
            break;
        case KeyEvent.VK_CONTROL:
            keyFire = false;
            fireBullet();
            break;
        }
    }
```

```
/******************************************************
 * mouse events passed by game engine
 * the game is not currently using mouse input
 ******************************************************/
public void gameMouseDown() { }
public void gameMouseUp() { }
public void gameMouseMove() { }
```

Asteroid Manipulation Methods

The asteroids are the most complicated part of *Galactic War*. First of all, there are *four types* of asteroids in the game, each with several different images available (which are chosen randomly when a new asteroid is created). I have written several methods for working with asteroids, mainly called from the collision events that occur. The larger asteroids are destroyed and replaced by smaller asteroids, while an explosion is animated over the old asteroid.

Figure 10.7 shows the game with bounding boxes turned on so you can see the dimensions of each sprite in the game. Note how even the explosions have a bounding box—they are included in collision testing as well, even though the game ignores them. All of the original asteroids have been destroyed and replaced with increasingly smaller ones. If you want to grab some powerups (something that will be added in the next chapter), you will have to be careful not to destroy all of the larger asteroids—the smaller ones are next to impossible to get around, and your ship will get hosed by them in short order if you let the guns go carelessly. As a result of this gameplay factor, this game involves some strategy.

This section of code marks the end of the game engine events. From this point forward, all of the methods are custom programmed and provide the real gameplay in *Galactic War*.

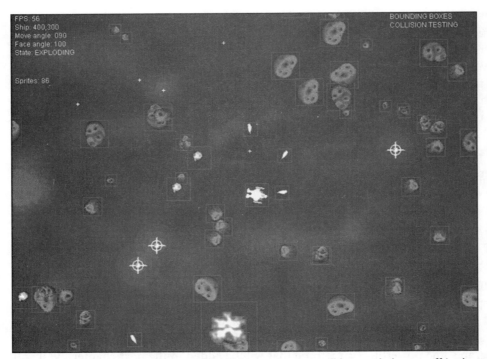

Figure 10.7 The bounding boxes and collision testing can still be toggled on or off in the game.

```
/*****************************************************
 * break up an asteroid into smaller pieces
 *****************************************************/
private void breakAsteroid(AnimatedSprite sprite) {
    switch(sprite.spriteType()) {
    case SPRITE_ASTEROID_BIG:
        //spawn medium asteroids over the old one
        spawnAsteroid(sprite);
        spawnAsteroid(sprite);
        spawnAsteroid(sprite);
        //draw big explosion
        startBigExplosion(sprite.position());
        break;
    case SPRITE_ASTEROID_MEDIUM:
        //spawn small asteroids over the old one
        spawnAsteroid(sprite);
        spawnAsteroid(sprite);
        spawnAsteroid(sprite);
        //draw small explosion
```

```
            startSmallExplosion(sprite.position());
            break;
        case SPRITE_ASTEROID_SMALL:
            //spawn tiny asteroids over the old one
            spawnAsteroid(sprite);
            spawnAsteroid(sprite);
            spawnAsteroid(sprite);
            //draw small explosion
            startSmallExplosion(sprite.position());
            break;
        case SPRITE_ASTEROID_TINY:
            //spawn a random powerup
            spawnPowerup(sprite);
            //draw small explosion
            startSmallExplosion(sprite.position());
            break;
    }
}


/*****************************************************
 * spawn a smaller asteroid based on passed sprite
 *****************************************************/
private void spawnAsteroid(AnimatedSprite sprite) {
    //create a new asteroid sprite
    AnimatedSprite ast = new AnimatedSprite(this, graphics());
    ast.setAlive(true);

    //set pseudo-random position around source sprite
    int w = sprite.getBounds().width;
    int h = sprite.getBounds().height;
    double x = sprite.position().X() + w/2 + rand.nextInt(20)-40;
    double y = sprite.position().Y() + h/2 + rand.nextInt(20)-40;
    ast.setPosition(new Point2D(x,y));

    //set rotation and direction angles
    ast.setFaceAngle(rand.nextInt(360));
    ast.setMoveAngle(rand.nextInt(360));
    ast.setRotationRate(rand.nextDouble());

    //set velocity based on movement direction
    double ang = ast.moveAngle() - 90;
    double velx = calcAngleMoveX(ang);
```

```
            double vely = calcAngleMoveY(ang);
            ast.setVelocity(new Point2D(velx, vely));

            //set some size-specific properties
            switch(sprite.spriteType()) {
            case SPRITE_ASTEROID_BIG:
                ast.setSpriteType(SPRITE_ASTEROID_MEDIUM);

                //pick one of the random asteroid images
                int i = rand.nextInt(2);
                ast.setImage(medAsteroids[i].getImage());
                ast.setFrameWidth(medAsteroids[i].width());
                ast.setFrameHeight(medAsteroids[i].height());

                break;
            case SPRITE_ASTEROID_MEDIUM:
                ast.setSpriteType(SPRITE_ASTEROID_SMALL);

                //pick one of the random asteroid images
                i = rand.nextInt(3);
                ast.setImage(smlAsteroids[i].getImage());
                ast.setFrameWidth(smlAsteroids[i].width());
                ast.setFrameHeight(smlAsteroids[i].height());
                break;

            case SPRITE_ASTEROID_SMALL:
                ast.setSpriteType(SPRITE_ASTEROID_TINY);

                //pick one of the random asteroid images
                i = rand.nextInt(4);
                ast.setImage(tnyAsteroids[i].getImage());
                ast.setFrameWidth(tnyAsteroids[i].width());
                ast.setFrameHeight(tnyAsteroids[i].height());
                break;
            }

            //add the new asteroid to the sprite list
            sprites().add(ast);
        }
```

```
/****************************************************
 * create a random powerup at the supplied sprite location
 * (this will be implemented in the next chapter)
 ****************************************************/
private void spawnPowerup(AnimatedSprite sprite) {
}


/****************************************************
 * create a random "big" asteroid
 ****************************************************/
public void createAsteroid() {
    //create a new asteroid sprite
    AnimatedSprite ast = new AnimatedSprite(this, graphics());
    ast.setAlive(true);
    ast.setSpriteType(SPRITE_ASTEROID_BIG);

    //pick one of the random asteroid images
    int i = rand.nextInt(5);
    ast.setImage(bigAsteroids[i].getImage());
    ast.setFrameWidth(bigAsteroids[i].width());
    ast.setFrameHeight(bigAsteroids[i].height());

    //set to a random position on the screen
    int x = rand.nextInt(SCREENWIDTH-128);
    int y = rand.nextInt(SCREENHEIGHT-128);
    ast.setPosition(new Point2D(x, y));

    //set rotation and direction angles
    ast.setFaceAngle(rand.nextInt(360));
    ast.setMoveAngle(rand.nextInt(360));
    ast.setRotationRate(rand.nextDouble());

    //set velocity based on movement direction
    double ang = ast.moveAngle() - 90;
    double velx = calcAngleMoveX(ang);
    double vely = calcAngleMoveY(ang);
    ast.setVelocity(new Point2D(velx, vely));

    //add the new asteroid to the sprite list
    sprites().add(ast);
}
```

```
/*****************************************************
 * returns true if passed sprite type is an asteroid type
 *****************************************************/
private boolean isAsteroid(int spriteType) {
    switch(spriteType) {
    case SPRITE_ASTEROID_BIG:
    case SPRITE_ASTEROID_MEDIUM:
    case SPRITE_ASTEROID_SMALL:
    case SPRITE_ASTEROID_TINY:
        return true;
    default:
        return false;
    }
}
```

Handling Multiple Key Presses

I spent a lot of time trying to incorporate a multiple key press system into the game engine itself, but this proved to be too troublesome. As a result, the main game keeps track of key presses and releases using global boolean variables. Since only a handful of keys are ever used in an arcade-style game like this, a more complex form of key handler is not necessary. As it is implemented here, the engine calls a few events and passes the key code when a key is pressed or released so that you don't have to bother decoding the KeyEvent, MouseEvent, or MouseMotionEvent classes.

```
/*****************************************************
 * process keys that have been pressed
 *****************************************************/
public void checkInput() {
    //the ship is always the first sprite in the linked list
    AnimatedSprite ship = (AnimatedSprite)sprites().get(0);
    if (keyLeft) {
        //left arrow rotates ship left 5 degrees
        ship.setFaceAngle(ship.faceAngle() - SHIPROTATION);
        if (ship.faceAngle() < 0)
            ship.setFaceAngle(360 - SHIPROTATION);
    }
    else if (keyRight) {
        //right arrow rotates ship right 5 degrees
        ship.setFaceAngle(ship.faceAngle() + SHIPROTATION);
        if (ship.faceAngle() > 360)
            ship.setFaceAngle(SHIPROTATION);
    }
```

```
    if (keyUp) {
        //up arrow applies thrust to ship
        ship.setImage(shipImage[1].getImage());
        applyThrust();
    }
    else
        //set ship image to normal non-thrust image
        ship.setImage(shipImage[0].getImage());
}
```

Moving the Space Ship

The space ship in *Galactic War* is rotated using the left and right arrow keys, and thrust is applied by pressing the up arrow key. The applyThrust() method handles the acceleration of the ship while keeping the ship within a reasonable velocity threshold.

```
/*****************************************************
 * increase the thrust of the ship based on facing angle
 *****************************************************/
public void applyThrust() {
    //the ship is always the first sprite in the linked list
    AnimatedSprite ship = (AnimatedSprite)sprites().get(0);

    //up arrow adds thrust to ship (1/10 normal speed)
    ship.setMoveAngle(ship.faceAngle() - 90);

    //calculate the X and Y velocity based on angle
    double velx = ship.velocity().X();
    velx += calcAngleMoveX(ship.moveAngle()) * ACCELERATION;
    if (velx < -10) velx = -10;
    else if (velx > 10) velx = 10;
    double vely = ship.velocity().Y();
    vely += calcAngleMoveY(ship.moveAngle()) * ACCELERATION;
    if (vely < -10) vely = -10;
    else if (vely > 10) vely = 10;
    ship.setVelocity(new Point2D(velx, vely));
}
```

Firing Weapons

The most significant area of improvement for the game is in the weaponry department, so some time will be spent in the next chapter adding powerups to the game. You will be able to grab powerup icons that are dropped by exploding asteroids, which will then enhance the ship in various ways. The current version of the game here has not changed

from the previous chapter, except that it now functions with the game engine. The
Ctrl key is used to fire weapons, but you can change this to another key if you want by
examining the key handlers.

```
/*****************************************************
 * fire a bullet from the ship's position and orientation
 *****************************************************/
public void fireBullet() {
    //the ship is always the first sprite in the linked list
    AnimatedSprite ship = (AnimatedSprite)sprites().get(0);

    //create the new bullet sprite
    AnimatedSprite bullet = new AnimatedSprite(this,graphics());
    bullet.setImage(bulletImage.getImage());
    bullet.setFrameWidth(bulletImage.width());
    bullet.setFrameHeight(bulletImage.height());
    bullet.setSpriteType(SPRITE_BULLET);
    bullet.setAlive(true);
    bullet.setLifespan(200);
    bullet.setFaceAngle(ship.faceAngle());
    bullet.setMoveAngle(ship.faceAngle() - 90);

    //set the bullet's starting position
    double x = ship.center().X() - bullet.imageWidth()/2;
    double y = ship.center().Y() - bullet.imageHeight()/2;
    bullet.setPosition(new Point2D(x,y));

    //set the bullet's velocity
    double angle = bullet.moveAngle();
    double svx = calcAngleMoveX(angle) * BULLET_SPEED;
    double svy = calcAngleMoveY(angle) * BULLET_SPEED;
    bullet.setVelocity(new Point2D(svx, svy));

    //add bullet to the sprite list
    sprites().add(bullet);
}
```

Blowing Stuff Up

Explosions are fun, at least in a video game (probably not in real life!). There are two main
methods for starting explosions. I could have come up with a craftier way to do this, but
decided to just write two similar methods: one for initiating large explosions and another
for smaller explosions. They use images stored in the explosions array (of ImageEntity

objects). There are currently only two explosion animations. The large explosion is used when you hit a large asteroid. The small explosion is drawn when you hit smaller asteroids. I think the result looks pretty good.

Since there are a *lot* of small asteroids and bullets flying every which way, you don't want too complex of an explosion sucking up the game's resources when there could be a couple dozen such explosions animating at a time. Check out Figure 10.8. The large explosion's frames are 96 x 96 pixels in size and there are 16 frames; the small explosion has 8 frames, and each one is only 40 x 40 pixels in size. The big explosion is used for the ship and large asteroids. This should be used sparingly because it is such a large image.

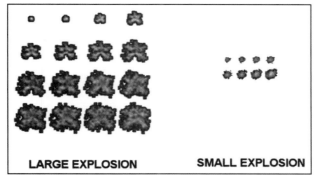

Figure 10.8 The two explosion animations compared side by side.

```
/******************************************************
 * launch a big explosion at the passed location
 ******************************************************/
public void startBigExplosion(Point2D point) {
    //create a new explosion at the passed location
    AnimatedSprite expl = new AnimatedSprite(this,graphics());
    expl.setSpriteType(SPRITE_EXPLOSION);
    expl.setAlive(true);
    expl.setAnimImage(explosions[0].getImage());
    expl.setTotalFrames(16);
    expl.setColumns(4);
    expl.setFrameWidth(96);
    expl.setFrameHeight(96);
    expl.setFrameDelay(2);
    expl.setPosition(point);
```

```
        //add the new explosion to the sprite list
        sprites().add(expl);
    }


    /****************************************************
     * launch a small explosion at the passed location
     ****************************************************/
    public void startSmallExplosion(Point2D point) {
        //create a new explosion at the passed location
        AnimatedSprite expl = new AnimatedSprite(this,graphics());
        expl.setSpriteType(SPRITE_EXPLOSION);
        expl.setAlive(true);
        expl.setAnimImage(explosions[1].getImage());
        expl.setTotalFrames(8);
        expl.setColumns(4);
        expl.setFrameWidth(40);
        expl.setFrameHeight(40);
        expl.setFrameDelay(2);
        expl.setPosition(point);

        //add the new explosion to the sprite list
        sprites().add(expl);
    }
```

Additional Game Logic

The last method in the game is called warp(), and it has the duty of making sprites wrap around the edges of the screen (right, left, top, and bottom). This is kind of a strange occurrence if you think about it, but a lot of games use this technique. The idea is that this makes an otherwise small playing field appear larger because objects can just travel through *ether-space* behind the monitor and magically re-appear on the other side, otherwise unscathed. It helps to contain the gameplay when a scrolling game world is not a goal for the game.

```
    /****************************************************
     * cause sprite to warp around the edges of the screen
     ****************************************************/
    public void warp(AnimatedSprite spr) {
        //create some shortcut variables
        int w = spr.frameWidth()-1;
        int h = spr.frameHeight()-1;
```

```
        //wrap the sprite around the screen edges
        if (spr.position().X() < 0-w)
            spr.position().setX(SCREENWIDTH);
        else if (spr.position().X() > SCREENWIDTH)
            spr.position().setX(0-w);
        if (spr.position().Y() < 0-h)
            spr.position().setY(SCREENHEIGHT);
        else if (spr.position().Y() > SCREENHEIGHT)
            spr.position().setY(0-h);
    }
}
```

What You Have Learned

This was a code-heavy chapter that involved significant changes to the coding model we've been following in each chapter up to this point. Now that *Galactic War* is event-driven and makes use of a sprite engine, the game has many more upgrade possibilities than it might have had before (where each new sprite had to be implemented from scratch). Here are the key topics you learned:

- How to create an event-driven game engine
- How to use the new Game class
- How to handle all sprites uniformly, regardless of type
- How to adapt *Galactic War* to an event-driven game

Review Questions

The following questions will help you to determine how well you have learned the subjects discussed in this chapter.

1. What is the name of the new game engine class developed in this chapter?
2. How many sprites can the new engine handle on the screen simultaneously?
3. Which of the four key classes in the game engine handles image loading?
4. How many different asteroid sizes does the game use?
5. True or False: Collisions are handled inside the game engine.
6. What type of object is animImage, a private variable in AnimatedSprit?
7. Which class is responsible for rendering a single frame of an animation in AnimatedSprite?
8. What is the maximum velocity value for the player's space ship?

9. What class does the game/sprite engine pass in some of its events?

10. What is the name of the support method in `AnimatedSprite` that returns a properly formed URL for a file to be loaded?

On Your Own

The following exercises will help you to see how well you have integrated the new material in this chapter with your existing knowledge of Java game programming.

1. The game currently has a toggle key (C) that turns collision testing on or off for all the sprites in the game. Devise a way to turn off collision testing for just the player's space ship, but not for any other sprites.

2. There are currently two methods used to start an explosion—a custom method for large explosions and another one for small explosions. These methods do the same thing, but they use a few different properties. How could you revise one of them to handle both cases for a large or small explosion with a single method?

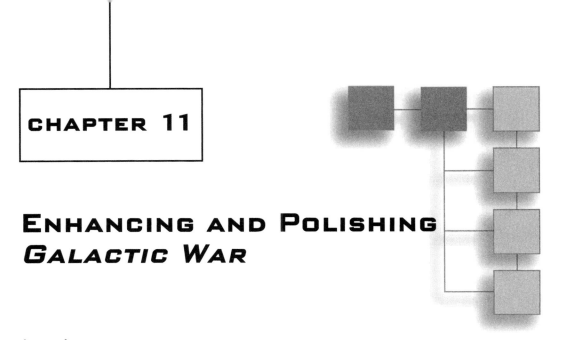

CHAPTER 11

ENHANCING AND POLISHING GALACTIC WAR

T he things you have learned in this book all culminate in this last chapter involving *Galactic War*. The game will be enhanced, polished, and ready for a production environment at the end of this chapter. All that will remain to do is to package up the entire game, resources and all, into a JAR file for distribution on the Web (which is covered in the next and final chapter of the book). Here are the key topics of interest in this chapter:

- Adding powerups to the game
- Implementing a global game state with a start and end screen
- Polishing the game and preparing it for production

Let's Talk About Powerups

Let's face it, *Galactic War* is a difficult game. It's nearly impossible to clear the asteroids with the weapon we've been using up to this point—a single pea shooter, for the most part. I want to totally enhance the game in this chapter and make it ready for prime time—for distribution on the Web. To meet that lofty goal, there are quite a few things to cover in this chapter. I'll itemize what I'd like to accomplish:

- Add powerups to upgrade the ship's weapons system
- Add powerups to restore health and shields
- Add powerups to gain extra score points

Figure 11.1 shows the six powerups that will be added to the game in this chapter.

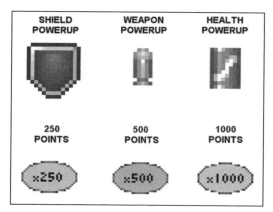

Figure 11.1 *Galactic War* has six different powerups that enhance the ship and increase your score.

tip

The complete version of the game is available on my Web site. Since I am continuing to improve the game, it may be somewhat different by the time you read this. Go here: www.jharbour.com/begjava5/GalacticWar.

Ship and Bonus Point Powerups

There are three different powerups that simply increase your score for 250, 500, and 1000 points. These powerups are released randomly when you destroy a tiny asteroid—the last stage of the asteroid's deterioration after the large, medium, and small stages.

The shield powerup will increase your shield strength by 1/4 (not the full refill that you were expecting?). Likewise, the cola can increases your ship's health by 1/4, up to the maximum value displayed in the health bar at the top of the screen. Figure 11.2 shows the three states the ship can take on during gameplay. Wait, the ship doesn't have any shields! Oh, right; that's a feature we'll add to the game in this chapter as well.

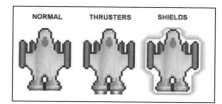

Figure 11.2 There are now three modes for the ship: normal, thrusters, and shields.

Weapon Upgrades

The weapon upgrade powerup is by far the most interesting new feature of the game, and it is very welcome given how difficult it is to stay alive in this game! You can earn up to five levels of weapon upgrades in this game. I had my son, Jeremiah, help me design the weapon patterns for each upgrade, and the result is shown in Figure 11.3.

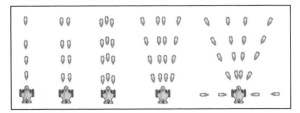

Figure 11.3 The five levels of weapon upgrades for your ship.

The upgrades were implemented a little differently than our design here, but the result is unmistakable. The biggest difference is upgrade level five: rather than firing side to side, the two additional shots go upward at a slight angle. I made this adjustment while playing the game when it seemed to be more effective than firing them at 90-degree angles. Let's take a tour of the five weapon upgrades as they were implemented in the game.

Standard Weapon

The standard weapon is shown being fired in Figure 11.4. Note the single bullet icon in the upper right corner of the screen showing the current weapon upgrade level.

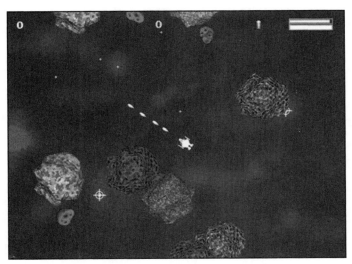

Figure 11.4 The standard weapon is a single bullet.

Weapon Level 2

The first weapon upgrade allows the ship to fire two shots at the same time, as shown in Figure 11.5. There are now two bullet icons at the upper right. After play testing the game for a while, I decided to make this the starting weapon level. You can still lose this by getting hit and then drop down to the standard weapon if you aren't careful.

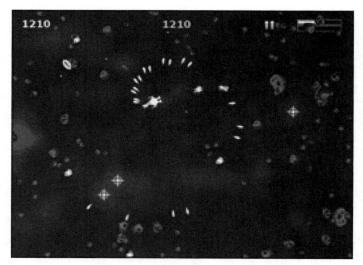

Figure 11.5 Two bullets definitely do a lot more damage!

Weapon Level 3

Weapon upgrade level three allows the ship to fire three shots at the same time, as shown in Figure 11.6. There are now three bullet icons at the upper right.

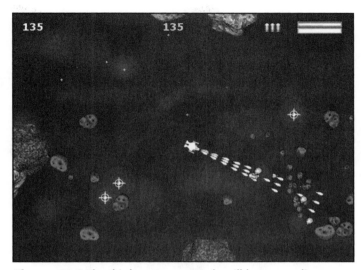

Figure 11.6 The third weapon upgrade will keep you alive much longer.

Weapon Level 4

The fourth weapon upgrade gives you four shots at a time, spreading out at slightly wider angles than the previous level, meting out massive damage to the horde of asteroids, as shown in Figure 11.7.

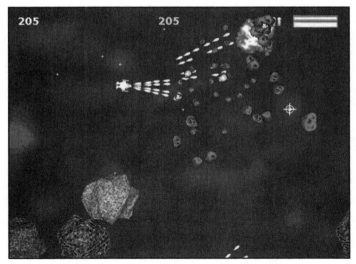

Figure 11.7 Four shots at a time is good for your self-confidence.

Weapon Level 5

Heavy gunner! Weapon level five is truly staggering, delivering massive amounts of fire-power to the ship. Take care, though—if you get hit, your ship is taken down a notch to level four again. The angles of spread at level five are slightly wider than level four, and two additional shots fire out roughly sideways from the ship (see Figure 11.8).

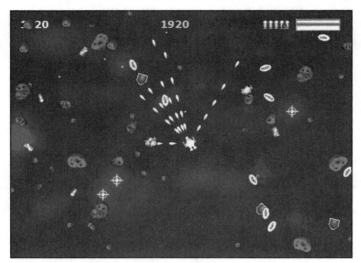

Figure 11.8 Weapon upgrade level five gives your ship six projectiles!

Enhancing *Galactic War*

I'm going to start at the top of the GalacticWar.java file and note the changes made as we move down through the source code. We'll take a look at a few screenshots along the way to explain what's happening in the code. As you can clearly see in the pages that follow, the new game engine (via the Game class) makes enhancements incredibly easy to add to the game.

tip

If you run into any problems updating the source code with the new improvements, I recommend you open up the complete Galactic War project, located on the CD-ROM in \sources\chapter11.

New Sprite Types

The first change to the program involves adding some new sprite type definitions in GalacticWar.java. Near the top of the program listing is a set of sprite types. Add the new items shown in bold text.

```
//sprite types
final int SPRITE_SHIP = 1;
final int SPRITE_ASTEROID_BIG = 10;
final int SPRITE_ASTEROID_MEDIUM = 11;
final int SPRITE_ASTEROID_SMALL = 12;
final int SPRITE_ASTEROID_TINY = 13;
final int SPRITE_BULLET = 100;
final int SPRITE_EXPLOSION = 200;
final int SPRITE_POWERUP_SHIELD = 300;
final int SPRITE_POWERUP_HEALTH = 301;
final int SPRITE_POWERUP_250 = 302;
final int SPRITE_POWERUP_500 = 303;
final int SPRITE_POWERUP_1000 = 304;
final int SPRITE_POWERUP_GUN = 305;
```

New Game States

In order to give the game the ability to start, play, and end (with the option to restart), we need to add some conditional gameplay states and make use of the pause property in the sprite engine (found in the Game class). Add the following lines just below the new sprite definitions, above the toggle variables. The new code is shown in bold.

```
//game states
final int GAME_MENU = 0;
final int GAME_RUNNING = 1;
final int GAME_OVER = 2;

//various toggles
boolean showBounds = false;
boolean collisionTesting = true;
```

When the game first starts up, you see the title screen, which is shown in Figure 11.9. This screen shows the keys you press to control the ship.

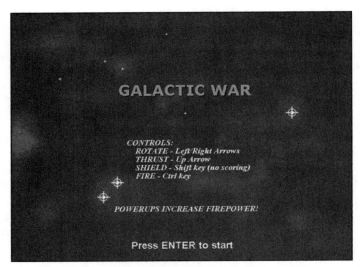

Figure 11.9 The title screen of *Galactic War* displays the key controls.

New Sprite Images

Now let's add some new sprite image definitions using the ImageEntity class. The ship has a new shield feature, and we have a whole bunch of new images for powerups and the updated user interface (such as the health and shield meters).

Scroll down a bit more to the block of code showing definitions for all of the ImageEntity objects used in the game. Add the new code shown in bold. (Note also the minor change to the shipImage array, which now has three elements.)

```
//define the images used in the game
ImageEntity background;
ImageEntity bulletImage;
ImageEntity[] bigAsteroids = new ImageEntity[5];
ImageEntity[] medAsteroids = new ImageEntity[2];
ImageEntity[] smlAsteroids = new ImageEntity[3];
ImageEntity[] tnyAsteroids = new ImageEntity[4];
ImageEntity[] explosions = new ImageEntity[2];
ImageEntity[] shipImage = new ImageEntity[3];
ImageEntity[] barImage = new ImageEntity[2];
ImageEntity barFrame;
ImageEntity powerupShield;
ImageEntity powerupHealth;
ImageEntity powerup250;
ImageEntity powerup500;
ImageEntity powerup1000;
ImageEntity powerupGun;
```

Health/Shield Meters, Score, Firepower, and Game State Variables

Now let's add some global variables to keep track of such things as the ship's health, shield power, game state, as well as more obvious things like current score, high score, and weapon upgrade level. Add the following code after the image definitions, before the Random line. New code is shown in bold.

```
//health/shield meters and score
int health = 20;
int shield = 20;
int score = 0;
int highscore = 0;
int firepower = 1;
int gameState = GAME_MENU;

//create a random number generator
Random rand = new Random();
```

New Input Keys

We need to add support for the new shield ability. I've defined the Shift key to activate the ship's shield, but you may change this key if you prefer a different one. Locate the key input tracking variables a few lines below the last change you just made, and note the new variable added in bold.

The collision toggle and bounding box toggle are both still active in the game. Although they were used for testing, they are now known as undocumented *hidden cheats* in the game!

```
//some key input tracking variables
boolean keyLeft, keyRight, keyUp, keyFire, keyB, keyC, keyShield;
```

Sound and Music Objects

Immediately below the key tracking variable definitions, add the following code for the sound and music objects (or make sure the code looks like this, if it differs in your source code listing). Note changes in bold.

```
//some key input tracking variables
boolean keyLeft, keyRight, keyUp, keyFire, keyB, keyC, keyShield;

//sound effects and music
MidiSequence music = new MidiSequence();
SoundClip shoot = new SoundClip();
SoundClip explosion = new SoundClip();
```

Loading Media Files

Unfortunately, all of these new features come with a price—load times. The game loads up very fast on your local PC, but can take 10 to 20 seconds to load from a Web site, depending on your connection speed. All the images and sounds used in this game are fairly small because they are stored in the compressed PNG format. The biggest file is the background, which is about 300 KB. All remaining image and sound files are well under 100 KB, and most of them are in the 1–10 KB range, which is extremely small indeed. I suspect that without the background image and the large explosion, the game would load up almost instantly. When packaged into a JAR (which is covered in the next chapter), the entire game is 600 KB.

Let's add all of the new code to gameStartup() to load all of the new images, sounds, and music in the game. There are also some gameplay-related changes in this method that you should look out for. All new code and changes are highlighted in bold.

```
void gameStartup() {
    //load sounds and music
    music.load("music.mid");
    shoot.load("shoot.au");
    explosion.load("explode.au");

    //load the health/shield bars
    barFrame = new ImageEntity(this);
    barFrame.load("barframe.png");
    barImage[0] = new ImageEntity(this);
    barImage[0].load("bar_health.png");
    barImage[1] = new ImageEntity(this);
    barImage[1].load("bar_shield.png");

    //load powerups
    powerupShield = new ImageEntity(this);
    powerupShield.load("powerup_shield2.png");
    powerupHealth = new ImageEntity(this);
    powerupHealth.load("powerup_cola.png");
    powerup250 = new ImageEntity(this);
    powerup250.load("powerup_250.png");
    powerup500 = new ImageEntity(this);
    powerup500.load("powerup_500.png");
    powerup1000 = new ImageEntity(this);
    powerup1000.load("powerup_1000.png");
    powerupGun = new ImageEntity(this);
    powerupGun.load("powerup_gun.png");
```

```
//load the background image
background = new ImageEntity(this);
background.load("bluespace.png");

//create the ship sprite--first in the sprite list
shipImage[0] = new ImageEntity(this);
shipImage[0].load("spaceship.png");
shipImage[1] = new ImageEntity(this);
shipImage[1].load("ship_thrust.png");
shipImage[2] = new ImageEntity(this);
shipImage[2].load("ship_shield.png");

AnimatedSprite ship = new AnimatedSprite(this, graphics());
ship.setSpriteType(SPRITE_SHIP);
ship.setImage(shipImage[0].getImage());
ship.setFrameWidth(ship.imageWidth());
ship.setFrameHeight(ship.imageHeight());
ship.setPosition(new Point2D(SCREENWIDTH/2, SCREENHEIGHT/2));
ship.setAlive(true);
//start ship off as invulnerable
ship.setState(STATE_EXPLODING);
collisionTimer = System.currentTimeMillis();
sprites().add(ship);

//load the bullet sprite image
bulletImage = new ImageEntity(this);
bulletImage.load("plasmashot.png");

//load the explosion sprite image
explosions[0] = new ImageEntity(this);
explosions[0].load("explosion.png");
explosions[1] = new ImageEntity(this);
explosions[1].load("explosion2.png");

//load the big asteroid images (5 total)
for (int n = 0; n<5; n++) {
    bigAsteroids[n] = new ImageEntity(this);
    String fn = "asteroid" + (n+1) + ".png";
    bigAsteroids[n].load(fn);
}
//load the medium asteroid images (2 total)
for (int n = 0; n<2; n++) {
```

```
        medAsteroids[n] = new ImageEntity(this);
        String fn = "medium" + (n+1) + ".png";
        medAsteroids[n].load(fn);
    }
    //load the small asteroid images (3 total)
    for (int n = 0; n<3; n++) {
        smlAsteroids[n] = new ImageEntity(this);
        String fn = "small" + (n+1) + ".png";
        smlAsteroids[n].load(fn);
    }
    //load the tiny asteroid images (4 total)
    for (int n = 0; n<4; n++) {
        tnyAsteroids[n] = new ImageEntity(this);
        String fn = "tiny" + (n+1) + ".png";
        tnyAsteroids[n].load(fn);
    }


    //start off in pause mode
    pauseGame();


  //delete this block of code, which has been moved to another method
/**** moved to resetGame
    //create the random asteroid sprites
    for (int n = 0; n<ASTEROIDS; n++) {
        createAsteroid();
    }
*/
    }
```

Game State Issue—Resetting the Game

The game used to just start up with asteroids flying at your ship, without any chance to prepare yourself! To avoid this problem, I've added an overall state system to the game, which now starts off in GAME_MENU mode. During normal gameplay, the state is GAME_PLAYING. When your ship blows up, the state is GAME_OVER. To make it possible to restart the game after dying (in which case, the high score is retained), we need a way to reset the key variables and objects—but the game should *not* reload any files! Add the resetGame() method just below gameStartup().

```
private void resetGame() {
    //restart the music soundtrack
    music.setLooping(true);
    music.play();
```

```
//save the ship for the restart
AnimatedSprite ship = (AnimatedSprite) sprites().get(0);

//wipe out the sprite list to start over!
sprites().clear();

//add the saved ship to the sprite list
ship.setPosition(new Point2D(SCREENWIDTH/2, SCREENHEIGHT/2));
ship.setAlive(true);
ship.setState(STATE_EXPLODING);
collisionTimer = System.currentTimeMillis();
ship.setVelocity(new Point2D(0, 0));
sprites().add(ship);

//create the random asteroid sprites
for (int n = 0; n<ASTEROIDS; n++) {
    createAsteroid();
}

//reset variables
health = 20;
shield = 20;
score = 0;
firepower = 2;
}
```

Detecting the "Game Over" State

The next method in the source code listing is gameTimedUpdate(), an event passed by the parent Game class. We need to add a bit of code here to handle the GAME_OVER state, which occurs when there is only one sprite left in the game—the ship. Figure 11.10 shows the game in this state after the health meter has dropped to zero.

Figure 11.10 If your health drops to zero, the game is over—you lose!

```
void gameTimedUpdate() {
    checkInput();

    if (!gamePaused() && sprites().size() == 1) {
        resetGame();
        gameState = GAME_OVER;
    }
}
```

Screen Refresh Updates

I've made a whole bunch of changes to the game screen, which is refreshed regularly during the applet's update() and paint() events. I've removed the testing/debugging displays, which showed the ship's vitals and other things. We want the game screen to look nice now, without any clutter. Since there are so many changes involved, you may want to just delete any commented-out code and rewrite this method as indicated. I will show new or changed code in bold and deleted code in italics.

```
void gameRefreshScreen() {
    Graphics2D g2d = graphics();

//*** REMOVE OR COMMENT OUT THIS BLOCK
        //the ship is always the first sprite in the linked list
    AnimatedSprite ship = (AnimatedSprite)sprites().get(0);
******/
```

```
                    //draw the background
                    g2d.drawImage(background.getImage(),0,0,SCREENWIDTH-1,SCREENHEIGHT-1,this);


//*** REMOVE OR COMMENT OUT THIS BLOCK
/*        //print status information on the screen
          g2d.setColor(Color.WHITE);
          g2d.drawString("FPS: " + frameRate(), 5, 10);
          long x = Math.round(ship.position().X());
          long y = Math.round(ship.position().Y());
          g2d.drawString("Ship: " + x + "," + y , 5, 25);
          g2d.drawString("Move angle: " + Math.round(ship.moveAngle())+90, 5, 40);
          g2d.drawString("Face angle: " +  Math.round(ship.faceAngle()), 5, 55);
          if (ship.state()==STATE_NORMAL)
              g2d.drawString("State: NORMAL", 5, 70);
          else if (ship.state()==STATE_COLLIDED)
              g2d.drawString("State: COLLIDED", 5, 70);
          else if (ship.state()==STATE_EXPLODING)
              g2d.drawString("State: EXPLODING", 5, 70);
          g2d.drawString("Sprites: " + sprites().size(), 5, 120);

          if (showBounds) {
              g2d.setColor(Color.GREEN);
              g2d.drawString("BOUNDING BOXES", SCREENWIDTH-150, 10);
          }
          if (collisionTesting) {
              g2d.setColor(Color.GREEN);
              g2d.drawString("COLLISION TESTING", SCREENWIDTH-150, 25);
          }
******/


          //what is the game state?
          if (gameState == GAME_MENU) {
              g2d.setFont(new Font("Verdana", Font.BOLD, 36));
              g2d.setColor(Color.BLACK);
              g2d.drawString("GALACTIC WAR", 252, 202);
              g2d.setColor(new Color(200,30,30));
              g2d.drawString("GALACTIC WAR", 250, 200);

              int x = 270, y = 15;
              g2d.setFont(new Font("Times New Roman", Font.ITALIC | Font.BOLD, 20));
              g2d.setColor(Color.YELLOW);
              g2d.drawString("CONTROLS:", x, ++y*20);
```

```
            g2d.drawString("ROTATE - Left/Right Arrows", x+20, ++y*20);
            g2d.drawString("THRUST - Up Arrow", x+20, ++y*20);
            g2d.drawString("SHIELD - Shift key (no scoring)", x+20, ++y*20);
            g2d.drawString("FIRE - Ctrl key", x+20, ++y*20);

            g2d.setColor(Color.WHITE);
            g2d.drawString("POWERUPS INCREASE FIREPOWER!", 240, 480);

            g2d.setFont(new Font("Ariel", Font.BOLD, 24));
            g2d.setColor(Color.ORANGE);
            g2d.drawString("Press ENTER to start", 280, 570);
        }
        else if (gameState == GAME_RUNNING) {
            //draw health/shield bars and meters
            g2d.drawImage(barFrame.getImage(), SCREENWIDTH - 132, 18, this);
            for (int n = 0; n < health; n++) {
                int dx = SCREENWIDTH - 130 + n * 5;
                g2d.drawImage(barImage[0].getImage(), dx, 20, this);
            }
            g2d.drawImage(barFrame.getImage(), SCREENWIDTH - 132, 33, this);
            for (int n = 0; n < shield; n++) {
                int dx = SCREENWIDTH - 130 + n * 5;
                g2d.drawImage(barImage[1].getImage(), dx, 35, this);
            }

            //draw the bullet upgrades
            for (int n = 0; n < firepower; n++) {
                int dx = SCREENWIDTH - 220 + n * 13;
                g2d.drawImage(powerupGun.getImage(), dx, 17, this);
            }

            //display the score
            g2d.setFont(new Font("Verdana", Font.BOLD, 24));
            g2d.setColor(Color.WHITE);
            g2d.drawString("" + score, 20, 40);
            g2d.setColor(Color.RED);
            g2d.drawString("" + highscore, 350, 40);
        }
        else if (gameState == GAME_OVER) {
            g2d.setFont(new Font("Verdana", Font.BOLD, 36));
            g2d.setColor(new Color(200, 30, 30));
            g2d.drawString("GAME OVER", 270, 200);
```

```
        g2d.setFont(new Font("Arial", Font.CENTER_BASELINE, 24));
        g2d.setColor(Color.ORANGE);
        g2d.drawString("Press ENTER to restart", 260, 500);
    }
}
```

Preparing to End

The gameShutdown() event comes next. As you'll recall, this method was left empty in the previous chapter, but now we need to use it properly. A well-behaved Java program will free up resources before the program ends. In the case of *Galactic War*, I prefer to rely on Java's built-in garbage collector to free up resources automatically. However, it is necessary to shut off the music and any sound effects currently playing before the applet ends because sometimes a MIDI sequence will keep playing after the game has ended.

```
void gameShutdown() {
    music.stop();
    shoot.stop();
    explosion.stop();
}
```

Updating New Sprites

Next up is the spriteUpdate() event method. There are a lot of new additions here but no changes, as we have all these new powerups that need to be handled when they appear on the screen. The most important thing to do here is to warp the powerups along with everything else in the game. Then, in addition, the powerups need to *wobble*, or alternate the rotation back and forth, so they stand out from the other sprites.

Just as an example, take a look at Figure 11.11. This zoom-in of the ship firing shows how much the sprite engine is handling at one time. In this figure, I count 60 sprites in just this small portion of the screen (which, granted, is where most of the action is currently taking place). All of the asteroids are rotating by some random value. The flaming bullets are rotated and adjusted every time they move along their paths. The ship rotates with user input. Every time you destroy a tiny sprite, an 8-frame animation is played. That's a lot of action! It's a good thing we developed the sprite engine in the last chapter, or none of this would have been possible using the old method of handling sprites with arrays. (Oh, and in case you were wondering—the bullets have not passed through any of those tiny sprites, they have just been spawned by the destruction of a larger sprite and will soon be annihilated by the incoming fire.)

Figure 11.11 There are a lot of sprites in any normal game, but this is only 1/4 of the screen.

The new code in spriteUpdate(), marked in bold, adds additional cases to the switch statement for dealing with the powerups.

```
public void spriteUpdate(AnimatedSprite sprite) {
    switch(sprite.spriteType()) {
    case SPRITE_SHIP:
        warp(sprite);
        break;
    case SPRITE_BULLET:
        warp(sprite);
        break;
    case SPRITE_EXPLOSION:
        if (sprite.currentFrame() == sprite.totalFrames()-1) {
            sprite.setAlive(false);
        }
        break;
    case SPRITE_ASTEROID_BIG:
    case SPRITE_ASTEROID_MEDIUM:
    case SPRITE_ASTEROID_SMALL:
    case SPRITE_ASTEROID_TINY:
        warp(sprite);
        break;
    case SPRITE_POWERUP_SHIELD:
    case SPRITE_POWERUP_HEALTH:
    case SPRITE_POWERUP_250:
```

```
        case SPRITE_POWERUP_500:
        case SPRITE_POWERUP_1000:
        case SPRITE_POWERUP_GUN:
            warp(sprite);
            //make powerup animation wobble
            double rot = sprite.rotationRate();
            if (sprite.faceAngle() > 350) {
                sprite.setRotationRate(rot * -1);
                sprite.setFaceAngle(350);
            }
            else if (sprite.faceAngle() < 10) {
                sprite.setRotationRate(rot * -1);
                sprite.setFaceAngle(10);
            }
            break;
    }
}
```

Grabbing Powerups

Next in the source code listing is the `spriteCollision()` event. All we need to do here is
handle all the new powerups that are in the game; this means that only the ship should
collide with the powerups. I've moved the test for the collision testing toggle to the top
of this method, out of the keyboard handling code, because it belongs here instead. Some
new lines have been added to increase the score whenever a bullet hits an asteroid and to
deal with collisions when the shield is up. Note changes in bold, as usual.

```
public void spriteCollision(AnimatedSprite spr1, AnimatedSprite spr2) {
    //jump out quickly if collisions are off
    if (!collisionTesting) return;

    //figure out what type of sprite has collided
    switch(spr1.spriteType()) {
    case SPRITE_BULLET:
        //did bullet hit an asteroid?
        if (isAsteroid(spr2.spriteType())) {
            bumpScore(5);
            spr1.setAlive(false);
            spr2.setAlive(false);
            breakAsteroid(spr2);
        }
        break;
    case SPRITE_SHIP:
```

```
            //did asteroid crash into the ship?
            if (isAsteroid(spr2.spriteType())) {
                if (spr1.state() == STATE_NORMAL) {
                    if (keyShield) {
                        shield -= 1;
                    }
                    else {
                        collisionTimer = System.currentTimeMillis();
                        spr1.setVelocity(new Point2D(0, 0));
                        double x = spr1.position().X() - 10;
                        double y = spr1.position().Y() - 10;
                        startBigExplosion(new Point2D(x, y));
                        spr1.setState(STATE_EXPLODING);
                        //reduce ship health after a hit
                        health -= 1;
                        if (health < 0) {
                            gameState = GAME_OVER;
                        }
                        //lose firepower when you get hit
                        firepower--;
                        if (firepower < 1) firepower = 1;
                    }
                    spr2.setAlive(false);
                    breakAsteroid(spr2);
                }
                //make ship temporarily invulnerable
                else if (spr1.state() == STATE_EXPLODING) {
                    if (collisionTimer + 3000 <
                        System.currentTimeMillis()) {
                        spr1.setState(STATE_NORMAL);
                    }
                }
            }
            break;

        case SPRITE_POWERUP_SHIELD:
            if (spr2.spriteType()==SPRITE_SHIP) {
                shield += 5;
                if (shield > 20) shield = 20;
                spr1.setAlive(false);
            }
            break;
```

```
    case SPRITE_POWERUP_HEALTH:
        if (spr2.spriteType()—SPRITE_SHIP) {
            health += 5;
            if (health > 20) health = 20;
            spr1.setAlive(false);
        }
        break;

    case SPRITE_POWERUP_250:
        if (spr2.spriteType()—SPRITE_SHIP) {
            bumpScore(250);
            spr1.setAlive(false);
        }
        break;

    case SPRITE_POWERUP_500:
        if (spr2.spriteType()—SPRITE_SHIP) {
            bumpScore(500);
            spr1.setAlive(false);
        }
        break;

    case SPRITE_POWERUP_1000:
        if (spr2.spriteType()—SPRITE_SHIP) {
            bumpScore(1000);
            spr1.setAlive(false);
        }
        break;

    case SPRITE_POWERUP_GUN:
        if (spr2.spriteType()—SPRITE_SHIP) {
            firepower++;
            if (firepower > 5) firepower = 5;
            spr1.setAlive(false);
        }
        break;
    }
}
```

New Input Keys

The game now uses the Shift key to engage the ship's shields, and the Enter key to continue when the game is in the GAME_MENU or GAME_OVER state. There's also a way to exit out of the game now: when the game is running, you can hit Escape to end the game (see Figure 11.12).

Figure 11.12 The Escape key will end the game immediately and allow you to start over.

Here are the new key handlers in bold.

```
public void gameKeyDown(int keyCode) {
    switch(keyCode) {
    case KeyEvent.VK_LEFT:
        keyLeft = true;
        break;
    case KeyEvent.VK_RIGHT:
        keyRight = true;
        break;
    case KeyEvent.VK_UP:
        keyUp = true;
        break;
    case KeyEvent.VK_CONTROL:
        keyFire = true;
        break;
```

```
        case KeyEvent.VK_B:
            //toggle bounding rectangles
            showBounds = !showBounds;
            break;
        case KeyEvent.VK_C:
            //toggle collision testing
            collisionTesting = !collisionTesting;
            break;
        case KeyEvent.VK_SHIFT:
            if ((!keyUp) && (shield > 0))
                keyShield = true;
            else
                keyShield = false;
            break;
        case KeyEvent.VK_ENTER:
            if (gameState == GAME_MENU) {
                resetGame();
                resumeGame();
                gameState = GAME_RUNNING;
            }
            else if (gameState == GAME_OVER) {
                resetGame();
                resumeGame();
                gameState = GAME_RUNNING;
            }
            break;
        case KeyEvent.VK_ESCAPE:
            if (gameState == GAME_RUNNING) {
                pauseGame();
                gameState = GAME_OVER;
            }
            break;
        }
    }
```

Now let's add a single new case to the gameKeyUp() event as well.

```
public void gameKeyUp(int keyCode) {
    switch(keyCode) {
    case KeyEvent.VK_LEFT:
        keyLeft = false;
        break;
```

```
        case KeyEvent.VK_RIGHT:
            keyRight = false;
            break;
        case KeyEvent.VK_UP:
            keyUp = false;
            break;
        case KeyEvent.VK_CONTROL:
            keyFire = false;
            fireBullet();
            break;
        case KeyEvent.VK_SHIFT:
            keyShield = false;
            break;
        }
    }
```

Spawning Powerups

In the previous chapter we added a new method to the game called spawnPowerup(), which was left empty at the time. Due to that foresight, we do not have to make any changes to the breakAsteroid() method that makes this call. Instead, here is the fully functional spawnPowerup(). At the top of the code, a random percentage determines whether the powerup is actually created. I have it currently set to 12 percent, which provides some fair gameplay. If you want to make the game more difficult, reduce this value. To make it easier, increase it.

Even though 12 percent doesn't sound like very many powerups, keep in mind that every large asteroid produces three "mediums," which each produces three "smalls," which each produces three "tinys" (see Figure 11.13). That's a whopping 27 tiny asteroids for every large one, and since the game starts out with 10 large ones, well, you can do that kind of math. In a single game session, 12 percent will generate about 30 powerups! I think this value should be reduced to about 20 to make the game a bit more challenging; but each powerup has a limited lifetime, so it's possible in the heat of battle that the player will only manage to grab a few of them.

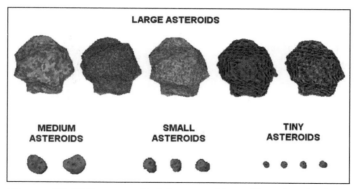

Figure 11.13 Here are all of the asteroids you'll run into in the game (pun intended).

The spawnPowerup() method creates a single powerup sprite with some standard properties that all powerups share, and then it sets the specific properties using a random number. Since there are six powerups, this random number determines the type of powerup.

```
private void spawnPowerup(AnimatedSprite sprite) {
    //only a few tiny sprites spit out a powerup
    int n = rand.nextInt(100);
    if (n > 12) return;

    //use this powerup sprite
    AnimatedSprite spr = new AnimatedSprite(this, graphics());
    spr.setRotationRate(8);
    spr.setPosition(sprite.position());
    double velx = rand.nextDouble();
    double vely = rand.nextDouble();
    spr.setVelocity(new Point2D(velx, vely));
    spr.setLifespan(1500);
    spr.setAlive(true);

    //customize the sprite based on powerup type
    switch(rand.nextInt(6)) {
    case 0:
        //create a new shield powerup sprite
        spr.setImage(powerupShield.getImage());
        spr.setSpriteType(SPRITE_POWERUP_SHIELD);
        sprites().add(spr);
        break;
    case 1:
        //create a new health powerup sprite
```

```
            spr.setImage(powerupHealth.getImage());
            spr.setSpriteType(SPRITE_POWERUP_HEALTH);
            sprites().add(spr);
            break;
        case 2:
            //create a new 250-point powerup sprite
            spr.setImage(powerup250.getImage());
            spr.setSpriteType(SPRITE_POWERUP_250);
            sprites().add(spr);
            break;
        case 3:
            //create a new 500-point powerup sprite
            spr.setImage(powerup500.getImage());
            spr.setSpriteType(SPRITE_POWERUP_500);
            sprites().add(spr);
            break;
        case 4:
            //create a new 1000-point powerup sprite
            spr.setImage(powerup1000.getImage());
            spr.setSpriteType(SPRITE_POWERUP_1000);
            sprites().add(spr);
            break;
        case 5:
            //create a new gun powerup sprite
            spr.setImage(powerupGun.getImage());
            spr.setSpriteType(SPRITE_POWERUP_GUN);
            sprites().add(spr);
            break;
    }
}
```

Making the Shield Work

Although the key events turn the ship's shield on or off, the real work is done in the checkInput() method shown here. Let's take a close-up look at the shield in action. Figure 11.14 shows the ship bombarded with asteroids, but the shield is taking all of the impacts and protecting the ship (at least until the shield runs out!).

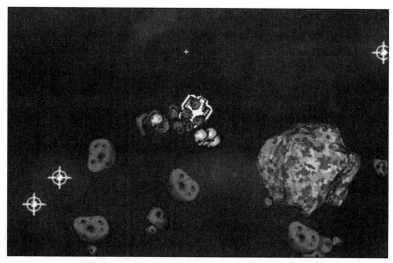

Figure 11.14 This close-up view shows multiple asteroids impacting the ship's shields (and breaking apart into small asteroids or just blowing up).

We also need to make a change to the new global game state so it will ignore input events unless the game is running—in other words, it should ignore gameplay input changes when in the GAME_MENU or GAME_OVER state. The new code is shown in bold.

```
public void checkInput() {
    if (gameState != GAME_RUNNING) return;

    //the ship is always the first sprite in the linked list
    AnimatedSprite ship = (AnimatedSprite)sprites().get(0);
    if (keyLeft) {
        //left arrow rotates ship left 5 degrees
        ship.setFaceAngle(ship.faceAngle() - SHIPROTATION);
        if (ship.faceAngle() < 0)
            ship.setFaceAngle(360 - SHIPROTATION);

    } else if (keyRight) {
        //right arrow rotates ship right 5 degrees
        ship.setFaceAngle(ship.faceAngle() + SHIPROTATION);
        if (ship.faceAngle() > 360)
            ship.setFaceAngle(SHIPROTATION);
    }
```

```
        if (keyUp) {
            //up arrow applies thrust to ship
            ship.setImage(shipImage[1].getImage());
            applyThrust();
        }
        else if (keyShield) {
            ship.setImage(shipImage[2].getImage());
        }
        else
            //set ship image to normal non-thrust image
            ship.setImage(shipImage[0].getImage());
    }
```

Making Use of Weapon Upgrade Powerups

The new weapon upgrades are awesome, as you saw earlier in the chapter—wouldn't you agree? This is the most interesting new gameplay feature, without a doubt. Each time you get a weapon upgrade, it adds another gun to your ship. However, if your ship gets hit, you lose an upgrade, so it's pretty tough to keep those upgrades. The good news is, when you get level four or five guns, your ship is so powerful that it's fairly easy to clear out the asteroids in short order.

To support weapon upgrades, the code in fireBullet() has been completely rewritten, and two new support methods were needed: adjustDirection() and stockBullet(). The new "bullets" emerge from the center of the ship, and then spread out in various patterns, based on the upgrade level (which is in a variable called firepower). I'll show you the new code for fireBullet() first.

```
public void fireBullet() {
    //create the new bullet sprite
    AnimatedSprite[] bullets = new AnimatedSprite[6];

    switch(firepower) {
    case 1:
        bullets[0] = stockBullet();
        sprites().add(bullets[0]);
        break;
    case 2:
        bullets[0] = stockBullet();
        adjustDirection(bullets[0], -4);
        sprites().add(bullets[0]);
```

```
        bullets[1] - stockBullet();
        adjustDirection(bullets[1], 4);
        sprites().add(bullets[1]);
        break;
case 3:
        bullets[0] - stockBullet();
        adjustDirection(bullets[0], -4);
        sprites().add(bullets[0]);

        bullets[1] - stockBullet();
        sprites().add(bullets[1]);

        bullets[2] - stockBullet();
        adjustDirection(bullets[2], 4);
        sprites().add(bullets[2]);
        break;
case 4:
        bullets[0] - stockBullet();
        adjustDirection(bullets[0], -5);
        sprites().add(bullets[0]);

        bullets[1] - stockBullet();
        adjustDirection(bullets[1], 5);
        sprites().add(bullets[1]);

        bullets[2] - stockBullet();
        adjustDirection(bullets[2], -10);
        sprites().add(bullets[2]);

        bullets[3] - stockBullet();
        adjustDirection(bullets[3], 10);
        sprites().add(bullets[3]);
        break;
case 5:
        bullets[0] - stockBullet();
        adjustDirection(bullets[0], -6);
        sprites().add(bullets[0]);

        bullets[1] - stockBullet();
        adjustDirection(bullets[1], 6);
        sprites().add(bullets[1]);
```

```
        bullets[2] = stockBullet();
        adjustDirection(bullets[2], -15);
        sprites().add(bullets[2]);

        bullets[3] = stockBullet();
        adjustDirection(bullets[3], 15);
        sprites().add(bullets[3]);

        bullets[4] = stockBullet();
        adjustDirection(bullets[4], -60);
        sprites().add(bullets[4]);

        bullets[5] = stockBullet();
        adjustDirection(bullets[5], 60);
        sprites().add(bullets[5]);
        break;
    }
    shoot.play();
}
```

Here's the new `adjustDirection()` support method, which basically just cuts down on the amount of code in `fireBullet()` because this code is repeated for every single bullet launched. This method is new, so you should add it below the `fireBullet()` method in your code listing for GalacticWar.java.

```
private void adjustDirection(AnimatedSprite sprite, double angle) {
    angle = sprite.faceAngle() + angle;
    if (angle < 0) angle += 360;
    else if (angle > 360) angle -= 360;
    sprite.setFaceAngle(angle);
    sprite.setMoveAngle(sprite.faceAngle()-90);
    angle = sprite.moveAngle();
    double svx = calcAngleMoveX(angle) * BULLET_SPEED;
    double svy = calcAngleMoveY(angle) * BULLET_SPEED;
    sprite.setVelocity(new Point2D(svx, svy));
}
```

The next support method that helps out `fireBullet()` is called `stockBullet()`. This method creates a stock bullet sprite with all of the standard values needed to fire a single bullet from the center of the ship. The custom upgraded bullets are modified from this stock bullet to create the various firepower patterns you see in the game. This method returns a new `AnimatedSprite` object.

```
private AnimatedSprite stockBullet() {
    //the ship is always the first sprite in the linked list
    AnimatedSprite ship = (AnimatedSprite)sprites().get(0);

    AnimatedSprite bul = new AnimatedSprite(this, graphics());
    bul.setAlive(true);
    bul.setImage(bulletImage.getImage());
    bul.setFrameWidth(bulletImage.width());
    bul.setFrameHeight(bulletImage.height());
    bul.setSpriteType(SPRITE_BULLET);
    bul.setLifespan(90);
    bul.setFaceAngle(ship.faceAngle());
    bul.setMoveAngle(ship.faceAngle() - 90);
    //set the bullet's velocity
    double angle = bul.moveAngle();
    double svx = calcAngleMoveX(angle) * BULLET_SPEED;
    double svy = calcAngleMoveY(angle) * BULLET_SPEED;
    bul.setVelocity(new Point2D(svx, svy));
    //set the bullet's starting position
    double x = ship.center().X() - bul.imageWidth()/2;
    double y = ship.center().Y() - bul.imageHeight()/2;
    bul.setPosition(new Point2D(x,y));

    return bul;
}
```

Tallying the Score

The final change to the *Galactic War* source code is the addition of a new method called
bumpScore(). This is called in the collision routine to increase the player's score for every
asteroid hit by a weapon (collisions with the ship don't count).

```
public void bumpScore(int howmuch) {
    score += howmuch;
    if (score > highscore)
        highscore = score;
}
```

312 Chapter 11 ■ Enhancing and Polishing *Galactic War*

What You Have Learned

This has certainly been an eye-opening chapter! It's amazing what is possible now that we have a sprite engine with such dynamic sprite-handling capabilities. It's now possible, as you have seen, to add new powerups and entirely new gameplay elements by simply adding new cases to the `switch` statements in the key event methods, as well as adding the few lines of code to load new images. The end result is now a fully polished, retail-quality game that's ready to take on any game in the Web-based casual game market.

Here are the key topics you learned:

- How to add powerups to the game
- How to enhance gameplay with new features
- How to fire a spread of bullets at various angles
- How to add a game state to give the game a start and ending

Review Questions

The following questions will help you to determine how well you have learned the subjects discussed in this chapter.

1. What method in GalacticWar.java makes it possible to add powerups to the game when a tiny asteroid is destroyed?

2. What construct does the sprite engine (in Game.java) use to manage the sprites?

3. How many weapon upgrades are available now in *Galactic War*?

4. How many different point-value powerups are there in the game?

5. What method in GalacticWar.java returns a stock bullet sprite object, which is then tweaked to produce the upgraded bullet spreads?

6. How many different asteroid images are there in `Galactic War`?

7. If you wanted to add another weapon upgrade to the game, which method would you need to modify?

8. How many sprites is the sprite engine capable of handling at a time?

9. How many bullets are fired at a time with the fifth level weapon upgrade?

10. What is the name of the static `int` that represents the game state when the game is running normally?

On Your Own

There are so many possibilities with this game, I hardly know where to start. Since I consider the game finished, in the sense that it is sufficiently stocked with features and gameplay elements to meet the goals I laid out for this book, I will just make some suggestions for the game.

I would like to add a black hole that randomly crosses the screen from time to time, sucking in everything it touches. Wouldn't that be cool? I have the animated black hole sprite already available—look for it in \media\images on the CD-ROM.

Another great feature would be to have an alien spacecraft come onto the screen from time to time and shoot at the player. To keep the alien ship from getting hit by asteroids, the ship would engage a shield whenever it collides with an asteroid; otherwise, it would have to navigate through the asteroid field, and that's some code I would not care to write! The UFO ship image and shield version are also available on the CD-ROM in \media\images, so you can give this new feature a shot if you want.

Here is yet another idea to improve gameplay, since the game is *really* hard. The game could start off with a single big asteroid for "Level 1" and then add an additional big asteroid to each level the player completes. Although the game can handle an unlimited number of sprites, I would end the game at level 10 to keep it reasonable. Since the game currently just throws ten asteroids at the player from the start, switching to a level-based system would greatly improve the fun factor!

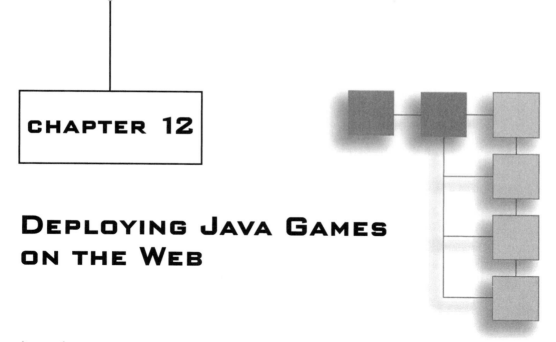

CHAPTER 12

Deploying Java Games on the Web

T his chapter finishes the book by explaining the all-important subject of how to deploy your Java applet-based games to the Web. I assume you already have some knowledge about how to access a Web server using FTP to copy your game to a Web server. I will show you how to prepare the applet so that it will run from a Web page. You will also learn how to use the Java Archive tool to bundle your entire game (with class files and all media files together) in a Java archive file.

- Packaging an applet in a Java Archive (JAR)
- Using the JAR command-line program
- Packaging *Galactic War* into a JAR file
- Creating a host html file for the applet

Packaging an Applet in a Java Archive (JAR)

The Java Development Kit (JDK) comes with a command-line tool called jar.exe that is used to create Java Archive files. JARs, as they are known, use the ZIP compression method when storing files. JARs can greatly reduce the size of a Java applet—which is crucial for Web deployment.

To use the JAR tool, you will need to open a Command Prompt window (also known as a *shell* in some operating systems), and then set the path to the JDK if it is not already set. By default, on a Windows system, the JDK is installed at C:\Program Files\Java, and under this folder there will be a folder containing the Java Development Kit (JDK) and the Java Runtime Environment (JRE). You need to set the path to include the \bin folder located in the JDK. This will differ depending on the version of JDK you have installed. Currently on my system, the jar.exe tool is located here:

`C:\Program Files\Java\jdk1.5.0_06\bin`

You can open the Command Prompt by going to Start, Program Files, Accessories. You can also run cmd.exe manually using Start, Run. On Linux and Mac systems, the JDK is usually already added to the path when it is installed.

Using the jar.exe Program

The JAR tool is a bit finicky. If you don't use the parameters exactly right and in the correct order, JAR will complain and fail to create the JAR file you wanted it to create. The order of the parameters should not be significant, but it is in this case. The general syntax of the JAR command can be viewed by typing JAR at the command line. The output looks something like Figure 12.1.

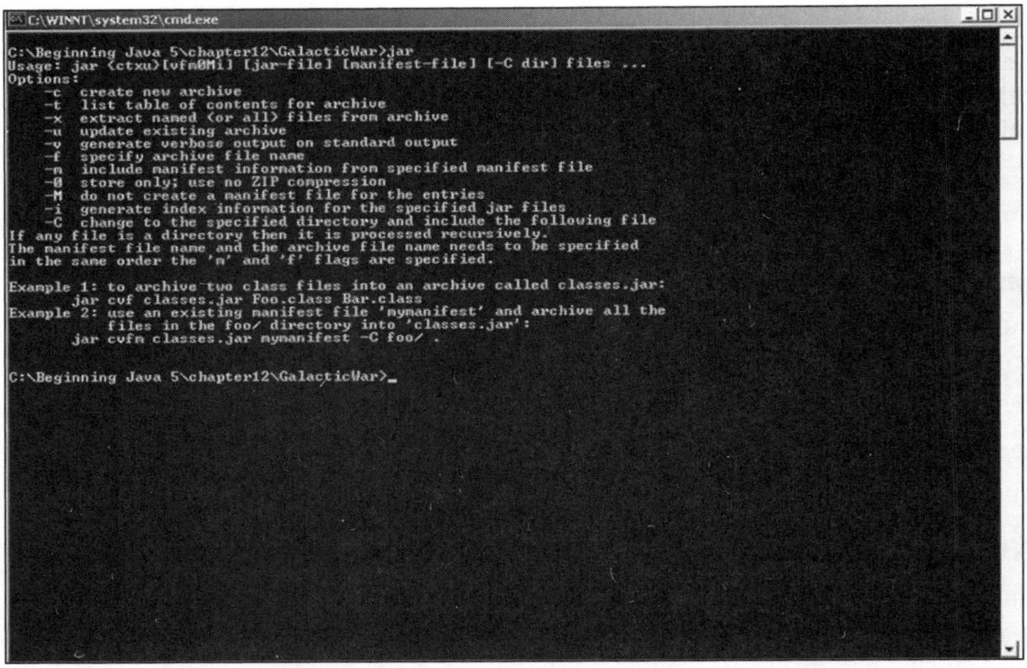

Figure 12.1 Verifying that the JAR program is available at the command prompt.

Creating a New JAR File

The parameters in this Help listing are deceptive. Not only should you *not* use the dash (–), but these parameters *must* be specified in a specific order. For instance, we use the "c" parameter to tell JAR to create a new JAR file. But this parameter must be used along with "f" to specify the file name. I can't imagine a situation where you would want to use the JAR tool without using a JAR file, but that's just me I guess. After the "cf" parameters, you specify the JAR file name, and then the files you want to add. Here is an example:

```
jar cf test.jar *.class
```

This command will create a new JAR file called test.jar and add all .class files found in the current folder to the JAR file. After doing so, if the JAR tool successfully created the new JAR file, it will simply exit and not print anything out. (So remember, no display equals no problems.)

Listing the Contents of a JAR File

To display the contents of a JAR file, use the "tf" parameter, like so:

```
jar tf test.jar
```

You can also include the "v" option to display the contents of the JAR file with details. This option also works when creating a new JAR file, but you must be careful to include the "v" option after the "c" or "t" parameter. Here's an example of both cases:

```
jar cvf test.jar *.class
jar tvf test.jar
```

Extracting Files from a JAR File

You can extract a single file or all files from a JAR file using the "x" option, like this:

```
jar xvf test.jar *.*
```

Updating a JAR File

You can update a JAR file using the "u" parameter. Any files you specify will replace existing files in the archive, and any new files will be added.

```
jar uvf test.jar HelloWorld.class
```

Manifest Files

Java archives can include a manifest file that tells the JRE the name of the .class file it should run (automatically) when it opens the JAR file. Since this is a fairly common occurrence, and manifest files are a cinch, it makes sense to include one in a JAR file that will run on the Web. The general format of the manifest file looks like this:

```
Main-Class: Filename
```

You should not include the .class extension. There are more options for manifest files, but this is the only one you need to be concerned with when the goal is to run an applet stored in a JAR file on the Web. Be sure to add a blank line after this single line in the manifest file or the JAR tool will complain.

To use a manifest file when creating a new archive, you can use the "m" parameter option. Just be sure that this is the *last* letter in the options you include.

```
jar cvfm test.jar manifest.txt *.class *.png
```

note

Given the Java community's obsession with clichés, I'm surprised the JAR program was not called MUG instead, since one does not usually drink a hot beverage from a JAR.

Packaging *Galactic War* in a Java Archive

The JAR program is fairly easy to use once you get used to its specific requirements. Now let's use this tool to package *Galactic War* into a Java archive. This will save a little space and will keep the game together in a single file so you won't leave any media files behind when copying the game or uploading it to a Web site.

caution

You must load files in a certain way in your code so that the JRE will know how to read them from a JAR file when you have deployed the applet to a Web site. I've shown you a couple of different ways to load images and other media files in this book.

The method you must use when a game is deployed in a JAR uses the java.net.URL class and the getResource() method to create a URL that you can pass to the appropriate image or sound loader. The getResource() method is available from this.getClass(). This method will correctly pull a media file from the local file system or from a JAR file when resources are stored within a JAR. Here is an example:

```
URL url = this.getClass().getResource(filename);
```

The first order of business is to copy your project folder to a new location so you don't accidentally mess up the original. Since I've been using JBuilder in this book, the class files and all media files have been stored inside the classes folder within each project folder. So, in Chapter 11, the class and media files were all located in GalacticWar\classes, while the source code was in GalacticWar\src. The JBuilder project files are located in the main folder, GalacticWar. I've copied the classes folder to a new location and left the project and source files behind. The new folder (now in Chapter12 on the CD-ROM) is simply called GalacticWar, and it contains the classes and media files for the game. Essentially, this new folder contains the run-time files for the game.

Reviewing the Project Files

Now let's create a Java archive to contain the files needed by this game. The manifest.txt file and index.html file (covered next) are found in the GalacticWar folder. I have copied all of the *Galactic War* media and class files into a folder called GalacticWar\project. Included are 30 image (PNG) files, two audio files, and one MIDI file. In addition, we have these nine Java class files:

- AnimatedSprite.class
- BaseGameEntity.class
- Game.class
- ImageEntity.class
- Point2D.class
- Sprite.class
- GalacticWar.class
- MidiSequence.class
- SoundClip.class

That's a lot of files for a single game! The last thing I want to do is deploy this game to a Web server by copying all 42 files along with index.html, although that is definitely a workable option. In fact, if you just edit the HTML file (which you'll learn to do here shortly), you can simply copy these files to a Web site and run the game over the Web. But a Java archive works so much better, and it saves some space too.

Building the Java Archive

Using the CD command in the command prompt, I've changed the current folder to \Beginning Java 5\chapter12\GalacticWar (this may be slightly different on your system). You can perform this step from any folder where your project files are located. I've copied all of the class and media files to a subfolder called project to keep things tidy. So, all I have in this main GalacticWar folder is index.html, manifest.txt, and the project subfolder (see Figure 12.2).

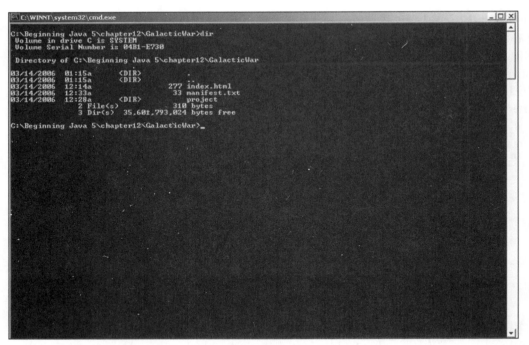

Figure 12.2 Listing the contents of the GalacticWar folder.

The manifest.txt file for *Galactic War* contains this line:

```
Main-Class: GalacticWar
```

This tells the JRE which of the .class files to open up and start running after opening the JAR file. (Be sure to include a blank line after the Main-Class property line.)

You will need to use an optional parameter of the JAR program that lets you specify a subfolder where the actual files are located. You don't want to just tell it to include .\project*.* because that will add .\project to the internal structure of the JAR file. Instead, you want to grab all the files inside of .\project, but not include the folder name. The option is "C" (uppercase is important). Here's the command to create the GalacticWar.jar file:

```
jar cvfm GalacticWar.jar manifest.txt -C project *.*
```

This line tells JAR to create a new Java archive called GalacticWar.jar, to include the manifest information stored in manifest.txt, to use the project subfolder, and to add all files in that subfolder to the JAR file. Figure 12.3 shows the output of the command.

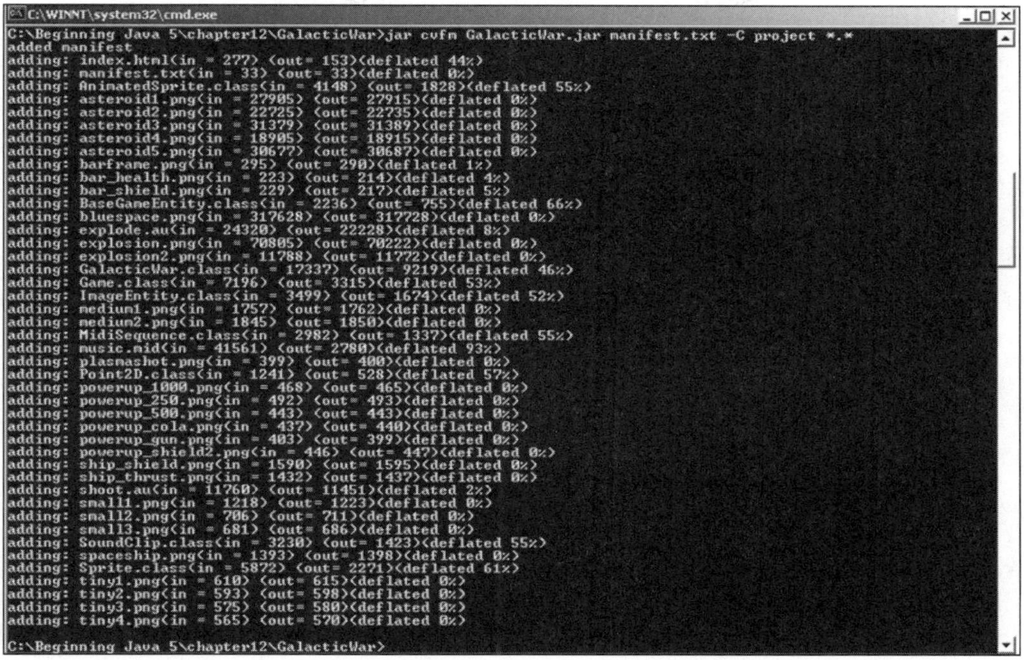

Figure 12.3 Verifying that the JAR program is available at the command prompt.

If these additional steps get on your nerves, just lump everything together in a single folder and run the JAR program in the same folder as all your Java project's files, without using the C option, like so:

```
jar cvfm GalacticWar.jar manifest.txt *.*
```

Creating an HTML Host File for Your Applet

HTML is short for *hyper-text markup language*, and it is the water flowing through the World Wide Web. To run a Java applet on the Web, you have to *embed* the applet inside a Web page. This involves creating an HTML file with an `<applet>` tag that specifies the details about how to run the applet and where it is contained.

A Simple HTML File

The most basic format for an HTML file that will host an applet looks like the following code. This code assumes that a file called game.class is available in the same Web folder as the HTML file.

```
<html><head>
<title>This is my game</title>
</head>
<body>
<applet code = game.class
 width=800 height=600>
</applet>
</body></html>
```

The key to running an applet inside a Java archive is to add another option within the `<applet>` tag called `archive`.

```
<applet code=game.class
 archive=game.jar
 width=800 height=600>
</applet>
```

The Web page file is usually called "index.html" because that is the name of a file that Web servers will send the Web browser automatically if you don't specify the HTML file directly. For instance, when you go to www.jharbour.com, the Web server used to deliver index.html automatically. (Now my Web server delivers a different file, called default.aspx, because I've converted the site to ASP.NET, but you get the idea.) You can create this simple HTML file using a text editor like Notepad (as shown in Figure 12.4).

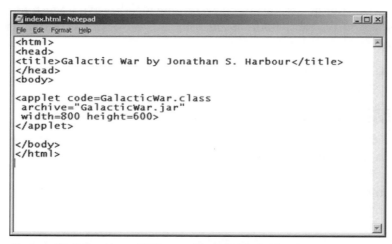

Figure 12.4 Creating a Web page file called index.html.

Testing the Deployed Applet Game

When you have the HTML host file and a JAR file ready to go, it's time to upload them to your Web server. I've created a folder on my Web server called /begjava5/GalacticWar/ that I'll use for the *Galactic War* files. The index.html and GalacticWar.jar files are both uploaded to http://www.jharbour.com/begjava5/GalacticWar and are ready to run from this location. When you hit this URL, the Web browser fires up the JRE, which displays an attractive logo image and a progress bar while it downloads the JAR file (see Figure 12.5).

Figure 12.5 The JRE displays this image and progress bar while the JAR file is being downloaded.

tip

The great thing about an applet is that your Web browser will store it in the Web cache. That is why the applet seems to just open up immediately when you go to the same URL again. The applet does not need to be downloaded again when it is stored in the local Web cache.

When the applet has completely downloaded to your local system, it will access the files in the JAR locally rather than hitting the Web server for every file. Remember the list of 42 media files in *Galactic War*? If the game were deployed to the Web server with all of those individual files, the applet would have to grab every single file individually over the Internet. That's a lot of file transfers! But when your applet is stored in a JAR, that single JAR file is downloaded to your PC and the applet runs from there. All media files are drawn directly from the JAR file instead of from the Web server. If all goes well during the downloading of the JAR file, the game should come up as shown in Figure 12.6.

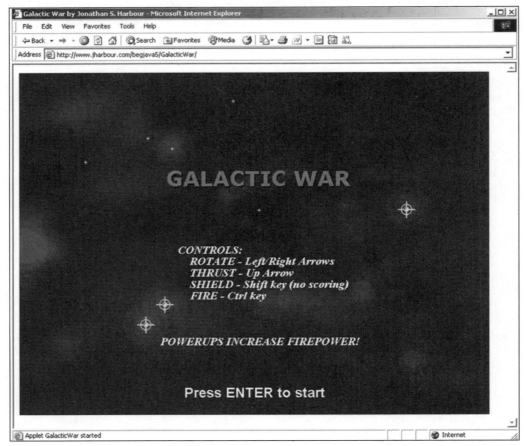

Figure 12.6 Galactic War is now running on a real Web server from within an efficient JAR file.

Epilogue

This concludes the final chapter of the book! I hope you have enjoyed this book as much as I enjoyed writing it. I'll admit, it was quite a challenge! For a while I didn't think this *Galactic War* game would ever see the light of day. There are so many advanced topics that we didn't have time to cover in this book, the likes of which a die-hard Java programmer would have liked to see. However, I believe a completely functional game, created from scratch and actually finished within the pages of a book, is far more educational than any so-called "advanced" material we might have looked at instead. My hope is that you have learned enough from this book to build your own Java applet-based games and that you will create the next blockbuster game for the online casual game market. Good luck!

What You Have Learned

Java applets can grow quite large when you are writing a game because most games use dozens of media files. By packaging a Java applet-based game into a Java Archive (JAR) file, you dramatically improve the time it takes to download and run the game from a Web server. You also cut down on the number of transfers that must be made when individual files are stored directly on the server instead of inside an archive file.

Here are the key topics you learned:

- Packaging an applet inside a Java archive
- Creating an HTML host file for your applet
- Running the applet from a Web site

Review Questions

The following questions will help you to determine how well you have learned the subjects discussed in this chapter.

1. What does the acronym JAR stand for?
2. What is the name of the program used to work with JAR files?
3. What types of files can be stored inside a JAR file?
4. What compression method does the JAR format use?
5. What method must you use in conjunction with the `java.net.URL` class for loading media files when an applet has been deployed in a JAR file?
6. What command would you enter to create a new JAR file, called test.jar, that contains all files in the current folder?
7. What command would you enter to create the same archive but also include a manifest file called manifest.txt?

8. What command would you enter to list the contents of a file called MyGame.jar with verbose listing enabled?

9. What JAR parameter option causes files to be added from a different folder without adding the folder name to the files stored in the archive?

10. What type of Web server do you need to host a Java applet-based game?

PART III

APPENDICES

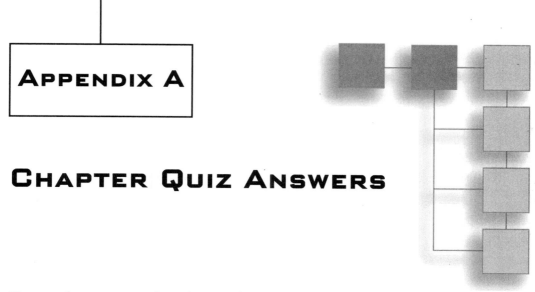

Appendix A

Chapter Quiz Answers

Here are the answers to the quizzes at the end of each chapter.

Chapter 1

1. What does the acronym JDK stand for?

   Answer: Java Development Kit

2. What version of the JDK are we focusing on in this book?

   Answer: 1.5 or Java 5

3. What is the name of the company that created JBuilder?

   Answer: Borland

4. Where on the Web will you find the free version of JBuilder 2005?

   Answer: www.borland.com

5. What is the free version of JBuilder called?

   Answer: Foundation

6. Where on the Web is the primary download site for the JDK?

   Answer: http://java.sun.com

7. What type of Java program do you run with the java.exe tool?

   Answer: application or service

8. What type of Java program runs in a web browser?

   Answer: applet

9. What is the name of the command-line tool used to run a Web-based Java program?

Answer: appletviewer.exe

10. What is the name of the parameter passed to the paint() event method?

Answer: Graphics *or* Graphics g

Chapter 2

1. What is the name of the JDK tool used to compile Java programs?

Answer: javac.exe

2. Which JDK command-line tool is used to run a Java application?

Answer: java.exe

3. Which JDK command-line tool is used to run a Java applet?

Answer: appletviewer.exe

4. What version of Borland JBuilder did you learn about in this chapter?

Answer: JBuilder 2005

5. Encapsulation, polymorphism, and inheritance are the keys to what programming methodology?

Answer: OOP: Object-Oriented Programming

6. What's the main difference between a Java application and an applet?

Answer: applets run in a Web browser

7. Which method of the Graphics class can you use to print a text message on the screen?

Answer: drawString()

8. How many bits make up a Java integer (the *int* data type)?

Answer: 32

9. How many bits are there in a Java long integer (the *long* data type)?

Answer: 64

10. What programming language was Java based on?

Answer: C++

Chapter 3

1. What is the name of the method used to enable keyboard events in your program?
   Answer: addKeyListener

2. What is the name of the keyboard event interface?
   Answer: KeyListener

3. What is the virtual key code for the Enter key?
   Answer: VK_ENTER

4. Which keyboard event will tell you the code of a pressed key?
   Answer: keyPressed

5. Which keyboard event will tell you when a key has been released?
   Answer: keyReleased

6. Which keyboard event will tell you the character of a pressed key?
   Answer: keyTyped

7. Which KeyEvent method returns a key code value?
   Answer: getKeyCode

8. What is the name of the method used to enable mouse motion events?
   Answer: addMouseMotionListener

9. What is the name of the class used as a parameter for all mouse event methods?
   Answer: MouseEvent

10. Which mouse event reports the actual movement of the mouse?
    Answer: mouseMoved

Chapter 4

1. What is the name of Java's digital sound system class?
   Answer: AudioSystem

2. What is the name of Java's MIDI music system class?
   Answer: MidiSystem

3. Which Java class handles the loading of a sample file?
   Answer: AudioInputStream

4. Which Java class handles the loading of a MIDI file?

   Answer: Sequencer

5. What type of exception error will Java generate when it cannot load a sound file?

   Answer: UnsupportedAudioFileException

6. Which method of the MIDI system returns the sequencer object?

   Answer: getSequencer

7. What is the main Java class hierarchy for the audio system class?

   Answer: javax.sound.sampled

8. What is the main Java class hierarchy for the MIDI system class?

   Answer: javax.sound.midi

9. What three digital sound file formats does Java support?

   Answer: AIFF, AU, and WAV

10. What rare exception error will occur when no MIDI sequencer is available?

    Answer: MidiUnavailableException

Chapter 5

1. What is the name of the method that calculates the velocity for X?

   Answer: calcAngleMoveX

2. What is the base class from which Ship, Asteroid, and Bullet are inherited?

   Answer: BaseVectorShape

3. What classic Atari game inspired the game developed in this chapter?

   Answer: Asteroids

4. What type of collision testing does this game use?

   Answer: bounding rectangle

5. What method of the Shape class does this game use for collision testing?

   Answer: contains

6. What geometric shape class is used in the Ship and Asteroid classes?

   Answer: Polygon

7. What geometric shape class does the Bullet class use?

   Answer: Rectangle

8. Which applet event actually draws the screen?

    Answer: `paint`

9. What is the name of the interface class used to add threading support to the game?

    Answer: `Runnable`

10. What math function does `calcAngleMoveX` use to calculate the X velocity?

    Answer: cosine

Chapter 6

1. What is the primary class we've been using to manipulate vector graphics in this chapter?

    Answer: `Graphics2D`

2. Where is a good source of free game art on the Web that was recommended in this chapter?

    Answer: www.reinerstileset.de

3. What `Graphics2D` method is used to draw an image?

    Answer: `drawImage()`

4. Which Java class contains the `getImage()` method?

    Answer: `java.awt` *or* `java.awt.Image`

5. What class makes it possible to perform translation, rotation, and scaling of shapes and images?

    Answer: `AffineTransform`

6. Which Graphics2D method draws a polygon?

    Answer: `draw`

7. Which transform method moves a shape or image to a new location?

    Answer: `translate`

8. What method initializes the keyboard listener interface?

    Answer: `addKeyListener`

9. What method in the `Random` class returns a double-precision floating-point value?

    Answer: `nextDouble`

10. Which KeyListener event detects key presses?

    Answer: `keyPressed`

Chapter 7

1. What is the name of the game that was created in this chapter from a previous project?

   Answer: Galactic War

2. What is the name of the base class used to create game objects?

   Answer: `BaseGameEntity`

3. What is the name of the class that handles vector-based graphics?

   Answer: `VectorEntity`

4. What is the new class that was created in this chapter to handle bitmap images?

   Answer: `ImageEntity`

5. Which method do we use to load a bitmap image in an applet?

   Answer: `getImage`

6. What is the name of the method that returns the directory containing the applet (or HTML container) file?

   Answer: `getCodeBase()`

7. What is the name of the method that returns the entire URL string including the applet (or HTML container) file?

   Answer: `getDocumentBase()`

8. What class do you use to store a bitmap image?

   Answer: `Image`

9. Which `Graphics2D` method is used to draw a bitmap image?

   Answer: `drawImage`

10. What is the name of the custom method that calculates the X velocity based on the angle that an object is facing?

    Answer: `calcAngleMoveX`

Chapter 8

1. What is the name of the support class created in this chapter to help the `Sprite` class manage position and velocity?

   Answer: `Point2D`

2. During which keyboard event should you disable a keypress variable, when detecting multiple key presses with global variables?

   Answer: `keyReleased`

3. What are the three types of parameters you can pass to the `collidesWith()` method?

   Answer: `Rectangle`, `Sprite`, *and* `Point2D`

4. What Java class provides an alternate method for loading images that is not tied to the applet?

   Answer: `Toolkit`

5. Which Java package do you need to import in order to use the `Graphics2D` class?

   Answer: `java.awt`

6. What numeric data type does the `Point2D` class (created in this chapter) use for internal storage of the X and Y values?

   Answer: `double`

7. What data types can the `Point2D` class work with at the constructor level?

   Answer: `int`, `float`, *or* `double`

8. Which sprite property determines the angle at which the sprite will move?

   Answer: `moveAngle`

9. Which sprite property determines at which angle an image is pointed, regardless of movement direction?

   Answer: `faceAngle`

10. What is the transparency layer in a PNG file called?

    Answer: mask

Chapter 9

1. What is the name of the animation class created in this chapter?

   Answer: `AnimatedSprite`

2. Which class does the new animation class inherit from?

   Answer: `Sprite`

3. How many frames of animation were there in the animated ball sprite?

   Answer: 64

4. What do you call an animation that is stored inside many files?
   Answer: sequence

5. What do you call an animation that is all stored in a single file?
   Answer: tiled

6. Which sprite state constant should you look for when a collision has occurred?
   Answer: `STATE_COLLIDED`

7. What is the name of the normal sprite state constant?
   Answer: `STATE_NORMAL`

8. Which sprite state constant gets set when a sprite is in the process of blowing up?
   Answer: `STATE_EXPLODING`

9. What is the name of the method developed for the AnimationTest program that draws a single frame in an animation strip?
   Answer: `drawFrame`

10. What is the name of the new collision handler for the player's ship?
    Answer: `handleShipCollisions`

Chapter 10

1. What is the name of the new game engine class developed in this chapter?
   Answer: `Game`

2. How many sprites can the new engine handle on the screen simultaneously?
   Answer: unlimited (with available memory)

3. Which of the four key classes in the game engine handles image loading?
   Answer: `ImageEntity`

4. How many different asteroid sizes does the game use?
   Answer: 4

5. True or False: Collisions are handled inside the game engine.
   Answer: False: Collisions are only detected, not handled.

6. What type of object is `animImage`, a private variable in `AnimatedSprite`?
   Answer: `ImageEntity`

7. Which class is responsible for rendering a single frame of an animation in `AnimatedSprite`?

   Answer: `Sprite` *(which, in turn, uses* `ImageEntity`*)*

8. What is the maximum velocity value for the player's space ship?

   Answer: 10

9. What class does the game/sprite engine pass in some of its events?

   Answer: `AnimatedSprite`

10. What is the name of the support method in `AnimatedSprite` that returns a properly formed URL for a file to be loaded?

    Answer: `getURL`

Chapter 11

1. What method in GalacticWar.java makes it possible to add powerups to the game when a tiny asteroid is destroyed?

   Answer: `spawnPowerup()`

2. What construct does the sprite engine (in Game.java) use to manage the sprites?

   Answer: `LinkedList`

3. How many weapon upgrades are available now in *Galactic War*?

   Answer: 5

4. How many different point-value powerups are there in the game?

   Answer: 3

5. What method in GalacticWar.java returns a stock bullet sprite object, which is then tweaked to produce the upgraded bullet spreads?

   Answer: `stockBullet()`

6. How many different asteroid images are there in Galactic War?

   Answer: 14

7. If you wanted to add another weapon upgrade to the game, which method would you need to modify?

   Answer: `fireBullet()`

8. How many sprites is the sprite engine capable of handling at a time?

   Answer: unlimited (with available memory)

9. How many bullets are fired at a time with the fifth level weapon upgrade?

Answer: 6

10. What is the name of the static int that represents the game state when the game is running normally?

Answer: GAME_RUNNING

Chapter 12

1. What does the acronym JAR stand for?

Answer: Java Archive

2. What is the name of the program used to work with JAR files?

Answer: jar.exe

3. What types of files can be stored inside a JAR file?

Answer: Any type of file

4. What compression method does the JAR format use?

Answer: ZIP compression

5. What method must you use in conjunction with the java.net.URL class for loading media files when an applet has been deployed in a JAR file?

Answer: getResource()

6. What command would you enter to create a new JAR file, called test.jar, that contains all files in the current folder?

Answer: jar cf test.jar *.*

7. What command would you enter to create the same archive but also include a manifest file called manifest.txt?

Answer: jar cfm test.jar manifest.txt *.*

8. What command would you enter to list the contents of a file called MyGame.jar with verbose listing enabled?

Answer: jar tvf MyGame.jar

9. What JAR parameter option causes files to be added from a different folder without adding the folder name to the files stored in the archive?

Answer: C

10. What type of Web server do you need to host a Java applet-based game?

Answer: Any server will do; applets are client-side programs.

APPENDIX B

RECOMMENDED BOOKS AND WEB SITES

With the click of a button (okay, and some keystrokes) you can find just about everything on the Internet, from how to cook Mandarin chicken to implementing the latest 3-D technology in your games. To make it just a little easier for you, here is a collection of sites I greatly recommend if you are interested in game development or computing in general—and my favorite, computer humor. Have fun on the Net.

Support on the Web

Sun Microsystems (the company that created Java) has an extensive Web site devoted to Java development at http://java.sun.com. Your best reference for the Java language will be the JDK documentation. This is available as a separate download from the JDK at the Sun Developer Network (SDN) Web site: http://java.sun.com/docs. This documentation is fully hyperlinked and searchable, and will be invaluable as you are writing Java code.

Borland also provides an extensive Web site for Java programming using JBuilder and other software development tools at http://www.borland.com.

I have set up a Web site to provide support for this book online. The site features an overview of the book, sample programs and screenshots, and corrections to the book. The main support site for this book: www.jharbour.com/begjava5.

In addition, I have set up an online forum dedicated to game development and focused on providing additional support for this book from other readers and fans of Java games. The online forum can be found here :www.jharbour.com/forums.

Thomson / Course Technology has an extensive Web site listing an awesome collection of game development books at www.courseptr.com. Thomson / Course Technology became involved in game development when it acquired Premier Press. Now that Charles River Media (formerly Premier Press' main competitor) is a part of the Thomson family of companies, Thomson is the industry-leading game development publisher. This Web site is more comprehensive and tailored to game development than Amazon.com.

Game Development and Programming

There are hundreds, if not thousands, of game development sites on the Internet. Some are good, some bad, but in my personal opinion, all in the following list fall into the first category. Not all of these are related to Java, but you will find a lot of useful information from game development discussions and articles *not* specifically written for Java. Since C++ and Java are so similar, you should be able to glean useful techniques for your Java games from any C++ tutorial or article.

University of Advancing Technology (UAT): www.uat.edu

GameDev LCC: www.gamedev.net

FlipCode: www.flipcode.com/

Game Developers Search Engine: www.gdse.com/

CFXWeb: www.cfxweb.net/

CodeGuru: www.codeguru.com

Programmers Heaven: www.programmersheaven.com

AngelCode.com: www.angelcode.com

OpenGL: www.opengl.org

IsoHex: www.isohex.net/

NeHe Productions: http://nehe.gamedev.net/

NeXe: http://nexe.gamedev.net/

Game Developer: www.gamedeveloper.net/

Wotsit's Format: www.wotsit.org/

News, Reviews, and Download Sites

Keeping up with all that is happening is a daunting task. New things happen every minute all over the world, and hopefully, the next set of links will help you keep up-to-date with it all:

Games Domain: www.gamesdomain.com

Blue's News: www.bluesnews.com

Happy Puppy: www.happypuppy.com

Download.com: www.download.com

Tucows: www.tucows.com

Slashdot: http://slashdot.org

Engines

Sometimes you should not try to reinvent the wheel. There are several good engines, both 2-D and 3-D out there. Below are some of the engines I have had the pleasure (or pain) to work with that I want to recommend to you. Some are expensive, but then again, some are free. See which is best for you and start developing. Again, these are not directly related to Java, but to C++, and it's a good idea to broaden your horizons as much as possible.

Garage Games' Torque Engine: www.garagegames.com

LithTech: www.lithtech.com

CDX: www.cdx.sk

Jet3D: www.jet3d.com

Genesis3D: www.genesis3d.com

RenderWare: www.renderware.com

Crystal Space: http://crystal.linuxgames.com

Independent Game Developers

You know, almost everyone started as you are starting, by reading books and magazines or getting code listings from friends or relatives. Some of the developers listed here struggled hard to get where they are now, and some are still struggling. Visit them, give them your support, and who knows, in the next book, it may be your site listed here.

Longbow Digital Arts: www.longbowdigitalarts.com/

Spin Studios: www.spin-studios.com/

Positech Computing Ltd: www.positech.co.uk/

Samu Games: www.samugames.com/

QUANTA Entertainment: www.quanta-entertainment.com/

Satellite Moon: www.satellitemoon.com/

Myopic Rhino Games: www.myopicrhino.com/

Industry

If you want to be in the business, you need to know the business. Reading magazines and visiting association meetings will help you for sure. The following list contains links to both physical and online magazines, trade associations, conferences, and developers associations.

Game Developers Magazine: www.gdmag.com

GamaSutra: www.gamasutra.com

International Game Developers Association: www.igda.com

Game Developers Conference: www.gdconf.com

Game Developers Conference Europe: www.gdc-europe.com/

Association of Shareware Professionals: www.asp-shareware.org/

RealGames: www.real.com/games

Computer Humor

Forget about Jerry Seinfeld and Ray Romano—now *this* is what I call real humor. The following online humor sites will keep you laughing for hours on end if you have some time to kill.

Home Star Runner: www.homestarrunner.com

User Friendly: www.userfriendly.org

Geeks!: www.happychaos.com/geeks/

Off the Mark: www.offthemark.com/computers.htm

Player Versus Player: www.pvponline.com

(My favorite comic of all time is at http://homestarrunner.com/sbemail94.html. Oh man, I start laughing just thinking about this one).

Noteworthy Books

This is a list of books with a short description for each. They are either books I have written (plug!) or that I highly recommend because I've found them useful, relaxing, funny, or essential on many an occasion. This list is not specifically geared toward Java programming.

Beginner's Guide to DarkBASIC Game Programming

Jonathan S. Harbour, Joshua R. Smith; Premier Press; ISBN 1-59200-009-6

This book provides a good introduction to programming Direct3D, the 3-D graphics component of DirectX, using the C language. The second edition is coming out soon, which will focus on all the latest features of Dark Basic Professional.

Beginning Game Programming

Jonathan S. Harbour; Course Technology; ISBN 1-59200-585-3

This book teaches basic game programming using Visual C++ and DirectX 9. Keep a look out for the second edition, due out in 2006. This new edition will focus more on creating games and less time on the DirectX SDK.

C Programming for the Absolute Beginner

Michael Vine; Premier Press; ISBN 1-931841-52-7

This book teaches C programming using the free GCC compiler as its development platform, which is the same compiler used to write Game Boy programs! As such, I highly recommend this starter book if you are just learning the C language. It sticks to just the basics. You will learn the fundamentals of the C language without any distracting material or commentary. It includes just the fundamentals of what you need to be a successful C programmer.

C++ Programming for the Absolute Beginner

Dirk Henkemans and Mark Lee; Premier Press; ISBN 1-931841-43-8

If you are new to programming with C++ and you are looking for a solid introduction, this is the book for you. This book will teach you the skills you need for practical C++ programming applications, and how you can put these skills to use in real-world scenarios.

Game Design: The Art & Business of Creating Games

Bob Bates; Premier Press; ISBN 0-7615-3165-3

This very readable and informative book is a great resource for learning how to design games—the high-level process of planning the game prior to starting work on the source code or artwork.

Game Programming All in One, Second Edition

Jonathan S. Harbour; Course Technology; ISBN 1-59200-383-4

This book explains how to create nice-quality arcade style games using the awesome cross-platform Allegro game library. Topics covered include tile-based scrolling, animated sprites, level editing, and the development of several complete arcade games. Look for the third edition in 2006.

High Score! The Illustrated History of Electronic Games, 2nd Edition

Rusel DeMaria, Johnny L. Wilson; McGraw-Hill/Osborne; ISBN 0-07-222428-2

This is a gem of a book that covers the entire video game industry, including arcade machines, consoles, and computer games. It is jam-packed with wonderful interviews with famous game developers and is chock full of color photographs.

The Java Programming Language (Fourth Edition)

James Gosling, et al.; Addison-Wesley; ISBN 0-32134-498-06

This reference for the Java language was co-authored by the man who invented the Java language at Sun Microsystems. The fourth edition includes material from the latest version, J2SE 5.0.

J2ME Game Programming

Martin Wells; Course Technology; ISBN 1-59200-118-1

This book will teach you how to use the Java 2 Micro Edition to program games for cell phones and other portable devices using the Java language.

Java Programming for the Absolute Beginner

Joseph Russell; Course Technology; ISBN 0-7615-3522-5

Looking for a good introduction to the Java language? Look no further! This book will provide you with all the information you need to get started programming in Java. A revised second edition will be available in Summer of 2006.

Microsoft C# Programming for the Absolute Beginner

Andy Harris; Premier Press; ISBN 1-931841-16-0

Using game creation as a teaching tool, this book not only teaches C#, but also the fundamental programming concepts you need to grasp in order to learn any computer language. You will be able to take the skills you learn from this book and apply them to your own situations. *Microsoft C# Programming for the Absolute Beginner* is a unique book aimed at the novice programmer. Developed by computer science instructors, this series is the ideal tool for anyone with little-to-no programming experience.

Microsoft Visual Basic .NET Programming for the Absolute Beginner

Jonathan S. Harbour; Premier Press; ISBN 1-59200-002-9

Whether you are new to programming with Visual Basic .NET or you are upgrading from Visual Basic 6.0 and looking for solid introduction, this is the book for you. It teaches the basics of Visual Basic .NET by working through simple games that you will learn to create.

Visual Basic Game Programming for Teens

Jonathan S. Harbour; Course Technology; ISBN 1-59200-587-X

This book is not about programming in Visual Basic or DirectX, although it uses these tools to good effect. The point of this book is to explain how to program a simple role-playing game using a tile-based scrolling game world and sprites.

Visual Basic Game Programming with DirectX

Jonathan S. Harbour; Premier Press; ISBN 1-931841-25-X

This book is a comprehensive programmer's tutorial and a reference for everything related to programming games with Visual Basic. After a complete explanation of the Windows API graphics device interface meant to supercharge 2-D sprite programming for normal applications, the book delves into DirectX 7.0 and 8.1, covering every component of DirectX in detail, including Direct3D. Four complete games are included, demonstrating the code developed in the book.

INDEX

try...catch error handler, sound clips, 89-90
try...catch...finally error handler, sound clips, 90

U

Unreal Engine 3, casual games, 10
Unsupported AudioFileException, unsupported file format, 83
update() method
    explosion enhancements, 26
    Galactic War game enhancements, 206-208
    screen refreshing, 114-115
    SimpleLoop program, 153-154
updateAsteroids() method, 120-121, 211
updateBullets() method, 120, 210-211
updateShip() method, 119-120, 209-211
user interfaces, listener methods, 62

V

variables
    animationDirection, 222-223
    collisionTesting, 202-204
    currentFrame, 222
    initializing, 76
    showBounds, 202-204
    static keyword, 234
    totalFrames, 222
vector arrays, Ship class, 108-109
vector classes, Galactic War game, 165-167
vector graphics
    Asteroids-style game, 104-106
    bounding rectangles, 106, 108-112
    defined, 104
    identity transform, 115-116
    Java 2-D programming, 131-140
    random shapes, 132-134
velocity
    advanced movement algorithm, 123, 125-126
    asteroid updating, 211
    bullet updating, 210-211
    defined, 125

getRotationVelocity() method, 111
    Ship class, 108-109
    Sprite class, 192
versions
    Java development history, 19-21
    JDK selection, 67
vertices, polygon shapes, 135
virtual key codes
    KeyEvent class, 63
    platform-neutral key values, 71

W

warp() method, Galactic War, 278-279
weapons
    firing, 275-276
    upgrade powerups, 283-286, 308-311
Web deployment
    HTML host files, 321-324
    JAR applet packaging, 315-321
Web hosting, applet requirements, 38-39
Web sites
    Audacity, 81
    Borland, 15
    Java Sound API, 82
    JDK (Java Development Kit), 15
    Mappy, 49
    Paint Shop Pro, 185
    Reiner Prokein, 141, 199
    supercomputer information, 40
windows, refreshing, 76, 114-115, 117, 259-261
wizards
    Applet, 29-30, 68
    Class, 54-56
    New JDK, 17-18
    Project, 27-28, 65-68
wrapping, sound clips, 90

X

Xbox Live Arcade, 9-10